WOMEN WHO SEXUALLY ABUSE CHILDREN

WILEY SERIES

in

CHILD CARE AND PROTECTION

Series Editors

Kevin D. Browne
School of Psychology
The University of Birmingham, UK

Margaret A. Lynch
Newcomen Centre
Guy's Hospital, London, UK

The Child Care and Protection Series aims to further the understanding of health, psychosocial and cultural factors that influence the development of the child, early interactions and the formation of relationships in and outside the family. This international series will cover the psychological as well as the physical welfare of the child and will consider protection from all forms of maltreatment.

The series is intended to become essential reading for all professionals concerned with the welfare and protection of children and their families. All books in the series will have a practice orientation with referenced information from theory and research.

Published

Dorota Iwaniec — The Emotionally Abused and Neglected Child: Identification, Assessment, and Intervention

Ann Buchanan — Cycles of Child Maltreatment: Facts, Fallacies and Interventions

Jacqui Saradjian — Women who Sexually Abuse Children: From Research to Practice

Forthcoming

Leonard Dalgleish — Risk and Decision in Child Protection

Michelle Aldridge — Interviewing Children: A Guide to Child Care and Forensic Practitioners

Potential authors are invited to submit ideas and proposals for publications for the series to either of the series editors or to Comfort Jegede, Publishing Editor, John Wiley & Sons Ltd, Baffins Lane, Chichester, West Sussex PO19 1UD, UK.

WOMEN WHO SEXUALLY ABUSE CHILDREN

From Research to Clinical Practice

Jacqui Saradjian
Leeds Community Mental Health Trust, UK

in association with

Helga Hanks
St James University Hospital, Leeds, UK

H HAVERING COLLEGE
OF FURTHER & HIGHER EDUCATION

LEARNING RESOURCES
CENTRE

JOHN WILEY & SONS
Chichester · New York · Toronto · Brisbane · Singapore

Q

304.1536

156664
6 537375

Copyright © 1996 by John Wiley & Sons Ltd,
Baffins Lane, Chichester,
West Sussex PO19 1UD, England

National   01243 779777
International (+44) 1243 779777
e-mail (for orders and customer service enquiries):
cs-books@wiley.co.uk
Visit our Home Page on http://www.wiley.co.uk
or http://www.wiley.com

Reprinted December 1997

All Rights Reserved. No part of this book may be reproduced, stored in a retrieval
system, or transmitted, in any form or by any means, electronic, mechanical,
photocopying, recording, scanning or otherwise, except under the terms of the
Copyright, Designs and Patents Act 1988 or under the terms of a licence issued by the
Copyright Licensing Agency, 90 Tottenham Court Road, London W1P 9HE, UK, without
the permission in writing of the Publisher.

Other Wiley Editorial Offices

John Wiley & Sons, Inc., 605 Third Avenue,
New York, NY 10158-0012, USA

Jacaranda Wiley Ltd, 33 Park Road, Milton,
Queensland 4064, Australia

John Wiley & Sons (Canada) Ltd, 22 Worcester Road,
Rexdale, Ontario M9W 1L1, Canada

John Wiley & Sons (Asia) Pte Ltd, 2 Clementi Loop #02-01,
Jin Xing Distripark, Singapore 129809

Library of Congress Cataloging-in-Publication Data

Saradjian, Jacqui,
    Women who sexually abuse children: from research to clinical
practice/Jacqui Saradjian: in association with Helga Hanks.
       p. cm.
    Includes bibliographical references and index.
    ISBN 0-471-96072-1 (pbk. : alk. paper)
    1. Women child molesters—Great Britain. 2. Women child
molesters—Rehabilitation—Great Britain. I. Hanks, Helga G. I.
II. Title.
HV6570.4.G7S37   1996
364. 1´536—dc20   96-32161
                                                              CIP

British Library Cataloguing in Publication Data

A catalogue record for this book is available from the British Library

ISBN 0-471-96072-1

Typeset in 10/12pt Palatino from the author's disks by Vision Typesetting, Manchester
Printed and bound in Great Britain by Biddles Ltd, Guildford and King's Lynn
This book is printed on acid-free paper responsibly manufactured from sustainable
forestation, for which at least two trees are planted for each one used for paper
production.

For my son Adam, who has taught me more about a good relationship between a mother and her child than any academic text ever could

CONTENTS

ABOUT THE AUTHOR

Jacqui Saradjian—Clinical Psychology, High Royds Hospital, Menston, Near Ilkley, West Yorkshire. LS29 6AQ

Jacqui Saradjian is a Clinical Psychologist working for Leeds Community Mental Health Trust. She began her research into women who sexually abused children while an undergraduate and postgraduate at Leeds University and has continued this research over the past four years.

Her current post involves carrying out risk assessments of sexual offenders, assessing the therapeutic needs of survivors and offenders of sexual abuse and undertaking therapy with both survivors and perpetrators. She has carried out training on this topic throughout this country and presented this research at conferences throughout the British Isles and abroad.

SERIES PREFACE

The **Wiley Series in Child Care and Protection**, is a new series of books primarily written for all professionals in research and practice concerned with the care, welfare and protection of children and their families.

The aim of the series is to publish books on child care and protection covering both the psychological and physical welfare of the child and to include legal and social policy aspects. The series was prompted by the need to view child protection within the wider concepts of child care and social welfare. After three decades of remarkable growth in child protection work, which has led to widespread public awareness and professional understanding of child maltreatment, it has become increasingly recognised that child protection is enhanced by the improvements in the welfare of families and the promotion of positive parenting and child care. Indeed, child care, family welfare and effective child protection are inter-linked and cannot be separated.

For example, the inability of maltreating parents to adaptively interact with their children is seen by many professionals as being representative of a general lack of interpersonal skills. Abusive and neglective parents often share a common pattern of social isolation, adverse living conditions, poor work history and few friendships with others outside the home. This isolation means that parents unable to cope are usually unwilling, or unable, to seek help by themselves from outside agencies who could provide assistance or emotional support. If such parents do interact with others they are most likely to choose those with similar problems to themselves, thereby gaining no experience of alternative parenting styles or positive coping strategies and continuing to be ineffective in promoting the optimal development of their children. Hence, child protection is multi-faceted involving many different aspects of child care and the social welfare of families.

Books in the series will be from a wide range of disciplines and each book will be encouraged to link research and practice to inform, in an easily accessible way, professionals, policy makers and the public in general. In this way it is hoped to further the knowledge and understanding of health, psychosocial and cultural factors that influence the development of the child, early interactions and the formation of relationships in and outside the family.

In this landmark book, Jacqui Saradjian explores the lives of women who sexually abuse children. Based on her own interviews with 50 women, this is a significant contribution to the knowledge needed to protect children from an often unacknowledged form of child abuse. The interviews yielded so much rich material that the production of a concise book of this size has been a particular challenge.

The book has had a seven-year gestation period which started with Jacqui's tentative steps as an undergraduate to come to grips with the concept of women as sexual abusers. This initial interest, inspired by Helga Hanks, herself an acknowledged child protection pioneer, went on to form the subject of Jacqui's MSc research and to become an area in which she has become a skilled clinician. This ensured the book was written with the practitioner in mind.

Insights gained from sensitive and thorough research are shared with the reader in a non-sensational way, the intention being to promote a therapeutic approach to recognition and intervention for both the women themselves and their victims. The book goes on to examine possible theoretical models developed from research and clinical experience. These models may prove useful in understanding the underlying dynamics which result in women sexually abusing children and in pointing the way to appropriate assessment and therapeutic intervention.

The editors wish to acknowledge their thanks to Helga Hanks for her supervision, wisdom and support. Recognising the importance of publishing on this, for some a contentious topic, Helga was a major motivating force behind the idea for the book and has remained closely involved throughout its preparation.

Margaret A. Lynch
Kevin D. Browne

OVERVIEW

In any field find the strangest thing and then explore it. (John A. Wheeler)

The sexual abuse of a child always takes place in secrecy. This secrecy is maintained by an enforced conspiracy of silence. When that secret is disclosed, the reaction to that disclosure will determine not only whether that abuse continues, but also whether the victims and the perpetrators get the help they need. This scenario is reflected in society as a whole. Mehan and Ward (1975) propose that the reporting and interpretation of such social phenomena as child abuse is culturally based. Although the evidence that women sexually abuse children has been available for many years, it is only within the last decade that as a society we have begun to accept that this occurs and to explore it.

The overwhelming aim for me in writing this book has been to assist child protection. It is hoped that by raising awareness of the possibility of women sexually abusing children, providing information as to the ways in which they can and do sexually abuse, and considering possible aetiologies and motivations, more effective assessments and interventions can be made. Thus it will be possible to hear children and adult survivors who tell us that this has been their experience and we shall also be able to contemplate assessing the risk a woman poses and what interventions can be made to reduce that risk and thus protect children. While raising this awareness, there is however no attempt to suggest equivalence of numbers with male offenders. While socialisation of males in our current society tends to reinforce sexually aggressive behaviour, socialisation of women inhibits it. For women to sexually offend against children they have to deviate greatly from the accepted schema of femaleness (see Chapter 1). Thus it is extremely unlikely that as many women as men will be found to be perpetrators of child sexual abuse. However, the number of children who are sexually abused by women is such a sizeable minority that work in this area is of vital importance.

This book draws on in-depth research and clinical experiences of therapeutic work carried out with more than 50 women who have sexually abused children. The research began in 1989 when I was an undergraduate psychologist. With Helga Hanks as my supervisor, I interviewed three women who had sexually abused children. Since I was an undergraduate this was a naïve piece of work as I did not ask any questions about the sexual acts or the women's sexual fantasies. After discussing my work with Hilary Eldridge at Gracewell, a centre working with primarily male sexual offenders, I rectified this deficit in the study. Only one of the original three women interviewed is included in the final data as she was the only one with whom I could set up a further interview. In my research for my masters degree with Jan Burns as my academic supervisor and Helga Hanks as a clinical supervisor, I interviewed a further nine women. Since qualifying as a clinical psychologist three years ago, I have carried out more than 40 interviews and clinical work with several women. For all of this work my supervisor has been Chris Grulich.

It is hoped that this will provide an original piece of work which will add to the currently available knowledge about women who sexually abuse children. Although what I am presenting here is information gathered from what to my knowledge is the largest sample of women offenders reported on in Britain to date, this is still a relatively small sample. This book forms part of the *beginning* of our attempts to understand women who sexually abuse children. There are many ways in which this research needs to be further expanded and developed. For example, there are no women from any ethnic group other than caucasian who were available and/or willing to take part in the project. There are no women with any form of disabilities either physical or cognitive; no older women; nor any women who primarily target children in their mid-childhood years. Yet women in all these groups are known to have sexually abused children.

Chapter 1 considers society's current responses to women who have been found to sexually abuse children. It looks at how the denial of women as sexual offenders against children, and the minimisation of the effects of that abuse, can cause additional problems for the victims of women perpetrators. In this chapter the difficulty of establishing the extent of the problem is considered.

Chapter 2 discusses the research methodology; how the information to be described in later chapters was collected and analysed. It also describes the demographic data of the women who took part in this study and also the acts the women perpetrated and the children they targeted.

Chapters 3 to 7 contain the detailed results from the research. Related topics will be grouped together in specific chapters: the women's own experience of childhood; relationships: how they view themselves and their relationships with partners and peers; stresses, social supports and coping mechanisms; the children whom the women target to sexually abuse; and the women's experience of sex. Each specific topic will be indicated by a bold heading followed by how and why this topic was explored. Under the title 'Findings' the general pattern of what was found will be presented. Those results specific to different groups of women will be indicated, e.g. *Women who initially target young children (Group A)*. This will enable someone interested in findings for a woman who has behaved in a specific way to access the information more easily. Where appropriate in the text, the theoretical implications of these findings will be considered under the heading Reflection and Comment.

Chapter 8 summarises these findings and describes typical characteristics of offenders and also describes women who do not conform to these current groupings as presented. Although these women are described as 'Atypical Offenders' it is suggested that many more women who behave in the manner described will come to light when sexual abuse by women is more widely recognised.

Chapter 9 will describe the lives and experiences of four particular women who have abused children. These are women who were involved in ritual abuse. As society has begun to hear about this form of abuse, which is characterised by extremely severe exploitation of children, it has been recognised that many of those involved as perpetrators are women (e.g. Finkelhor, 1988). Due to the fact that ritual abuse has engendered so much debate, this chapter will include some detailed discussion about this form of abuse. There will also be some exploration of the controversial issues with which, as professionals, we are still struggling. These issues are considered important as studying them sets the behaviours of the women perpetrators in context.

Chapter 10 offers a speculative theoretical model based on the findings from the research. While hypothesising on the dynamics involved in the perpetration of these acts, there is no way that it should be believed that the aim is to excuse the women's behaviours; whatever has occurred the women always had a choice and were always responsible for the exploitation of the children whom they hurt.

Chapters 11 and 12 address the important issue of risk assessment and the planning and process of therapeutic intervention. This issue is presented in such a way as to be of interest whatever the therapeutic orientation of the therapist.

The Final Words (Chapter 13) consist of three vignettes describing case studies of women who have become engaged in therapy with successful outcomes. Although not all interventions have had such positive outcomes, these are presented to offer encouragement that even women who have had very difficult lives and have coped with that by abusing children, can change.

CASE EXAMPLES

Throughout the text illustrative case examples will be provided. *Unless otherwise stated* these case examples are of women who have taken part in the research and/or I have seen for therapy. Also included are some of the stories of the victims of these women whom I have been able to interview. Everyone whose stories are included gave permission for these to be used provided their anonymity was assured. Thus case examples will be appropriately disguised and/or composite cases will be given based on actual cases in order further to protect confidentiality. Names (not their actual names) will be given for each woman offender so that connections can be made between the case examples to give a fuller picture of the different aspects of the women's lives.

ACKNOWLEDGEMENTS

There have been many people who have helped me greatly in the work presented in this book and to whom I am very grateful.

The person who has most influenced my psychological thinking and my whole approach to working with people is Chris Grulich, Consultant Clinical Psychologist, Leeds Community Mental Health. He has supported me through hearing the very difficult stories the women had to tell me, helped me maintain a sense of perspective in the world and given me the confidence to relate the stories as they are written in this book. It is no exaggeration to say that without his support, both practical and personal, the book would never have been completed. I also want to thank Hilary Eldridge, Clinical Director of the Faithfull Foundation. We have spent many hours sharing thoughts and insights about women who sexually abuse children. She has taught me a great deal and has been very generous in allowing me to use many of her ideas. Through her I have gained access to several of the women who agreed to their stories being included in this research. Other people have also been generous in allowing me to interview women with whom they have been working and in sharing their ideas with me. In particular Mimi Howett, Chartered Forensic Psychologist, was very important in helping me to get access to subjects and she was also influential in my thinking about some of the women offenders. There have been many others who have taught me over the years and whose synthesis of psychological thinking I have used in this work and to whom I am very grateful: particularly Peter Stratton, Jan Burns, Jenny Hewison, John Blundell, John Rodgers, and Jim Wright. I would also like to thank those people who have read chapters of the book, offered me encouragement and very useful comments (including on my spelling and grammar): particularly Sheelagh Rodgers and Alison Wilson, who have read the whole book, and Judith Jones, Gerrilyn Smith, Caroline Plimley, Stephen Morely, Beatrix Campbell, and members of the psychology department of Leeds Community Mental Health, who have each commented on specific chapters. I especially want to thank Sheila Youngson for all her support and importantly for her ability to be succinct, thus helping me cut down the first much too long draft of this book to a readable length. I am grateful to Margaret Lynch for editing the book and Wendy Hudlass at Wiley for having the courage to accept a book on such a potentially controversial issue. Finally, and most importantly, I would like to thank all the women who agreed to take part in this research; those who had sexually abused children and those who had not. Without their trust, cooperation and openness such a book could not exist.

Jacqui Saradjian

1

INTRODUCTION

- THE DENIAL OF 'NORMAL' WOMEN AS SEXUAL AGGRESSORS
- PSYCHOLOGICAL REASONS FOR ENGAGING IN DENIAL
- CONSEQUENCES OF THE DENIAL OF WOMEN AS PERPETRATORS OF CHILD SEXUAL ABUSE FOR THEIR VICTIMS
- TWO SPECIFIC RESPONSES OF VICTIMS WHEN THE PERPETRATOR OF CHILD SEXUAL ABUSE IS A WOMAN
- DEFINING SEXUAL ABUSE BY WOMEN
- WOMEN AS PERPETRATORS OF CHILD SEXUAL ABUSE: ESTIMATING THE EXTENT OF THE PROBLEM
- WOMEN WHO SEXUALLY ABUSE CHILDREN: WHAT THE LITERATURE TELLS US

---

the routine occurrence of child molestation remains a subject from which people prefer to avert their eyes. (Susan Brownmiller, 1975, p.272)

The history of the recognition of any form of child abuse can be seen as a series of stories that we have told ourselves which have allowed us to recognise some realities when we have become ready to do so, but not others. Over the last 10 to 20 years, the stories that have begun to be accepted about the sexual abuse of children have broadened radically and yet each new revelation encounters undiminished resistance.

THE DENIAL OF 'NORMAL' WOMEN AS SEXUAL AGGRESSORS

Secrecy and denial about sexual abuse are still common, particularly when the perpetrator of that abuse is a woman. Robert Wilkins (1990) gives a good example of such denial.

A respected child psychiatrist recently dismissed as 'an obvious fabrication' and a 'physical impossibility' the account of a 7-year-old boy who had described to his teacher how his mother had taken him to bed and placed his 'willy' in her 'fanny' and used her son as a masturbatory implement. (p.1153)

Society's construction of womanhood means that for women to be associated with sexual abuse against children is so contrary to the role set out for them that we try to deny that it occurs or when it does try and find some way to explain it away.

1. 'Inappropriate Affection'

Sexually abusive behaviour of women is often explained away as 'inappropriate affection' or by suggesting that women are 'naturally physically closer to children'. Mothers, in particular, are construed as a special and 'purer' form of womanhood; virtually asexual. One mother, described by Estella Welldon (1988), went to her doctor for help because of her preoccupation with her daughter which involved sexual contact between them. The doctor said that 'it is just natural for a mother to feel very fond of her children' (p.100).

As women in our culture are allowed a much larger scope of physical contact with children than men, confusion can arise as to whether contact with a child is in the normal range or is abusive. Anne Banning (1989) describes 'The Case of Rex'. Rex's mother described him as 'highly sexed' and as liking to fondle her breasts and give her tongue kisses. The mother kissed Rex's penis to comfort him and chased him naked, then, when catching him, biting his bare bottom. Rex was also sexually aggressive towards female children and had inappropriate sexual knowledge. However, the case was not registered as sexual abuse. When Anne Banning presents the identical scenario but with the sexes reversed—a father and a daughter—it is very clear the child is at risk.

2. Denying the Woman Has Full Responsibility for the Sexual Acts She Commits

When there is no alternative but to accept that a woman has sexually abused a child, then we find ways of reducing her responsibility for her behaviour.

Many women are initially coerced by men into sexually abusing children. In these cases, it is generally considered the interest comes from the male and that the female participates under duress. Of course in some cases this is what occurs but many of these women can and do subsequently sexually abuse children of their own volition. Other women who sexually abuse in conjunction with men do so as *equal* partners. One woman, interviewed for this research, targeted male paedophiles in order to jointly sexually abuse children, and another woman coerced a man into sexually abusing a child (see Chapter 8).

If a woman does sexually abuse a child as a sole perpetrator, another tactic used to deny she has full responsibility for her actions is to believe that at the time of her offences, she was somehow 'not in a normal state': for example, if she is mentally ill, of very low intelligence, or under the influence of some mind-altering substance. This belief would be supported by a review of the earlier academic literature citing women who sexually abuse children (Wahl, 1960; Kramer, 1980; Shengold, 1980; Holubinskyj & Foley, 1986; Chasnoff, Burns, Schnoll et al., 1986). Margolin (1986) clearly warned against generalising from these early case studies as it is often the most disturbed women who come to the attention of the authorities. She writes 'the cases are heavily weighted in favour of those who are having severe problems with their lives' (p.107).

In particular some women perpetrators were often judged to be psychotic on the basis of the sexual acts that a woman perpetrated rather than any considered psychiatric examination of her. This still occurs. One young patient hospitalised for severe depression and suicide attempts told the staff about his mother's sexual behaviour with him and pleaded with them not to let him go home. His disclosures were seen as part of his illness, until the mother was actually caught behaving sexually with her son. Although the staff knew the woman well, rather than challenging her about her behaviour, they attempted to admit her as it was decided she must have become psychotic. There is little doubt that *some* women who sexually abuse children are psychotic (e.g. Schreiber, 1973) and others are addicted to various substances (e.g. Chasnoff et al., 1986). What needs to be recognised is that no state of altered consciousness such as these women experience can be said to be *the cause* of the women sexually abusing children. This is a construction made in order to help to distance ourselves, our mothers, our sisters and our daughters from women who carry out these unspeakable acts. The vast majority of women who are diagnosed as being schizophrenic, alcoholic or addicted to any other form of substance, *do not* sexually abuse children. The vast majority of women who *do* sexually abuse children are *not* psychotic, drunken, or drugged when they commit these acts. This is reflected in more recent literature (McCarty, 1986; Faller, 1987; Marvasti, 1986; Krug, 1989; Welldon, 1988; Banning, 1989; Travin, Cullen & Protter, 1990; Speltz, Matthews & Mathews, 1989;

Matthews, Mathews & Speltz, 1991). Just as accounts of sexual abuse by 'normal' men were drastically underreported until there was public recognition that this occurred, so might also be the case for sexual abuse of children by women.

3. Construing a Woman Who Sexually Abuses Children As 'Evil' or 'Other'

If we cannot deny or reconstruct a woman's behaviour, excuse it or project the responsibility for her behaviour onto a man, then often greater anger is generated towards the woman. For a woman to become a sexual aggressor against a child or children, is seen as a greater deviation than if the same act/s were committed by a man. An illustration of society's increased abhorrence towards perverse behaviour on the part of women compared to men, is the case of Myra Hindley. Myra Hindley and her partner, Ian Brady, were convicted in 1965 of the abduction and murder of three children. There were tapes, photographs and journals that indicated that the children were also sexually assaulted. Very few male child-killers, not even her partner Ian Brady, have attracted such virulent hatred as Myra Hindley, yet the actual part she played in these offences has never been completely revealed. At the time of her trial, Myra Hindley said nothing. She refused to say what society wanted to hear, *whether it was the truth or not*: that she was forced by Brady, coerced into committing these offences, that she tried to protect the children but was helpless and could only do *his* will. If she had done so she would have protected our ideals of woman-hood and maybe would be free today. While not denying the seriousness or the perversity of her offences, it is argued that it is for going against the expectation of her as a woman, that she is still so condemned. As Cameron and Fraser (1987) conclude: 'Myra Hindley's real crime was hubris; she went against the sex role laid down by the gods and nature' (p.146).

PSYCHOLOGICAL REASONS FOR ENGAGING IN DENIAL

Most of the barriers that prevent the acceptance of women as perpetrators of child sexual abuse come from our society's construction of womanhood. All of us, through our interactions with the world, produce models or schema which help us to predict and interpret our experience (see Chapter 10). Basically these are guides which help us make sense of the world. Whether an experience is positive or negative, if it is not predictable within our schema, our sense of competence, and hence our security, is threatened

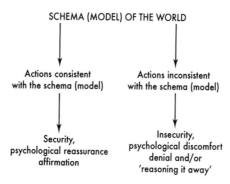

Figure 1.1:

and the natural human response to this is feelings of anxiety and/or anger (Figure 1.1).

Socialisation in today's culture leads to completely different models, and thus expectations, of men and women. Our construction of maleness readily accommodates a lack of expectation of men to be carers and nurturers, an expectation that men's needs should and will be catered for, including overt aggression, sexual initiation and even sexual assault. Consequently when a man sexually abuses a child, it does not dramatically change the generally held schema of men, as it is within the range of predictability. Conversely, socialisation facilitates the acceptance of a general schema of femaleness as being nurturing, protecting, and caring, there to meet the needs of others, often at personal expense, non-aggressive, and asexual, except in response to men's desires. Consequently, when a woman sexually abuses a child, it is perceived as so contrary to the acceptable socially constructed schema of femaleness that it is not predictable. This unpredictability makes us feel great psychological discomfort. Therefore we try to deny it or find some other explanation for it, as previously described, in order to maintain our security in our model of the world.

No matter how sexually aggressive the acts the women perpetrate are, attempts are made, unfortunately often by a professional, to reinterpret them as being 'a misguided extension of love'. Thus this reinterpretation is in keeping with the model of a woman as nurturant and caring. If we cannot deny that the acts that the women perpetrate are actually sexually motivated then responsibility is reattributed. If it cannot be attributed to the 'force of a man' (i.e. the woman was coerced into the behaviour) or to the fact that the woman is in some state of altered consciousness (i.e. that she is 'not in her right mind' mad, drunk, drugged, or of very low intelligence), then great anger towards the woman is aroused. We then attempt to maintain our schema by regarding her as virtually 'inhuman'.

CONSEQUENCES OF THE DENIAL OF WOMEN AS PERPETRATORS OF CHILD SEXUAL ABUSE FOR THEIR VICTIMS

I picked up a book in a shop and was at first ecstatic, and relieved, to at last see a book on sexual abuse that had a chapter in it entitled, 'Female Incest Perpetrators' [Russell, 1986]. As I began to read it, my anger mounted . . . it said 'not only was incestuous abuse by female perpetrators very rare, it also appears to be less serious and less traumatic than incestuous abuse by male perpetrators' [p.298]. I was sexually abused by my mother from before I can remember until I was 8 years old. I have spent the last 30 years, most of my adolescent and adult life, in and out of mental hospitals, in various states of psychic distress. At last I'm getting the help I need. I am now 43. (Linda is the daughter of Sophia who was interviewed for this research.)

There is no model of trauma that would indicate that sexual abuse perpetrated by a female would be any less traumatic than that perpetrated by a male. Yet it is frequently stated this is so, regardless of the fact that there have been very few studies to date that have considered the impact of sexual abuse according to the gender of the perpetrator and its interaction with the gender of the child. The general belief that sexual abuse by a male results in greater trauma than sexual abuse by a female perpetrator is widely held. Finkelhor (1984) reports on 521 parents asked about the seriousness of different experiences of sexual abuse. They perceived the actions of female perpetrators, with both male and female victims, as less abusive than those of male perpetrators.

The belief that to be sexually abused by a woman is less harmful than by a man is now known to be erroneous. The interviews with the survivors of the women perpetrators in this research as well as descriptions of the lives of other survivors of sexual abuse by female perpetrators (e.g. Elliot, 1993) indicate that these survivors suffer the same range of symptoms— psychological, behavioural and physical—as do victims of male perpetrators of child sexual abuse.

It can be argued that the very denial of the fact that women can and do sexually abuse children can compound the effects of that abuse for the victim. This argument is considered in relation to one of the most commonly applied models, the *Traumagenic Dynamics in the Impact of Child Sexual Abuse* (Browne & Finkelhor, 1986): *Traumatic sexualisation, Stigmatisation, Powerlessness, Betrayal.*

1. Traumatic Sexualisation

Traumatic sexualisation relates to how sexual abuse distorts the child's sexual development. Children can become confused between sex and affection. In the case of the female offender, with the social construction of women as carers, nurturers and asexual beings, the link for the child between care-getting, care-giving and sex is likely to be even more distorted. As women are perceived by society as ostensibly non-sexually aggressive beings, victims often employ the defence of construing themselves as the sexual aggressors, or at the very least 'equal partners' to protect the model of the asexual female carer. In the case of adolescent boys, this is supported by society who see them as 'lucky' or in some way to be envied for being sexually abused by an older woman, while the victims themselves feel great distress.

CASE EXAMPLE 1.1

A 14-year-old runaway boy was being sexually assaulted by a 39-year-old woman in return for a roof over his head. The investigating police officer said '. . . he fell right on his feet there didn't he . . . lucky sod'.

2. Stigmatisation

Stigmatisation relates to the negative messages the child receives through the interactions with the abuser, some explicit, some implicit, and the negative messages the child believes it receives from society. The child's rationalisations or attempts to understand his or her experiences will reflect society's perceptions. With abuse by women being perceived as very rare, and women, particularly mothers, being construed as generally 'good', both boys and girls may conclude that they bear even greater guilt in relation to the abuse, and a greater shame and a greater sense of their own 'badness'. The woman can actively encourage this belief. The other aspect of stigmatisation is that of feeling that the activity that is engaged in is deviant and taboo. This dynamic must be exacerbated when the perpetrator is a woman, especially if the perpetrator is the mother.

As sexual abuse by a female is less recognised by society, the need for secrecy and the fear of disbelief appear to be greater, even after the abuse is over. Very crucial for any victim is the reaction received at the time of disclosure. Victims of female perpetrators describe very damaging reactions of shock, disbelief, and minimalisation to disclosure of their abuse, including being told they must be confused about who the abuser was or what really had happened to them.

CASE EXAMPLE 1.2

When Linda tried to talk about being sexually abused by her mother in psychiatric hospital, she was told she was suffering from delusions and was medicated. Over the next 20 years Linda made three attempts at therapy. When she said her mother had sexually abused her, her first therapist referred her back to psychiatry; her second told her it was 'really her father but it was safer for her to believe that it was her mother' and her third told her she had false memories implanted by previous therapists.

3. Powerlessness

Powerlessness is caused when the needs and desires of the child are subsumed by those of the abuser, not least by the repeated invasion of the child's body. Thus the child feels no control over the environment, or even his or her own body. Fear from direct and/or indirect threats of the abuser also enhances the child's feelings of powerlessness. The degree of powerlessness a victim feels is exacerbated by how prolonged the abuse is, by having few other significant relationships, and by increased aggression, either physical or verbal. Our knowledge of female perpetrators would indicate they target a child and tend to abuse that child over a long period of time. They are often isolated, so the child seldom has any other significant relationships that are non-abusive. The feelings of powerlessness would be particularly profound if the abuser was the victim's mother or primary carer, as is so often the case with female offenders. Children see their parents as omnipotent. With victims of *intra-familial abuse* by females, if a child is sexually abused by a sole parent, or both parents, this omnipotence becomes malevolent. Thus the child develops the belief that the world is malevolent and s/he is powerless.

4. Betrayal

Betrayal is the realisation on the part of the child that someone who should care for them, and on whom they are dependent, causes them harm.

Betrayal is far greater if there is an expectation that the abuser should care for the child. Society's construction of females as trustworthy, carers, and non-abusers means that sexual abuse by a woman is likely to be perceived as even a greater betrayal than that by a man. One victim reflected the sentiments of several other victims when she stated: 'You expect it of men, don't you, you are aware, you know what men are like, but you'd never expect a woman to do that would you, I mean they just don't'. The degree of betrayal is related to the closeness of the relationship. The majority of women who sexually abuse children target those children who are closest to them, often their own. Thus the relationship betrayed is likely to be an important one. This sense of betrayal frequently leads to great anger on the part of victims of women who sexually abuse children.

TWO SPECIFIC RESPONSES OF VICTIMS WHEN THE PERPETRATOR OF CHILD SEXUAL ABUSE IS A WOMAN

1. Anger

Subjective reports from victims indicate that when both a male and a female have sexually abused a child, it is towards the woman they commonly feel most anger. Sgroi and Sargent (1993) comment on clients who had been sexually abused by both men and women:

> all seven of the adult female clients reported a perception that sexual abuse by a first degree female relative was the most shameful and damaging childhood victimisation they had suffered. (Sgroi & Sargent, 1993, p.23)

Similarly many of the victims of the women in this study who had been conjointly abused by a man and a woman described feeling more betrayed by, and holding more anger towards, the woman than the man.

CASE EXAMPLE 1.3

'She got away with it because she said he beat up on her ... well he did but that weren't no excuse ... she were just pathetic ... weak ... and I hate her. She let him do it to me and she did it too. It were disgusting ... really disgusting. I want her to die ... what he did was bad, but I'll never forgive her.' (Her father had had intercourse with her *before* he coerced her mother into abusing her. *On his explicit instructions* she had massaged her daughter's breasts, masturbated her and had performed cunnilingus on her.)

CASE EXAMPLE 1.4

'I never did anything to the kids unless he was there ... I was dead scared of him ... it repulsed me as much as it repulsed them. I just can't understand the kids reaction, two of them won't talk to either of us, I understand that but the other two ... John writes to him every week and he got Susan to go with him to see him in prison ... neither of them write to me, nor visit. I did get one letter ... It was full of hatred ... yet they're willing to see him.'

The aetiology of this anger is clearly very complex and warrants some reflection if insight is to be gained into the experiences of the victims. Anger is one of the emotions aroused when there is a perceived threat to an individual's basic survival needs; care-giving, care-receiving, competence and power (Gilbert, 1988). The experience of being sexually abused would threaten each of these basic needs and thus is likely to generate anger. Even very young sexually abused children who have experienced very little . cultural socialisation have been found to exhibit high levels of anger (Tufts, 1984). This anger tends to be directed towards the female whatever the role she plays in the abuse: sole perpetrator; co-perpetrator; coerced perpetrator; and even when the female is a non-abusing parent (Herman, 1981; DeYoung, 1982; Briere, 1984).

A possible explanation of the root and direction of this anger is proposed here. Sexual abuse is a source of great stress. When stress is experienced attachment figures are sought to alleviate that stress. If the primary attachment figure is emotionally unavailable, and thus relief of stress does not occur, anger and anxiety are evoked. Such anger towards an unavailable attachment figure has been observed even in very young children. The function of this anger is protest, to deter the attachment figure from the feared abandonment.

When a male abuses, the child experiences extreme stress but is rarely able to turn to the primary attachment figure (the mother) for comfort. Thus she is perceived by the child as being unavailable and anger is directed towards her. This does not occur in the reverse situation because when a woman sexually abuses a child, it is often the child to whom she is a primary attachment figure that she abuses. The child is also unlikely to have any expectations of the father as primary attachment figure, thus the anger is solely directed towards the female perpetrator. Often it may be too dangerous for this anger to be expressed at the time towards an adult on whom the child is dependent. Consequently it becomes internalised and repressed, resulting in various symptoms of distress.

2. Enmeshment and Identity

Another major issue for so many victims of women perpetrators of child sexual abuse was that of the difficulty in establishing personal identity and separation from the female abuser and primary caregiver. Enmeshment is particularly a problem for the victims when their abuser was their own mother. As the perpetrator and the primary attachment figure are usually one, this compounds a basic human dilemma—separating from mother. All the issues of separation and individuation each human infant experiences are even more complex when the mother is using the child's body as an extension of her own, to gratify some need within her. Several victims discussed their real suffering in dealing with the enmeshment they felt with their abuser. One young woman said, 'I feel totally swallowed up by her; I see her, smell her, feel her breath on my body', and a young man said 'Wherever I go, whatever I do, I still feel as if her body is engulfing mine'. One woman went through large amounts of plastic surgery to make herself physically different from her mother who sexually abused her. On two occasions I have been told of women who had been sexually abused by their mothers (not victims of the women in this study), wanting to have a 'sex-change'. This epitomises the difficulties these victims have in forming an identity separate from that of their abuser. Even physical separation can be extremely difficult to achieve. Conversely some victims repeatedly go back to their abusers, hoping for a positive response. Mahler and her colleagues (1975) describe the need for individuation, which is the developmental process of achieving intrapsychic autonomy and separation which involves differentiating and disengaging from the mother. Although these stages originate in infancy they continue throughout childhood. This process is often a source of difficulty for children of both sexes but will be specifically exacerbated by the mother's sexual abuse of the child. The inability to complete these developmental tasks leads to severe psychopathology which in adolescents and adults is often labelled as borderline personality disorder (Meissner, 1988). It can also lead to such a crisis of identity that a psychotic breakdown ensues.

DEFINING SEXUAL ABUSE BY WOMEN

That she might seduce a helpless child into sex play is unthinkable, and even if she did so, what harm could be done without a penis? (Mathis, 1972, p.54).

Due to the greater level of intimacy allowed to females than to males in relation to children, it has been found to be more helpful to be specific about the actual acts involved than to follow a general definition of child sexual abuse. Christine Lawson (1993) groups these acts into five specific categories: subtle, seductive, perverse, overt and sadistic. *These forms of abuse are not mutually exclusive, women may abuse in one or all of these ways or may progress from one form of abuse to another.*

> **Subtle abuse** is 'behaviours that may not be intentionally sexual in nature but serve to meet the parents' emotional needs and/or sexual needs at the expense of the child's emotional and or developmental needs' (Lawson, 1993, p. 265).

Examples of when subtle sexual abuse occurs include a woman frequently sharing a bed with a child, bathing or massaging a child of an age when it is inappropriate for her to do so, asking the child to massage or bath her, obsessively washing a child's genitals and/or repeatedly giving a child enemas. Valarie Sinason (October 1993) gave examples of the effects of subtle abuse by drawing causal connections between the disturbed and aggressive behaviour of adolescent boys and the fact that they were sleeping in their mothers' beds. Regardless of the fact that there appeared to be no overt sexual contact, the inappropriateness of this behaviour had considerable effects on the children's emotional adjustment.

CASE EXAMPLE 1.5

A 15-year-old boy was referred due to his very aggressive behaviour which had started when he was 10 years old. He had often hit his mother causing bruising, he had broken her ribs and had twice tried to strangle her. This aggression had generalised to other women. The mother, who had psoriasis and eczema, had been left by her violent husband when her son was nine. She then saw her son as her adult partner. He had slept in her bed in case she should feel ill in the night; she made him rub cream all over her naked body saying it was too difficult for her to do this, and also required him to help her in and out of the bath and to wash her. Although there was never any *overt* sexual intention in the acts, the boy disclosed feelings of sexual arousal while carrying out these tasks. He described feeling it was his duty to care for his mother and yet feeling disgusted by what he had to do. The combination of this arousal and disgust was very disturbing to him and led to his fury with his mother.

> **Seductive abuse** is defined as 'sexual stimulation that is inappropriate for the child's age and/or is motivated by the (woman's) sexual needs' (Lawson, 1993, p.266).

Behaviours may include exhibitionist displays of nudity or sexual behaviour, exposure to pornographic materials or exposure to seductive posing, gestures or verbal messages (Bolton, Morris & MacEachron, 1989, as quoted in Lawson, 1993).

CASE EXAMPLE 1.6

A man sought therapy for severe depression and his destructive relationships with women, in which he either treated them as a 'mother' or insisted they behave as a 'whore' and then physically and emotionally abused them. He disclosed that, aged 14, he had run away from home due to his stepmother's behaviour. She was only 22, and when his father (aged 40) was away on business, she would walk naked into his bedroom after he had gone to bed. She would stand stroking her breasts and clitoris and inserting her fingers into her vagina, telling him that he needed to know what a woman liked to have done to her so 'he would be a good lover and not a beast like his father'. As she was touching herself she would ask if he were aroused and how hard his penis was. The boy did frequently become aroused to the point of orgasm which upset him. He began barricading the door to his bedroom, however his stepmother continued the behaviour in other places. This led to the boy running away.

Perverse abuse occurs when the child's sexual development is distorted by the behaviours of the abuser.

For example, a male child being forced to wear female clothing; a child's sexual development being criticised; a child being made to feel their sexuality is something corrupt or to be afraid of.

CASE EXAMPLE 1.7

A woman was so afraid of her daughter's sexual maturity that she bound her developing breasts and insisted that she wear clothing more suitable for a much younger child. The mother refused to allow her daughter to go out anywhere without her and if she showed any interest in dressing more age appropriately, in using make-up or in boys, her mother became extremely angry, called her a whore and beat her. The daughter was a product of rape in the mother's adolescence for which she blamed herself. She was therefore determined that her daughter would not 'bring such an experience on herself'.

Overt sexual abuse is defined as overt sexual contact between a (woman) and (a child). 'Overt sexual abuse involves some form of coercion and or threats to discourage disclosure' (Lawson, 1993, p.266).

Behaviours include the full range of sexual behaviours: intercourse, attempted intercourse, fondling of the child's genitals, engaging the child in fondling the woman's genitals and/or breasts, cunnilingus, fellatio, anilingus, penetration of the vagina and/or anus by digits and/or objects, sexualised kissing and touching (Faller, 1987; Margolin, 1986; Speltz, Matthews & Mathews, 1989; Matthews, Matthews & Speltz, 1991; Bolton, Morris & MacEachron, 1989).

CASE EXAMPLE 1.8

'I used to go round to her when I truanted from school. She always had time for me and we'd get videos out and watch them on her TV. . .we didn't have a video at home. She'd get in crisps and pop. I began 'bunking-off'. . . until I was hardly at school. It started with us snuggling up watching a film and then she started playing with my hair, kissing my neck. . . . Then she began to get out films with more sex in them and the next thing we were doing it [having sex]. We did everything and if she ran out of ideas, we'd get out real sex films and do what we saw . . . I liked the attention and she made me feel very special. I was never comfortable with it though, I always felt dirty afterwards. If I started to tell her I didn't want to do it any more, she told me I must be homosexual so I felt I had to. If I didn't go round she told me she'd tell what we'd done. She said that people didn't understand relationships like ours and I'd go to prison. I believed her.' (The woman was 33 years old and the boy was 13.)

Sadistic sexual abuse includes (female) 'sexual behaviour that is intended to hurt the child and may be part of a general pattern of severe physical and emotional abuse' (Lawson, 1993, p.266).

Examples of sadistic sexual behaviour are insertion of objects into the vagina or anus; beating and/or bruising the child's genitals; rubbing and scrubbing the child's genitals until they are sore. The most extreme form of sadistic sexual abuse can involve cutting of the child's genitals.

CASE EXAMPLE 1.9

'The worst [sexual abuse] were when she were angry. It was always when she were angry but I never knew what made her angry. . . It were as if she wanted to tear me apart inside. She'd sometimes grab whatever were nearest to her and come at me. She'd insert anything into me 'down there', sometimes it were all her fingers, she'd push them at me really hard, sometimes it were a bottle neck or a brush handle, once or twice it were a knife and once rose stems. That were awful . . . I often bled but she never took me to the hospital or anything. I bled so often that when I started my periods I didn't realise, I just thought it were more bleeding from what she'd done.' (These activities had occurred from early infancy until she ran away from home when she was 12;

sometimes the abuse was overt and sometimes sadistic. The victim was frequently admitted to psychiatric hospitals suffering from severe depression. She took repeated overdoses, frequently self-mutilated her arms, legs and vagina and was addicted to a variety of psychotropic substances.)

WOMEN AS PERPETRATORS OF CHILD SEXUAL ABUSE: ESTIMATING THE EXTENT OF THE PROBLEM

A literature review to date has revealed no British or American study that has *specifically* addressed what percentage of children are sexually abused by a woman. The prevailing data are therefore a by-product of general sexual abuse prevalence studies which are beset by methodological hazards (Finkelhor, 1986). Hence what follows is a makeshift assessment and can only be considered as a tentative guide. Finkelhor and Russell (1984), surveying the data then available, concluded that of all children who had been sexually abused:

> The percentage of sexual contact by older females to be about 20% (range 14–27%) for male children and about 5% (range 0–10%) for female children. (Finkelhor & Russell, 1984, p.179)

To obtain some idea of what that means in actual numbers this finding needs to be considered in relation to the prevalence of child sexual abuse within the general population. Bagley and King (1990) reviewed the major prevalence studies to date, taking into account the principal sources of inconsistency of the work they reviewed. They concluded that:

> **Serious sexual abuse** in childhood (up to the age of 16 or 17) involving unwanted or coerced sexual contact occurs in *at least 15% of females* in the populations surveyed and *in at least 5% of males*. Because of various methodological factors, *these are likely to be the most conservative or minimum estimates.* (Bagley & King, 1990, p.70)

Although it is not statistically correct to do so, if these data are combined and translated into actual numbers, a very rough estimate can be obtained for the scale of the problem: one in every hundred girls and one in every hundred boys suffer *serious sexual assault* by an older female in childhood. These figures suggest that the belief that children are rarely sexually abused by women needs reconsideration, especially as this is certainly an underestimation due to low levels of disclosure.

Disclosure of child sexual abuse is less likely if people believe the experience is extraordinary in any way, or that they will not be believed, or if the abuser is particularly closely related. These are all factors particularly cogent to female perpetrators. Another factor contributing to the difficulty of establishing accurate prevalence rates is that of the tendency of human beings to repress incidents of severe trauma from conscious awareness, especially when that trauma begins at an early age. Some child victims of sexual abuse, in particular those whose abuse began at an early age, use unconscious techniques such as repression, depersonalisation, or the development of multiple personalities as survival mechanisms when faced with severely traumatic experiences (Cole & Putnam, 1992). There is a growing awareness of the number of infants that are sexually abused (e.g. MacFarlane & Waterman, 1986; Hanks, Hobbs & Wynne, 1988). Much of the knowledge that we have to date seems to point to the sexual abuse of a greater number of women's victims beginning in this age range (Faller, 1988; Speltz, Matthews & Mathews, 1989). Sexual abuse at this pre-verbal stage of development has powerful consequences for the child's development in fundamental areas such as sense of self, self-regulatory functions, trust in others and sensitivity in social relations (Cole & Putnam, 1992). Reporting of the occurrence of this abuse when older however, will be limited by the inability of pre-verbal infants to verbally process and conceptualise such a traumatic experience, thus it may remain outside their accessible consciousness.

Male victims also find it difficult to disclose any form of sexual abuse. Due to their socialisation to be sexual initiators they find it aversive to admit to sexual subjugation. This aversion is magnified if the abuser is a woman. Many boys, particularly those sexually abused as adolescents, cognitively reframe their experience as sexual exploration or even as being sexual aggressor, in an attempt to maintain consistency with this role of sexual initiator (Bolton, Morris and MacEachron, 1989).

CASE EXAMPLE 1.10

During a psychotic breakdown a young man of 17 repeatedly said he had 'raped' his mother. When all other symptoms abated, he continued to talk about the 'rape'. Several years later, and free of psychosis, he entered therapy, his symptoms still being related to the 'rapes' of his mother. He began to talk about sexual contact with his mother from the age of 10 when she had begun to massage his body. She told him that his body was changing, growing and developing, and she needed to make sure that his 'hormones were evenly distributed'. This led to her masturbating him, fellating him and eventually, in his early teens, to intercourse. The patient very slowly began to recognise that it was in fact his mother who had sexually assaulted him. He eventually chose to confront his mother who admitted to her behaviours.

There have been studies of special populations such as serial rapists (Burgess, Hazelwood, Rokous, et al., 1987); rapists (Petrovich & Templar, 1984) and incest offenders (MacFarlane, 1982) that have shown a high rate of sexual abusive experiences in childhood perpetrated by a woman (Saradjian, 1992). Studies of special populations, however, should not be generalised. For example, the high percentage of women perpetrators found in studies of sexual abuse of children in Day Care (Finkelhor, 1988) is unsurprising considering the vast majority of staff in Day Care are women.

No matter how we refine our studies or ask the question, it is highly unlikely that the number of children that are sexually abused by women will equal the number sexually abused by men, but the assumption that child sexual abuse is *solely* a male crime needs to be redressed. Tilman Furniss summed up the existing situation when he said: 'my feeling is that the total will turn out to be less than 50% of all abusers but less than 50% is a long way from the perceived wisdom of 2%' (Tilman Furniss, *The Spectator*, 1991).

WOMEN WHO SEXUALLY ABUSE CHILDREN: WHAT THE LITERATURE TELLS US

Much of the literature relating to women who sexually abuse children is in the form of case studies. As more women abusers are being recognised attempts have been made to group the women together to look at common characteristics. From the therapeutic work carried out in treatment centres with women who have sexually abused children, typologies of female offenders denoted by the primary mode of their abuse appear to be emerging. McCarty (1986) reviewed the case records of 26 women who had sexually abused children. Twelve of these women were independent offenders and nine were co-offenders with a male partner. Five women who did not actually sexually abuse children but were so collusive in facilitating the sexual abuse by men that they were convicted, were also included in the study. McCarty suggests relatively distinct patterns of behaviour and characteristics for independent perpetrators, co-offenders and accomplices. Similar typologies with more detailed findings have been reported by Speltz, Matthews and Mathews (1989; Matthews, Mathews & Speltz, 1991, $n = 16$). They were engaged in working therapeutically with women in the Genesis II Female Sex Offender Program. As a result of this work they proposed three distinct categories of female offenders: *male-coerced offenders, teacher-lovers* (primarily target adolescents), and *inter-generationally predisposed offenders* (primarily targeting very young children). Speltz, Matthews and Mathews (1989; Matthews, Mathews &

Table 1.1: Characteristics implicated to be of aetiological significance in the sexual abuse of children by women

CHARACTERISTIC OF THE WOMAN OR OF HER EXPERIENCE	LITERATURE THAT IMPLICATES THIS FACTOR
Low self-esteem, feelings of inadequacy and vulnerability	Groth (1982); Krug (1989); Speltz, Matthews & Mathews (1989); Matthews, Mathews & Speltz (1991); Travin, Cullen & Protter (1990); Rowan, Rowan & Langelier (1990); Faller (1987);
Troubled childhoods	McCarty (1986); Allen (1991); Speltz, Matthews & Mathews (1989); Matthews, Mathews & Speltz (1991); Travin, Cullen & Protter (1990); Rowan, Rowan & Langelier (1990)
Sexually abused as a child	McCarty (1986); Faller (1987 – 47.5%); Speltz, Matthews & Mathews (1989); Matthews, Mathews & Speltz (1991); Travin, Cullen & Protter (1990); Rowan, Rowan & Langelier (1990)
Lack nurturance	Groth (1982)
Need for nurturance and control is prominent	Krug 1989); Welldon (1988); Allen (1991)
Early marriage	Wahl (1960); McCarty (1986)
Close age gap between woman and child	Wahl (1960); Groth (1982); Faller (1987); Speltz, Matthews & Mathews (1989); Matthews, Mathews & Speltz (1991)
Experiences a sense of aloneness, isolation and separation from others	Groth (1982); McCarty (1986); Welldon (1988); Chasnoff et al. (1986); Travin, Cullen, & Protter (1990)
Woman alone or her partner away a great deal	Holubinskyj & Foley (1986); Kramer (1980); Krug (1989); Mayer (1983)
She seeks substitute gratification with the child	Shengold (1980); McCarty (1986); Wahl (1960); Margolis (1977); Mayer (1983); Krug (1989); Lidz & Lidz (1969)
Relationships with male peers are often negative and abusive	Speltz, Matthews & Mathews (1989); Matthews, Mathews & Speltz (1991); Allen (1991)

Table 1.1: (*continued*)

CHARACTERISTIC OF THE WOMAN OR OF HER EXPERIENCE	LITERATURE THAT IMPLICATES THIS FACTOR
History of indiscriminate or compulsive sexual activity	Groth (1982); Wahl (1960); Meiselman (1978); Speltz, Matthews & Mathews (1989); Matthews, Mathews & Speltz (1991); Allen (1991)
Severe psychological disturbance or mental illness	Wahl (1960); McCarty (1986–50%); Mayer (1983); Shengold (1980); Meiselman (1978); Kramer (1980); Holubinskyj & Foley (1986); Rowan, Rowan & Langelier (1990); Faller (1987–7.5%)
Women are addicted to psychotropic substances, e.g. alcohol, heroin, etc.	Groth (1982); Allen (1991); Speltz, Matthews & Mathews (1989); Matthews, Mathews & Speltz (1991); McCarty (1986–46%); Allen (1962); Faller (1987); Wahl (1960); Margolis (1977), Chasnoff et al. (1986); Meiselman (1978)
Mothers who abuse children treat them as extensions of themselves	McCarty (1986); Welldon (1988); Kramer (1980); Lidz & Lidz (1969)
The relationship is unsatisfactory and parasitic	Kramer (1980)
The child may be unwanted or the wrong sex	Welldon (1988); Kramer (1980)
The woman is 'stuck' in the relationship with her own mother	Welldon (1988)

Speltz, 1991) do suggest that severely psychologically disturbed offenders may be another category. However, although this is the group previously most commonly reported on in the professional literature—those women with a history of severe psychiatric or psychotic difficulties—there was only one woman that Speltz, Matthews and Mathews believe would have fitted into this category. As she dropped out of the treatment at an early stage, they felt that not enough was known about her to substantiate classification.

Research to date has indicated that the life histories of abusers, their relationships, and their social circumstances, are related to the genesis of sexually abusive behaviour. Throughout this literature various factors have been described that have been considered to contribute to the aetiology of child sexual abuse by women. Different factors have been highlighted that reflect the theoretical orientation of the writer/s. These are summarised in Table 1.1. It is clear that not all women who sexually abuse children display all the characteristics described in the table. It is also clear that multitudinous women exhibit these same characteristics who do not sexually abuse children. The aim has therefore been to discover if there is a particular combination of factors held by women who sexually abuse children that lead to the expression of this behaviour. The typologies and case studies previously presented are important in pointing to such factors. However, one of the main drawbacks has been the absence of control or comparison groups. It is only through the use of such groups that we can begin to understand how women who sexually abuse children differ from other women. Such knowledge would lead to more specific, appropriate and effective help to prevent women offending and reoffending.

WHO THE WOMEN WERE AND HOW THEY TOLD THEIR STORIES

- HOW THE STORIES WERE TOLD
- THE WOMEN WHO TOOK PART IN THE STUDY
- THE CHILDREN WHOM THE WOMEN SEXUALLY ABUSED AND THE ACTS PERPETRATED
- SUMMARY

HOW THE STORIES WERE TOLD

Working with sexual offenders is like walking unbeknown into a maze. One of the most effective tools to use is a map. The trick is to arrive at an accurate map. The offender's life history provides the map of meaning for sexually abusive behaviour. (Janis Bremer, 1989)

1. Rationale behind the Choice of Information Collected

Research with both juveniles and male offenders has indicated that the genesis of sexually abusive behaviour is related to the life history of the abuser. However, it is not solely what happens to people or the relationships they have that affects their lives, but each person's individual perception and interpretation of that experience. Kelly (1955) saw people as having individual construct systems which they applied to every experience. Thus two people may have similar objective experience but have very different subjective realities. The amalgamation of these factors, the experiences in conjunction with the individual's perception of those experiences, forms the basis of an individual's map of life.

In talking both to women who had, and to those who had not, sexually abused children, and getting sight of their maps, we can begin to identify the different routes that these women have taken, whether freely or enforced, that have brought some of them to sexually abuse children. In identifying the similarities and differences between the maps, it is hoped that it will be possible to ascertain whether a particular route leads to a particular form of sexual abuse of children and thus to the appropriate areas in which to effect intervention and prevention.

2. From Maps to Mathematical Analysis

As a therapist, my task is to develop a mutual language with each individual client, to enable her to see her own map. In doing so, she and I come to a shared understanding of how she came to think, feel and behave as she does, so that she may choose to change, or not, as she wishes. As a clinical researcher, my task is to translate the language of each client's map into the language of research, so that each individual's map becomes open to scientific analysis and hence comparable with the maps of other clients. In this way other researchers and therapists can gain a shared understanding of what these clients have in common, that makes them come to think, feel and behave as they do. Thus, using therapeutic techniques, we can gain information that can be analysed via research methods, giving theoretical insights that can in turn, improve the therapeutic process.

The map will of necessity be complex, if it is to be at all useful in helping us understand such a multifarious event as the sexual abuse of a child. It will require the teller to describe her journey as candidly as possible as well as detailing her interactions with many others she has encountered along her way.

The listener needs to be aware of the psychological processes involved in telling of such journeys and attempt to be an honest witness, taking a credulous approach as unimpeded as possible by preconceptions and a judgemental stance.

As these journeys are being described retrospectively, they will have inherent limitations. Therefore care must be taken to check the reliability of the information. The way in which the journeys are to be described is therefore guided by the researcher. The teller will be asked to describe each route in several ways, in order to check whether the map remains consistent.

In the language of researchers, this is called the technique of multiple methods; using more than one method, qualitative and/or quantitative, to obtain similar pieces of information, in doing so achieving a level of internal reliability. This 'is a form of triangulation in which different types of data provide cross-data validity checks' (Patton, 1990, p.238).

3. Methods of Collecting the Information

1. A structured interview was constructed on the basis of a review of the currently available literature relating to female perpetrators of child sexual abuse. This related to: relationships in childhood; abuse histories; education; work histories; relationships as adults; religious beliefs; stress; coping strategies; their health, both physical and mental; sexual behaviour and fantasy life; and their beliefs about and relationships with children.

2. The women were asked to fill in a rating scale—partially provided, partially derived from the woman—related to their perceptions of the children in their lives.

3. Repertory Grid (Kelly,1955) accessed a view of how the women saw themselves, as well as significant people in their lives.

4. The women's own sense of the level of stress that they experienced and the social support network available to them, was accessed via a Dependency Grid (Kelly, 1955)

5. As the abusive behaviour was sexual, it was felt it was important to look at the meaning of sex for the women. As no published test was available specifically related to this issue, one was constructed.

6. The Rosenberg Self-Esteem Questionnaire provided a further measure of the women's perception of self.

NB: Details of these questionnaires are provided in Appendix 3.

4. Analysis of the Information Collected—For the More Statistically Minded!

The Repertory Grid was analysed using the GRAN Computer Program for the Analysis of Repertory Grid Data devised by Leach (1988). The area of particular interest from the grid was the distances (Euclidean Distances) between particular elements. As the constructs were provided, a traditional construct analysis was not included but comparisons were made between the ratings given to specific constructs for specified elements. Non-parametric tests were used throughout to analyse the data. Being an independent groups design, the data were subjected to Kruskal–Wallis tests; with Dunn's post hoc multiple comparisons to establish where the differences between groups lay. The Level of Significance used was the conventionally accepted 5% ($p \leq 0.05$) which was adjusted appropriately for the multiple comparisons. The results of the 'What Sex Means' questionnaire are purely descriptive and should only be considered in this context.

THE WOMEN WHO TOOK PART IN THE STUDY

1. Criteria for Inclusion of the Women Offenders

A woman offender was included in the study if it had been substantiated that she had perpetrated a sexual act on a child. This substantiation was in line with that of Finkelhor (1988): 'the investigating agencies had decided that sexual abuse had occurred and that it had been perpetrated by the woman who was to be interviewed'. By the time the interview was carried out, all bar one offender had admitted to the sexual abuse she had perpetrated (this woman is described as 'an equal partner' in Chapter 9). All the women were known to the relevant child protection agencies.

2. How the Subjects Became Involved in the Study

Nationally known agencies who worked with victims and/or perpetrators of child sexual abuse were contacted and asked if any women perpetrators were known to them who would be willing to take part in the study. Many female perpetrators of child sexual abuse were contacted via this route. While attending conferences, both as a delegate and as a speaker, professionals talked of female perpetrators within various agencies— social services, probation, and mental health—and arranged for them to take part in the study. Four women perpetrators were accessed via adult survivors. Thus the women came from all parts of the British Isles. The sample could not have been randomly chosen due to the small number of women perpetrators currently known who would be willing and able to take part in the research.

3. The Allocation of Women to Specific Groups

Fifty women who were known to have sexually abused children are reported on in this text. They were divided into groups via the mode of the sexual abuse that they perpetrated, initially using the model devised by Speltz, Matthews and Mathews (1989; Matthews, Mathews & Speltz, 1991): Predisposed Offenders, *women who initially targeted very young children* Teacher-lover Offenders, *women who initially targeted adolescents*; and Male-coerced offenders, *women who were initially coerced into offending by men*. As the research progressed, it was recognised that these groups were not able to encompass all the women. Some women, ten in all, will be discussed separately as *'atypical perpetrators'*. In addition, four women were interviewed who had been involved as *perpetrators in the ritual abuse of children*. Such abuse is considered to be qualitatively different from other forms of sexual abuse (Youngson, 1994) and therefore this group of perpetrators will be deemed to be a separate group.

The women who had sexually abused children were each individually matched with another woman who would then become a member of the *comparison group*. The women were matched for race, age, marital status, sexual orientation, number of children, social class group, education level and years in employment. The women in the comparison group were wherever possible recruited from the same area as the offender. The women in the comparison group were accessed via the same professionals who were working with the women or from local schools or play groups via word of mouth.

The numbers involved in each of the groups

For this study therefore the groups that were used were:

Women who initially target young children
Group A (*n* = 14)
Women who initially target adolescent children
Group B (*n* = 10)
Women who were initially coerced into sexually abusing by men
Group C (*n* = 12)
Comparison group
Group D (*n* = 36)
Women who have not sexually abused children 'matched' with the perpetrators in Groups A, B, and C.

The main part of this book will concentrate on findings related to the women in the three groups of offenders—Groups A, B, and C—and the women in the comparison group. Due to the smaller number of atypical perpetrators and those women involved in ritual abuse, they could not be included in the comparative quantitative analysis but discussion of the findings related to these women will be presented in later chapters.

(i) 'Atypical' perpetrators
Equal co-perpetrators (*n*=2); Woman who coerced a man (*n*=1); Psychotic Offenders (*n*=2); Women who sexually abused in a dissociative state (*n*=2); Blurring sexual boundaries (*n*=3).

(ii) Perpetrators of ritual abuse of children (n=4)
Although the women were grouped on the basis of their known perpetrating behaviour, it should be emphasised that these may not be the only children that they have targeted to sexually abuse. As with male perpetrators, it should not be assumed that because a child is of a specific age and/or a specific gender the child will not be abused by the woman. All abusers may have preferred targets but may also sexually abuse other children.

4. Demographic Data—Areas on which the women had been matched

(a) Social class

The women who sexually abused children came from all social classes; one woman had been connected for many generations to the aristocracy, another woman had spent much of her childhood and adult life homeless. Most of the women's social situations were between these two extremes. As with male perpetrators, women in Social Groups IV and V are more likely to come into contact with the agencies alerted to the possibility of child sexual abuse.

CASE EXAMPLE 2.1

Sophia's father was a diplomat. They lived in a house that had been in her mother's family for many generations. They had always had servants and she had been primarily cared for by a nanny and had been sent away to school.

CASE EXAMPLE 2.2

Mary was abandoned by her mother and lived in her grandmother's home which was little more than a caravan. Her grandmother moved from one dreadful living situation to another depending on which man she was with. Sometimes her grandmother took Mary with her, sometimes she left her alone.

(b) Education levels

The large majority of women who sexually abused children left school at the earliest possible time, however almost half did achieve some academic qualification. Six women had university degrees, two of whom obtained their degrees after the abuse ended. Four women had been considered to have borderline intelligence levels. During the interviews it became clear that for at least three of these women, this was unlikely to be due to the effects of repeated trauma and/or poor educational opportunities. When such women are given a relatively abuse-free environment and constructive individual education, their cognitive abilities are seen to improve considerably.

CASE EXAMPLE 2.3

Mavis had always been considered to be 'slow'. She could barely read or write. When she entered prison having been convicted of sexually abusing her children, she was found to have an IQ of 67; the category of mild learning disabilities. As a child she often missed school due to the injuries she had sustained as a result of abuse by her father and brothers. In prison she flourished under the teaching she received and also spent time working through not only what she had done to her children but also the abuse she had experienced herself. Thus she had the emotional space to cognitively process information. She began to read books and express herself through her writings. When she left prison she could read and write as well as other adults and had also had one piece of her work published.

(c) Employment histories

Although many of the women who had sexually abused children were intellectually able, many were likely to have had relatively short employment histories, particularly the women who sexually abused very young children (Group A). Regardless of their level of education, most of the women who worked did poorly paid unskilled work. Some of the women who sexually abused children did have professional qualifications: one being a nurse, one a social worker and one a teacher.

(d) Race

All the women who took part in this study were caucasians.

(e) Marital status at the time of the abuse

The majority of women who were coerced into sexually abusing by men, co-habited with the man. The majority of the women who were sole perpetrators lived alone at the time when they were sexually abusing children.

THE CHILDREN WHOM THE WOMEN SEXUALLY ABUSED AND THE ACTS PERPETRATED

1. Relationship to the Perpetrator

The children the women were most likely to sexually abuse were their own children, the children most closely related to them or children to whom they were in a care-taking role. These findings are consistent with other studies that have identified women as perpetrators of child sexual abuse (Kercher & McShane, 1984; Faller, 1987; McCarty, 1986; Speltz, Matthews and Mathews, 1989; Matthews, Mathews & Speltz, 1991). Despite this consistency it may be a distortion, as it is presumed this would be the most disturbing form of sexual abuse by a woman and the most disturbing cases are more likely to be recognised.

Women who targeted adolescents appeared to be more likely to target children outside their own families. It may be significant however that these women were less likely to have access to 'appropriate' children within their own family.

Many of the women who had been coerced into sexually abusing children by men were specifically selected by the men because they had children who could be abused. Once coerced into abusing by the men, those women who went on to abuse independently almost always targeted their past victims; hence they too were more likely to sexually abuse their own children. Table 2.1 shows the minimum number of children known to be sexually abused by the women in this study. The + in Group A refers to a very prolific female perpetrator who had abused so many children she had lost count.

2. The Gender of the Victims

The women who sexually abused very young children were equally likely to target male and female children; some women sexually abused both. For some women the gender of the child was crucial, for others it was factors other than the gender of the child that led to the choice of a particular target. Conversely, the women who targeted adolescent children were very specific about the gender of the child that was targeted. In the cases studied, the gender of the target child is related to the woman's sexual orientation; women who identify as heterosexual, target males, women who identify as lesbians, target females. One woman, who could not take part in the research, did target both male and female adolescents. She

Table 2.1: Relationship of targets to the perpetrators

GROUP	MINIMUM NUMBER OF VICTIMS (KNOWN OF)	BIOLOGICAL CHILDREN	RELATED CHILDREN	UNRELATED CHILDREN	GENDER OF CHILDREN
A (n=14)	30+	25	2+	3+	♀ - 17 ♂ - 13
B (n=10)	13	3	2	8	♀ - 4 ♂ - 9
C (n=12)	25	16	7	2	♀ - 18 ♂ - 7
TOTAL	68+	64.7%	16.3%	19.1%	

orchestrated 'sex-games' at her house seeing herself as an equal with these children: 'one of the gang'.

When women were coerced into sexually abusing by men, the children they abused were those targeted and groomed by the men and hence, the male dictated the gender of the child. Those women who subsequently sexually abuse children alone were most likely to abuse those same children. The gender of the child thus tended to reflect the original targets of the abuse she was coerced into perpetrating.

3. Age of the Women When They Started Sexually Abusing Children

Women who sexually abuse very young children tended to be in their mid-teen years when they *began* to perpetrate sexual abuse. Two of these women admitted to imposing sexual acts on other children when they themselves were children. The women who sexually abused adolescents and the women who abused in conjunction with men were somewhat older when they began to perpetrate sexual abuse.

None of the women interviewed for this study admitted to beginning to sexually abuse children during their early adolescence, in the way that many male perpetrators do. As female adolescent abusers are known (e.g. Cavanagh-Johnson, 1989) this is likely to be a spurious finding due to the small numbers of women. It may, however, also reflect different patterns of male and female offending behaviour which is based on socialisation. This culture expects that in adolescence young men become sexual predators and females are passive in relationships (Smith, 1994). Most of the women in this study did not start perpetrating until they were placed in

Table 2.2: Age gap between the women offenders and the children that they sexually abuse

	GROUP A	GROUP B	GROUP C	GROUP D
Mean age gap between woman and the children they sexually abuse	18.0 yrs (range 15–25)	16.6 yrs (range 9–25)	18.5 yrs (range 15–29)	—
Mean age at which woman have their first child (where applicable)	17.5 yrs (range 15–22)	20.0 yrs (range 15–32)	18.9 yrs (range 15–26)	23.4 yrs (range 17–34)
Mean age of the woman's first pregnancy	15.4 yrs (range 12–19)	17.2 yrs (range 14–19)	16.8 yrs (range 14–22)	21.2 yrs (range 16–34)

a maternal role: having another human being lower in the hierarchy than themselves, or when they were many years older than their victims.

4. The Age Gap between the Women and the Children They Sexually Abuse

Several authors have found that there is a close age gap between the women and the children that they sexually abuse (Wahl, 1960; Groth, 1982; Faller, 1987; Speltz, Matthews & Mathews, 1989) Table 2.2.

As a result of matching subjects and comparison group for age and number of children with the women offenders, there was not a significant difference regarding the age gap between the women and their children. However, the offenders were more likely to become pregnant at an early age although these pregnancies may not have gone to term, some having been miscarried and others aborted. The fact there are no older women involved in this study is a distortion of the small sample. There is no reason to believe that at least some of these women would have continued to sexually abuse children had their behaviour not been exposed. One of the female offenders in this study had as a child been sexually abused by her grandmother.

CASE EXAMPLE 2.4

'My mother never wanted children but she was raped and I was born. She'd leave me with my gran while she went to work. Gran and I'd go to bed for our nap . . . We'd take our clothes off and I'd lie with my back to her. She'd rub my genitals, she'd then put her fingers inside me and push them in and out while she "rubbed herself"...We'd sleep with me sucking on her old wrinkled breasts. After I started school ... it happened in the holidays and whenever I stayed the night. It stopped when my gran died, she was 76 and I was eight years old.'

Considering most of the victims were the children of the women offenders there was a relatively close age gap between the women and the children they sexually abused. However, this is likely to be a distortion due to the small number of older women in the sample. Older women, including grandmothers, sexually abuse children yet these women very rarely come to professional attention. When they do, the abuse they perpetrate is even more likely to be denied, minimalised, and/or ignored than that of younger women. In cases in which there has been overwhelming evidence that grandmothers have perpetrated child sexual abuse, prosecutions were not brought. It is proposed that it is not the actual 'age-gap' that is important but that some part of the woman was emotionally congruent with the target child/ren.

5. The Acts

The acts the women committed against the children are detailed in Table 2.3. Of the 36 women, 14 admitted to gaining sexual arousal from the children's pain. This finding goes some way to dispelling the myth that sexual abuse by women is misconstrued as inappropriate expressions of affection. Nevertheless even the women who were sexually aroused by children's pain, at other times were 'gentle' and 'seductive' abusers. Women coerced into sexually abusing children by men were much more likely to participate in pornography than sole perpetrators. This may be because pornography reflects male sexuality and the use of pornography by men is seen as culturally acceptable.

CASE EXAMPLE 2.5

Carrie was groomed by a man many years her senior who made her feel 'loved for the first time in her life'. He said they needed 'more spice in their sex lives' and she agreed to get a 15-year-old girl to 'join-in' their love making. When her partner seemed to prefer this young woman to her, Carrie became 'jealous and angry' so when he suggested that the two of them 'imprison' this young woman and carry out sadistic sexual acts on her, Carrie readily agreed. For two days they incarcerated the young woman and inflicted extensive sexual acts and sexual torture on her. Carrie said she got enormous pleasure and arousal from this behaviour. They were imprisoned for the

Table 2.3: Sexual acts the women admit to having perpetrated

SEXUAL ACT	GROUP A (n=14)	GROUP B (n=10)	GROUP C (n=12)
Voyeurism	1	2	2
Exhibitionism	0	2	8
Child masturbates woman	7	7	6
Masturbation of child	9	8	9
Digital vaginal penetration	9	2	10
Object penetration	4	0	1
Oral sex	5	8	7
Anal penetration	5	1	6
Intercourse	3	6	4
Child pornography	0	0	5
Child prostitution	1	0	1
Sexual arousal from child's pain	9	0	5

offences. One year on Carrie said she still got very 'turned on' just thinking of the sexually sadistic acts and she kept thinking of how she could get to do it again.

6. The Frequency of Sexually Abusive Acts

Most women cited 'several times a week', as the frequency with which they engaged in sexual contact with a child, others that sexual contact occurred daily, others less than once a week.

7. The Duration of the Sexual Abuse

It is difficult to draw conclusions about the 'typical' length of time that a female perpetrator may sexually abuse a child as in all but a few of the cases under investigation the abuse was stopped, either due to discovery of the abuse or to the child escaping from the situation. Nevertheless some patterns have emerged from this study. As with all abusers, women can sexually abuse children in a single incident or repeatedly over a period of time. The finding that single incident abuse appears to be rare among women perpetrators may reflect underreporting of such acts.

The children who were sexually abused by their own mothers were likely to experience the longest duration of abuse, whether the mother was an independent or an initially coerced abuser (mean across all three groups 4.5 yrs compared to 0.8 yrs extra-familial). This is almost certainly because of the ease of accessibility of the child to the woman as well as the dependence of the child on the perpetrator. Recognition and/or disclosure is thus particularly difficult. The women who initially target very young children may continue to sexually abuse the child into adolescence and even adulthood.

CASE EXAMPLE 2.6

Vera sexually abused all five of her children, three boys and two girls, but stopped abusing three of her children when they were about six years of age. When she 'ran out' of young children she continued sexually abusing her youngest daughter until she ran away from home and her youngest son until his first ejaculation, when he was almost twelve. She describes her utter sexual repulsion towards him once this had occurred.

CASE EXAMPLE 2.7

Mavis sexually abused her son from the age of two until the age of fourteen when he was taken into care. He had mild learning disabilities, was extremely physically aggressive. By the time he was removed, she was having full sexual intercourse with him. She saw no connection between his problems and the fact that she was sexually abusing him. She said that if he had not been 'taken away', the sexual contact would have continued into adulthood.

The adolescent children targeted by women who were not their biological mothers were most likely to have the shortest period of being sexually abused. Because of their greater independence and freer access to other adults, the adolescent children are likely to end the abuse by eventually removing themselves in some way from the situation or disclosing the abuse to other adults. This was also true for adolescent targets of male-coerced offenders (see Table 2.4).

8. Grooming for Compliance and Preventing Disclosure

Grooming is the process by which sexual abusers ensure the compliance and the secrecy they need in order to engage in a sexual interaction with their chosen target (Eldridge, 1991). The women who sexually abuse very young children often begin the abuse when the child is so young that 'grooming for compliance' is not necessary as the children do not know any other form of treatment. Many of the women who abuse very young children describe also relying on the child's dependency on them to

Table 2.4: Age of perpetrators and targets and duration of abuse

GROUP	MEAN AGE WHEN THE WOMAN BEGAN SEXUALLY ABUSING	MEAN AGE OF THE CHILD WHEN THE ABUSE BEGAN	MEAN DURATION OF SEXUAL ABUSE (APPROX.)	MEAN NUMBER OF VICTIMS
A (n=14)	19.8 range (16–25)	1.47 years range (birth–5)	4.1 years range (single incident –12 years)	2.2 range (1–many)
B (n=10)	28.5 range (22–35)	12.3 years range (8–14)	2.3 years range (single incident –9 years)	1.3 range (1–3)
C (n=12)	26.1 range (17–38)	8.0 years range (birth–15)	2.9 years range (single incident –14 years)	2.08 range (1–8)

prevent disclosure. Some of these women also described threatening the child and/or were very sadistic and the children were terrified of the consequences of the abuse being discovered.

CASE EXAMPLE 2.8

A girl told her teacher how she had seen her mother and her brother Kevin (aged 14) 'doing naughties'. A professional describes Kevin's reaction to being questioned about the allegations. 'I've never seen a kid look so frightened. He actually wet himself. He became hysterical and babbled. He was convinced this was his end and his mother would now torture him to death.' Kevin had shared his mother's bed from when his father left when he was three until the abuse was discovered when he was fourteen. Sometimes the sexual interaction was 'loving and affectionate' and at others it was sadistic, depending on which fulfilled the mother's needs at that time.

Women who target adolescents described similar grooming processes to those of male perpetrators (Case Example 2.9). These women very rarely used violence or physical threats to prevent disclosure. This may be because, regardless of the age difference, adolescents, particularly adolescent boys, are likely to be as physically strong or even stronger than their abusers. The women were much more likely to constrain the child by use of bribery, coercion and the attribution of joint, and even greater responsibility to the child. Some women seem to explicitly assert that it is a mutual 'relationship', while at the same time employing various implied, rather than overt, prophecies of doom should the 'relationship' come to an end or they be found out.

CASE EXAMPLE 2.9

BEHAVIOUR	GROOMING TECHNIQUES
Nancy's abuse of her nephew began while 'baby-sitting' him and his three younger siblings. He had always been her favourite nephew and noticed how she was getting very excited about her baby-sitting evenings; constantly thinking of her nephew, fantasising 'a romance' between them.	Using fantasy to reduce her inhibitions.
She began to make even more of a fuss of him, buying him records he liked.	Bribery prior to the act.
She liked his company and 'got bored' on her own so she'd encourage him to stay up until just before she knew his parents would return at least 2 hours past his regular bedtime. Once or twice she brought alcohol with her and shared it with him. She began to act on her fantasies, talking to him about his girlfriends and sex; assuming a much greater depth of sexual knowledge and experience than he could possibly have had.	Compromising him and establishing a, relatively innocent, secret between them. Giving him the feeling of adulthood; equality. Developing a false sense of himself and his interest that would be difficult for him to deny and also reducing his inhibitions.
She'd always been very tactile with him from when he was a small child and this touching began to become more intimate, the reasons for this being attributed to *his* need.	Gradual increase in touching and developing of cognitive distortion of desire and hence guilt to the child.
With his parents she'd talk about how funny it was seeing him trying to act older when he was still such a child. She'd strongly place herself at their 'level' and 'distance herself from him' when they were all together.	Grooming the parents.

Once when kissing him goodnight, their lips 'accidentally' touched and she 'jokingly blamed him' for 'trying it on'.	Attribution of blame and desire to him.
The next time she built on this and actually did kiss him in a sexual manner while rubbing his penis and telling him he was really very aroused and wanted to have sex with her.	Further attribution of responsibility to the child.
The boy was actually rarely able to ejaculate and she used this as a lever to insist that she knew he wanted and needed her 'help'.	Attributing it to a need in him.
She developed the idea of 'their secret' saying how they'd both really get into 'big trouble' if anyone knew because they just wouldn't understand as they did not realise that he was as 'grown up' and as 'sexual' as she knew he was. At the same time, she implied threats of permanent impotency if they stopped.	Coercion and threats.

Women who were initially coerced into sexually abusing use male power to silence their victims, even when the women abused alone.

CASE EXAMPLE 2.10

When she wanted to do it to me, she'd say he'd told her to and I could never really be sure whether he had or not. She used to threaten me that . . . if I told anyone what was going on . . . I'd be in for 'it' and 'it' was really, really bad. I'd had 'it' before, and I never wanted to ever feel that bad again. The more I hurt the faster she'd 'come'. . . . she knew just how to hurt me and I knew that she'd really 'get off on' getting him to hurt me . . . I never would have told because I was just too scared.

9. How the Abuse Was Disclosed

Table 2.5 indicates the different ways in which the women's sexual contact with children ended. In all groups external intervention was most needed if the mother was the abuser. Two women, who were initially coerced into sexually abusing by men, ended the abuse themselves. They each reported it to the appropriate agencies and made sure the children were protected from the men involved.

Table 2.5: How the women's sexual contact with children ceased[a]

GROUP	WOMAN ENDED THE ABUSE	CHILD ENDED THE ABUSE	CHILD RAN AWAY	A CHILD DISCLOSED TO OTHERS/INVESTIGATION	A CHILD'S BEHAVIOUR LED TO DISCLOSURE	PHYSICAL EXAMINATION/INVESTIGATION	OTHER
A n=14	3	0	1	4	8	4	0
B n=10	0	5	2	3	3	0	0
C n=12	0	0	1	4	3	1	1 (photos) 1 (other children disclosed)

[a]There are more than 10 as the abuse for different children with the same perpetrator stopped in different ways.

SUMMARY

- Women of *any* age, social class group, intellectual ability, type of employment and marital status can sexually abuse children.
- The children they target are most likely to be children to whom they are in a maternal role.
- When they abuse very young children, the sex of the child that is abused does not appear to be crucial in the choice of target child.
- When adolescents are abused, the gender of the child appears to be an important aspect of the decision as to which child is targeted.
- Women tend to use similar tactics to men in grooming the child for compliance and disclosure; threat, coercion, care-giving, attribution of responsibility onto the child, fear of abandonment, etc.
- Women are likely to sexually abuse children in all the ways that a man does, except they have to penetrate the child with digits or objects instead of a penis. Women are capable of obtaining sexual gratification from sexual sadism with children.
- Women of any age can and do sexually abuse children. It is proposed that age difference is not the key issue but that *some* aspects of the woman offender are developmentally fixated, leading to emotional congruence with the child.
- Women tend to sexually abuse children over a long period of time, particularly if the target children are their biological children. This may be because of the increased dependency of children on the women who sexually abuse them and/or because the children have less conviction that they will be believed if they say that their abuser was a woman, and therefore are less likely to disclose abuse.

3

CHILDHOOD: THE FORMATIVE YEARS

- RELATIONSHIPS WITH PARENTS
- ABUSES EXPERIENCED IN CHILDHOOD
- RELATIONSHIPS WITH SIBLINGS
- RELATIONSHIPS WITH PEERS
- SUMMARY

Everything that the person later comes to believe, advocate and deem right is founded on the first formative experiences.
(Alice Miller, *Banished Knowledge*, 1990, p.5)

There is no psychologically viable theory of personality and behaviour that denies the influence of experience, particularly early experience. Everything that a person comes to know and believe about the self, about others, and about the world, comes from the history of their interactions with their environment and, more importantly, with the people within it. Although this process is continuous throughout life, and is dynamic and reflexive, the building blocks of the process are laid in childhood and, unless reassembled, become the foundations upon which the rest of the personality is built. This chapter aims to describe the women's perception's of some important aspects of their childhoods, so that it can be ascertained whether any particular set of building blocks was laid that could be the foundation from which a woman would sexually abuse children. The blocks that have been chosen for exploration are those that psychological theorists now consider to be the keystones of the early environment, the women's overall perception of their childhood experience, their relationships with their parents and/or other key adults, siblings and peers and whether or not they themselves experienced abuse in their childhood—sexual, physical or emotional abuse. The majority of the women who sexually abused children developed a perception of childhood as a stressful and difficult time. It must be recognised that several women within the comparison group also had extremely stressful childhoods but did not go on to sexually abuse children. This indicates that although the degree of stress may be important, specific aspects of that stress may be more predictive in the aetiology of this behaviour. There may also be aspects of a child life that facilitate the child's developing resilience to the experience of stress.

RELATIONSHIPS WITH PARENTS

Through the child's interactions with carers she develops mental templates on which she bases her expectations of adults, and on which her own behaviour, as an adult, is modelled. Many studies have reported that abusive parents had abnormal relationships with their own parents (Cicchetti & Rizley, 1981; Egeland, Jacobvitz & Sroufe, 1988; Rutter, 1989). However, not all children who have distorted relationships with their parents are likely to become abusive parents themselves and 'intergenerational discontinuities are at least as striking as continuities' (Rutter, 1989, p.321). The women's childhood relationships with their parents and parental figures were explored in order to consider in what areas, if any, the parenting the women abusers experienced differed from that of women in the comparison group.

1. The Women's Perceptions of their Parents

The women were asked to give three words to describe each of their parents or parental figures. Considering that none of the words were provided for the women, there was a remarkably consistent pattern of responses within each group of women offenders. The women in the comparison group provided a more heterogeneous range of descriptions. Every woman was also asked whether she had felt that each parent had been a 'good-enough' parent to her, that is, accepting that no parent is perfect was appropriately loving and caring. A comparison was also made between how the woman construed each of her actual parents and each of her ideal parents from the Repertory Grid (Table 3.1).

FINDINGS

Women who initially target young children (Group A). None of these women's mothers or their fathers were perceived by them to be at all similar to their ideal parents.

Table 3.1: The Women's perceptions of their parents/ parental figures

	GROUP A (n=14)	GROUP B (n=10)	GROUP C (n=12)	GROUP D (n=36)
Words used to describe mother/maternal figure	Distant, cold, domineering, demanding, did not love me, wanted to be close to her	Demanding, needy, strict, weak, more like a sister, couldn't cope	Rejecting, cold, selfish, mean, cruel, unloving, matriarchal but caring	Loving/caring hard-working, good, kind, fun, distant, weak, cold, ambivalent
Was your mother 'good-enough'?	YES: 0 NO: 14	YES: 0 NO: 10	YES: 1 NO: 11	YES: 27 NO: 9
Mean difference between mother and ideal mother (max 100)	52.3 (range 31–69)	34.5 (range 29–48)	60.3 (range 46–92)	18.4 (range 6–58)
Words used to describe father/paternal figure	Selfish, violent, oversexed, unstable, cruel	Often absent, hostile, selfish aggressive, rejecting	Loving, caring, kind, wonderful, as mother would let him be	Loving, strong, provider, cold, weekend-dad, strict, distant,
Was your father 'good-enough'?	YES: 0 NO: 14	YES: 0 NO: 10	YES: 12 NO: 0	YES: 20 NO: 16
Mean difference between father and ideal father (max=100)	71.4 (range 52–94)	50.4 (range 24–68)	40.2 (range 20–54)	26.7 (range 8–68)

Mothers. Not one of the women who initiated the sexual abuse of very young children felt, at the time of the interview, that either her mother or father had been 'good-enough' parents to her during her childhood. Interestingly, almost all spontaneously found reasons to excuse the mother for this, essentially blaming themselves as a child. These women's mothers were all described as 'not close' or 'distant'. Some of the women graphically described their feelings of needing to be close to their mothers and/or pleasing their mothers but 'not being able to be'. Four of the women described feeling very close to their mothers, as adults, in a way that they never did as children. When these beliefs are examined, to gain this 'closeness' the women had to negate themselves and do everything to please and appease their mothers and, from their descriptions, received virtually no care, support or affection in return. There tended to be many internal inconsistences in these women's descriptions of their relationships with their mothers.

CASE EXAMPLE 3.1

'Oh yeh . . . I'm close to me mam, very, very close to me mam . . . it's unbelievable, I find it hard to break away from me mam . . . I was too close to me mam . . .it used to get into situations that it were me mam or him [her partner] . . . I was so obsessed with me mam . . . still am . . . we're very close.' (This statement was totally inconsistent with the other aspects of this woman's assessment. She said that as a child there was no one at all whom she could go to when she felt upset and that she never remembered being cuddled by her mother, only being hit. She was very frightened of her mother. Regardless of her stated closeness to her mother, she rated herself as having experienced significant emotional abuse in her childhood, scoring 53 of a possible 60 on the scale. When filling in the Dependency Grid, relating to her adult social support networks, she *did not cite her mother once* as a person she could discuss, or rely on for help, with any problems there were.)

Fathers.   These women used extremely derogatory words to describe their fathers/father figures. The most positive description was: 'I suppose you could say he provided for us, but we had to pay for that, he was selfish, violent and treated us as if we were less than slaves.' Regardless of these derogatory statements, several of these women said that the negative contact with their father or father figure was the only recognition they received. They described seeking out their father, or father figure, however abusive he was and regarded this as further evidence of their own badness.

CASE EXAMPLE 3.2

When Connie was six, her mother escaped her very violent husband by leaving Connie to 'look after him as she had always done'. 'Looking after' her father meant calming his mood by allowing her father to be sexual with her, including fellatio and at a later stage intercourse. Connie 'looked after' her father and was subject to his moods and violence until she was twelve. He then moved a woman, with two young daughters, into the house and sent Connie to live with her mother, who sent back to her father. She began running away, and to survive, she prostituted herself. She said 'It was the career that I had been very well trained for by my parents'. (Connie sexually abused her youngest son from when he was six months until he was four years old.)

Women who initially target adolescents (Group B). The women who sexually abused adolescents rarely felt they had been parented by anyone when they were children. Each described in her individual way how she felt she had had to be 'the carer'. None believed they had had a 'good-enough' mother nor a 'good-enough' father. Neither mother or father was like their ideal parents.

Mothers. These women described their mothers as 'weak', 'needy' and 'demanding'. Mothers were seen more as peers than parents. Many of these women were responsible from a very young age for doing all the housework, cooking, shopping, caring for siblings as well as fulfilling their mothers' emotional needs.

Fathers. None of the women who targeted adolescents had a constant father or father figure throughout their childhoods. They all had contemptuous views of these men, mostly implanted by their mothers. Some women as young children had held very positive views of their fathers but had these feelings 'soured'.

CASE EXAMPLE 3.3

When Nancy was four, her father left her mother, herself and her older brother. Her only memories she has of him are of his violence. Throughout her childhood, when her mother could not cope she blamed Nancy's absent father, frequently launching into a tirade of abuse about him. Nancy had to totally agree with her mother in order to placate her. Nancy's mother had a series of many male partners who lived in the house, some for a night, some for a few weeks, and some for several months. Even when they were very young children, her mother would leave Nancy and her brother in the house alone and go out at night. Nancy doesn't remember when the housework and the care of her brother became her responsibility, but she also does not remember a time when she was not expected to do it. She would also steal money or food, to feed her brother and herself. Her brother never had to lift a finger to help and he was also violent towards Nancy. Whenever her mother was upset, she would confide in Nancy. At the same time, Nancy felt that her mother was 'never satisfied'. She would shout at Nancy, telling her how useless and selfish she was, and would always find fault with her. In her adolescence, her mother began to perceive Nancy as a rival for the attention of the men. This was exacerbated by several of her mother's men friends who behaved inappropriately with Nancy. The relationship deteriorated completely between mother and daughter when Nancy was raped on two separate occasions by one of her mother's lovers. When she eventually told her mother, rather than being angry with the man, she was furious with

Nancy. There followed a complete emotional coldness between them. As soon as she left school, her mother told Nancy to leave home.

Women who were initially coerced offenders (Group C). Each woman in this group said she had a far better relationship with her father than with her mother. Many of these women felt rejection by their mother and several saw themselves and their father as the 'couple'; forming an alliance against the perceived hostility of the mother and, in some cases, the other siblings.

Mothers.   Only one woman in this group felt that she had a 'good-enough' mother. She described her as 'strict, matriarchal but caring' and her father as 'a loving, kind, and wonderful man'.

Fathers.   Each woman who was initially coerced into sexually abusing children felt her father had been a 'good-enough' father. However the women's descriptions of their fathers were often of very 'idealised' images. When specific questions relating to the relationship were posed, the father's behaviour was far from the ideal that was portrayed. In several cases, behaviours described by the women as examples of his 'love' and her 'specialness', were overtly sexually abusive. In almost all cases, the women's transcripts present a confused and distorted picture of these men. Of the 14 women, 8 used the phrase 'I adored my father'. Any woman who did recognise faults in her father, attributed these behaviours either to the intervention or influence of her mother or to something very negative about herself. In many cases, it is likely the fathers were the architects of these beliefs, dividing the mother and child for their own purposes.

CASE EXAMPLE 3.4

One father who said that he was forbidden to share his wife's bed when he had been out drinking, on these occasions would get into his daughter's bed. He would always be naked and she would 'relieve him' (masturbate him). He would then snuggle up to her and go to sleep. This had occurred from when she was about three or four until she left home, at which time, it was occurring almost daily. The woman told this story solely in response to being asked to give an example to illustrate how close they were. She did not construe this behaviour as at all abusive; in fact quite the contrary, she said that she felt special as the father did not ever sleep in her sister's bed.

CASE EXAMPLE 3.5

Carrie was told by her father that her mother 'ran-off' soon after her second birthday because she hated her and did not want to be her mother. Carrie had always slept in her father's bed and had done 'as best as I could to make up for her leaving him'. She said, 'I would have done anything to make him happy'. Carrie said that she 'adored her father' but she often 'upset him' without meaning to and then she was very frightened he would leave her. In her mid-twenties this fear was especially bad as he got his first 'woman friend'. This 'woman-friend' was *10 years younger* than Carrie herself. At this time Carrie began to be groomed by a male acquaintance of her father's and became involved in the relationship with him that led to her offences. (See Case Example 2.9)

The comparison group (Group D). Several women in the comparison group felt they had had very poor relationships with one or other of their parents but only two felt they had neither a 'good-enough' mother or father. One of these women had spent much of her childhood in care and had formed some positive relationships with her carers. The other woman had been brought up by her aunt and uncle and had very good relationships with each of them.

2. Constancy of Relationships

Loss and disruption of relationships, particularly during childhood, is associated with various psychopathological symptoms (Bowlby, 1980; Reite & Field, 1985). Due to the utter dependency of children on their carers, any loss or separation from them has a distressing psychological effect on a child. It has also been demonstrated that such separation, without effective attenuation of this loss by substitute relationships, can lead to permanent effects on a developing nervous system (Gilbert, 1988, pp.128–134).

FINDINGS

Women in all groups, including the comparison group, experienced disturbances in their relationships with parental figures which were mainly due to breakdowns in the adults' relationships or an adult's inability to cope (Table 3.2).

Women who initially target young children (Group A). These women tended to have had very chaotic childhoods. Four of the women were left with their grandparents, for months and even years at a time, and periodically returned to live with their mothers/parents. One woman's mother put her into care every time her father left home and allowed her

Table 3.2: Women's home situations during their childhoods

	GROUP A (n=14)	GROUP B (n=10)	GROUP C (n=12)	GROUP D (n=36)
Parents stayed together throughout childhood	2 14.3%	0 0%	8 66.7%	16 44.4%
Parents together but father frequently away from home for long periods	3 21.4%	3 30%	1 8.3%	3 8.3%
Parents split up and child lived mostly with mother	2 14.3%	6 60%	1 8.3%	11 30.5%
Parents split up and child lived mostly with father	2 14.3%	0 0%	2 16.6%	1 2.7%
Father died, child lived with mother	0 0%	1 10%	0 0%	2 5.5%
Child spent much of childhood with people other than parents	5 35.7%	0 0%	0 0%	3 8.3%

back home so he could use her sexually for the periods when he returned.

Women who initially target adolescents (Group B). None of the women who sexually abused adolescents had lived with *both* their biological parents for the majority of their childhood years. The fathers were absent: two due to being frequently in hospital or ill in bed, the others having left the family. Four of the women had mothers who had a series of adult male partners and had been made to move from place to place, and were 'left' with various carers so that their mothers could pursue these relationships.

CASE EXAMPLE 3.6

'My mum was always off somewhere with some man she picked up . . . leave me with whoever would have me . . . she could be back the next day, sometimes it'd be a week or more . . . she didn't always tell me she was going, just leave a note to say to go to someone or other's . . . a few times, I'd just be waiting and she'd not come home at all and I didn't know who to go to so I'd be alone' (Melanie).

Women who were initially coerced offenders (Group C). The women who were initially coerced into abusing by men, *appear* to have had more stable childhoods. Of these women 75% lived with both their biological parents.

The comparison group (Group D). Overall the women in the comparison group had more stable relationships than the women sexual offenders. Even when parental relationships broke up, they were more likely to have had positive relationships with both parents. Those women who did have very complex and distressing living situations, did experience some positive relationship with at least one person other than a biological parent.

REFLECTION AND COMMENT

Three differences emerged between the women in the comparison group and the women in the offender groups who had had difficulties in their parental relationships:

1. The women in the comparison group were much more consistent in their reporting of their models of their parents.
2. The women in the comparison group tended to perceive the major responsibility for deficits in care as being their parents', whereas the women perpetrators attributed it to themselves as children.
3. Regardless of how bad the parenting within their family of origin the women in the comparison group, unlike the women offenders, each experienced some level of consistent positive parenting for some period during her childhood.

No parent, or parental substitute, is perfect but the women offenders as children were cared for by, at best, incompetent, and worst, actively malevolent, parents. Young vulnerable children, for psychological and physical survival, need to maintain a belief that at least one, if not both, parents are benevolent carers. Therefore to maintain some sense of the safety of having a benevolent carer, these women sought justifications and vindications for their parents' behaviours. In order to do this children have to find some way of rationalising their negative experiences of their carers. Some children do so by repression and denial of these experiences, some by excusing and justifying and each, to some extent, by internalising the belief that there is something bad or unworthy within herself that provokes the carer to behave destructively towards her. In doing this the child can preserve an image of a good carer and also maintain some small degree of control and power (Herman, 1992; Miller, 1991). The consequence of this behaviour is that the child has to embrace a totally negative sense of self and complex, confused and distorted models of parents, adults and adult behaviour. These models, on which the child's sense of survival is founded, are difficult to relinquish and are carried through life, influencing beliefs and behaviours.

As well as the losses of parental support due to emotional and physical unavailability to the child, many of the women offenders, particularly sole offenders, experienced major separations from parental figures. Any substitute relationships were at best inadequate and likely to exacerbate rather than ameliorate the effects of loss. Repetition of this scenario is likely to lead to passivity and eventually emotional despair for the child. The cognitive, emotional and physiological changes that are associated with such prolonged stress predispose the individual to psychopathological symptoms. In addition, the child learns that relationships are unreliable, uncontrollable and a source of stress, and she fails to learn that relationships can be a source of comfort, security, happiness and personal growth.

Each woman perpetrator as a child had to, at least partially, assume pseudo-adult roles in relation to her carers. These pseudo-adult roles entailed fulfilling the carers' physical needs, emotional needs and/or sexual needs. The internalised models of the relationships between children and parents that these women assimilated would therefore most likely include the belief that a child's *raison d'être* is to serve the needs of an adult, whatever those needs may be. Thus, unless these beliefs were radically challenged, as adults they too would have similar expectations of children with whom they had contact.

The relationships between those women who were coerced into sexually abusing children and their parents are of particular interest as these seem to be repeated in their relationships with the men who coerce them into sexually offending. It is proposed that such confused models of male figures, in conjunction with confused experiences of what is and is not 'caring' within a relationship, increased these particular women's vulnerability to involvement with men who treated women and children in an abusive manner. These women had internalised models of the mother/female role as negating the needs of a child and of men needing to be pleased and appeased in order to ensure affection, safety and protection. This combination would make a woman more readily accessible as a target for a man motivated to coerce a woman into sexually abusing children with him.

ABUSES EXPERIENCED IN CHILDHOOD

Abuse has been primarily delineated under the categories of physical, sexual and emotional abuses. No abuse, however, is unidimensional. When a child is being physically abused, the perpetrator may be experiencing sexual arousal, a state that will be perceptible at some level to the child. In the process of being sexually abused a child endures painful physical injuries. When a child is sexually and/or physically abused, apart from any bodily damage that may be sustained, the consequences for the child are emotional. Bodily damage is almost always reparable but it is the communications that the child receives about the self and other people through being sexually or physically abused, that produce the psychologically and emotionally damaging long-term effects. A child who is emotionally abused; a child who lacks affection, is neglected, is repeatedly denigrated and humiliated, will form a very poor self-image (Garbarino, 1986). Due to lack of age-appropriate care and protection, such a child becomes extremely vulnerable to experiencing physical harm and is also a prime target for grooming by sexual abusers. Mindful of these difficulties in exactly defining categories of abuse, the women were given definitions and asked to respond to that definition in terms of their own experience. In addition they were asked to recall any similar experiences which might not exactly fit the definition so that no aspect should be missed.

1. Physical Abuse

Definition used: Physically harmful actions directed towards the child causing actual bodily injuries such as bruises, cuts, burns, head injuries, fractures, abdominal injuries and poisoning.

FINDINGS

The women who sexually abused children were more likely than the women in the comparison group to have experienced physical abuse in their childhoods (Table 3.3).

Women who initially target very young children (Group A). Eight of the nine women who experienced physical abuse were physically abused regularly throughout their childhood and adolescence. Six of these women were physically abused by more than one person.

Table 3.3: The women's experience of physical abuse in childhood

	GROUP A (n=14)	GROUP B (n=10)	GROUP C (n=12)	GROUP D (n=36)
Experienced physical abuse as defined	9 (64%)	3 (30%)	3 (25%)	5 (14%)
Received appropriate treatment for injury	4 (43%)	1 (33%)	1 (33%)	4 (80%)
Smacking/hitting used for discipline	13 (93%)	8 (80%)	10 (75%)	29 (80%)

CASE EXAMPLE 3.7

Mary was severely physically abused throughout her childhood. She was beaten by her mother and grandmother and also by her older brothers. On one occasion one of her brothers deliberately held her leg against a bar of an electric fire. Mary also describes her mother 'trying to kill' her when she beat her until she lost consciousness. On another occasion her mother threw a tin at her head, cutting it so badly as to require hospital treatment of four weeks.

Women who initially target adolescents (Group B). Three of these women said they had been physically abused as children: one by her father, one by her mother and also her mother's lover, the third by her brother. Although many of the incidents were serious, the abuse was not a regular occurrence.

Women who are initially coerced into offending (Group C). Three women in this group described experiencing physical abuse at the hands of their mothers on a regular basis. Four other women describe 'being disciplined' by their fathers but even though each woman sustained injuries, none described it as abuse.

CASE EXAMPLE 3.8

Celia's father walked out when she was seven and never returned. Celia says,'I really, really loved my dad. . . . I didn't believe my mother when she said that he'd gone off with one of his women, I didn't believe . . . other relatives [who said he was] irresponsible, a gambler, a con-artist and a womaniser . . . I was his 'little angel'.' Celia was the eldest of four children. She'd always been her father's favourite and when he left she says she 'played up her mother something rotten' and that she 'became very rejecting of her'. She hit her very badly, often with objects. She had bruises and black eyes, her mother would stub her cigarettes on her, beat her with a belt, one occasion she broke her arm, and on another, broke her collar bone.

The comparison group (Group D). Five of the women in the comparison group also suffered physical abuse. For three of these women it was a relatively regular experience; for one the perpetrator was her mother, for one her father and the other her stepfather. Of the other two women, both experienced physical assaults as one-off experiences, each by her mother.

REFLECTION AND COMMENT

Every woman who was physically abused internalised the belief that she was weak in relation to her abuser and that there was something intrinsically bad about her that elicited these attacks. When injured, the women in the comparison group were more likely to receive appropriate care for their injuries. Therefore this indicated that there was someone who cared enough for them to see that these injuries were treated. Few of the women offenders received such care unless the injury was very serious. Interestingly, all three of the women in the comparison group who had experienced relatively regular and prolonged physical abuse, suffered from anxiety disorders in their late adolescence and/or adulthood. None of the women in any of the groups of female offenders who suffered comparable physically abusive experiences as a child suffered from such anxiety disorders. This indicates they found another way of dealing with the distress.

2. Sexual Abuse

Definition to be used: Each woman was asked about sexual activity or experience of any kind, other than self-masturbation, including any mutual sexual exploration between peers, before the age of 16. (Tables detailing the sexual abuse the women experienced in their childhood and their abusers are in Appendix 2.) Each experience was then discussed with the woman in terms of whether or not *she* perceived them as abusive.

FINDINGS

(a) The incidence of sexual abuse in the women's childhoods

All the women who sexually abused children as sole perpetrators (Groups A and B), were themselves sexually abused as children. Of the women who were initially coerced into sexually abusing children by men (Group C) 75% were sexually abused as children. Among the women in the comparison group 19% were sexually abused as children. The women who initially sexually abused young children in particular experienced profound sexual abuse from an early age and for many years during their childhood. For half of the women in this group, the sexual abuse by their childhood abuser continued into adulthood.

CASE EXAMPLE 3.9

Mavis, 36 when she was arrested, said 'The day I was arrested was the first day of my life that I can remember when I was not sexually assaulted'. Her father and, as they got older, her older brothers, sexually assaulted her daily. Even after her marriage to a violent man, both her father and her brothers would come to her home and force her to have sexual intercourse with them.

Four of these women were sexually assaulted on their wedding day by a person who had sexually abused them throughout their childhood. For example, Vera was told by her father as he raped her just before the ceremony that it was so that she would remember who she really belonged to.

(b) The women's perceptions of being sexually abused

At the time of the interview, all the women who had been sexually abused perceived that the experience was abusive. Nevertheless, several women who sexually abused children said that as a child, *the one person* that they felt important to, from whom they gained attention and any form of affection, was the person who sexually abused them. One woman in the comparison group also felt that she received attention and affection from the person who sexually abused her but he was not the sole source of these experiences throughout her childhood.

CASE EXAMPLE 3.10

When Karen was sexually abused by her mother, it was the only time that she received any physical touch or attention from her. Karen described feeling bereft when the abuse stopped. She sexually abused her own daughter in a similar manner to how she herself was abused: Karen did not remember a time when her mother did not 'sexually caress' her. When Karen was six, her mother moved a man into the house and Karen was moved into her own room. She says she 'felt devastated', and that she had done 'something wrong'. Her mother became cold and Karen felt alone. She said that she longed all her life for that closeness with her mother back again. As soon as her own daughter was born (her third child, the other two being boys, who were in care for neglect), she took her into her bed and sexually abused her. Karen said that at last she felt whole again and her daughter was the first person she had felt close to since her mother 'abandoned her'.

Women who initially target adolescents (Group B). These women were prone to minimise the abusiveness of their own sexual experiences in their adolescence. Despite being between 12 and 14 years of age and most of their abusers being more than 25 years older, most of the women believed when the 'relationship' started they were 'equal partners' and were 'in love'. Even when they began to feel unhappy, wanted to get out of the relationship and were unable to do so, they said that at the time they still believd the 'relationship' was not abusive.

Women who are initially coerced into offending (Group C). From the description of the activity that took place between themselves and their fathers, four of these women were experiencing incestuous contact but described it as love. Importantly, each of these women later justified the sexual interaction between her husband, herself and her children similarly: an expression of affection and closeness. With these exceptions, the other women in this group perceived the sexual experiences they had before the age of 16, with anyone more than five years older than them, as being imposed on them but also believed they were in some way responsible for that abuse.

(c) The women's perceptions of the reaction of others to the sexual abuse that they experienced

Before their behaviour was discovered, only one of the women perpetrators of child sexual abuse had told anyone about her childhood sexual victimisation who had believed her and/or acted appropriately. This woman told a counsellor, and for her therapy, kept a diary in which she wrote down parts of her experience. Her husband found her notes and used them as part of his coercion tactics. All of the women who initiated the sexual abuse of children had the belief that other adults in their lives knew they were being sexually abused and either condoned, colluded or even actively facilitated that abuse. Several women initially coerced into sexually abusing children also held these beliefs. Others who thought no one knew of the sexual abuse believed that even if they did know they would neither care nor make it stop. In contrast each of the women in the comparison group believed that no other adult knew of the sexual abuse she was enduring at the time it occurred, and if they did it would not be condoned.

CASE EXAMPLE 3.11

Theresa said she clearly remembers telling her mother about her grandmother's sexual behaviour with her and that she 'didn't like it'. She says her mother's reply was, 'Granny just wants a big cuddle . . . do what granny wants or she won't want you, and you'll have to stay in the house alone, when mummy works'.

CASE EXAMPLE 3.12

Two women who sexually abused adolescents, were themselves sexually abused by teachers (one by a female teacher, one by a male). Each *believed* other teachers knew about the 'relationships' and seemed both to condone and to encourage them. Both described it as being common knowledge at the school that the teachers took them to their homes, spent many breaks and lunchtimes together and that they had 'a special relationship' with them.

CASE EXAMPLE 3.13

When Celia was seven years old, she told her mother how a man had 'hurt' her. Her vagina was torn and bleeding and she was very bruised. Her mother told her that, it 'served her right', because she should 'never have been born'.

(d) Relationship between the sexual abuse that the women experienced and that they perpetrated

The sexual abuse that the women acting as sole perpetrators *originally* perpetrated tended to reflect in several ways the sexual abuse they themselves experienced as a child. Women who were initially coerced into sexually abusing by men, when they sexually abused as sole perpetrator tended initially to imitate the abuse they perpetrated when coerced.

(i) Age of children targeted
Women who initially target very young children (Group A) were themselves *initially* victims when they were very young, often within the family and for a long period of time. Women who initially target adolescents (Group B) were likely to have initially been victims of sexual abuse in their adolescent years, often by someone outside the family.

(ii) Targeting and grooming their victims
There was a strong correlation between the manner in which the women as children were targeted, groomed and silenced by their sexual victimisers and the manner in which they in turn targeted, groomed and silenced their sexual victims (see Chapter 2).

(iii) Acts experienced compared to acts perpetrated
In some cases but not all, the actual sexual acts the women perpetrated were similar to those perpetrated against them. Some women identically re-enacted the sexual abuse they had experienced as children.

CASE EXAMPLE 3.14

In the course of Sophia's therapy dealing with the abuse she perpetrated against her daughter, she began to get 'flashbacks' of herself being sexually abused. Initially she completely dismissed these flashbacks as they were of her grandfather doing to her exactly the same pattern of behaviours, including use of a particular object in a particular way, at the same time in the bedtime 'routine', that Sophia had done to her daughter. Her grandfather died when she was six. He had lived with them and she was his 'favourite, everyone had said so'. The flashbacks were persistent and she eventually went to see her cousin, also one of his grandchildren. Without giving her cousin any details, Sophia asked her if their grandfather had sexually abused her. She said 'Of course he did'. Sophia asked her cousin what she remembered him doing and her cousin described the exact same things, a particular and regular pattern of sexual activity, that she was remembering in her flashbacks: the exact same pattern of sexual activity that she had perpetrated on her daughter. *Sophia had re-enacted her own sexually abusive experience without any conscious memory of this abuse.*

CASE EXAMPLE 3.15

Carol was an only child. From birth she shared a bed with her father and mother. Carol said that she 'could tolerate being sexually abused by her father' but not by her mother. She felt that her mother had 'set her up' to be abused by her father. From 14 on, Carol was taken to sex parties by her parents. There she met her husband. She believed that he was a really loving person. He actually asked her permission to touch her and never did anything that she did not want. She agreed to marry him. Immediately his behaviour changed. He forced her to do all the things that she had refused him. Carol believed that he got an even greater thrill and satisfaction from knowing it was exactly what she did not like. Their first child was a daughter who 'naturally' shared their bed. When her partner started sexually abusing her and wanting Carol to join in, she said that she felt that it was a 'natural thing to do'. Carol had two other children, both sons, neither of whom had been sexually abused. While eventually admitting to the abuse of her daughter, she appeared genuinely shocked at the idea of sexually abusing her sons.

(iv) Seductive/Sadistic abuse
There was no direct correlation between the type of sexual abuse primarily experienced, seductive or sadistic, and that primarily perpetrated. Importantly, it was the women who were most frequently physically abused, and who had suffered the most severe emotional abuse as children, who were more likely to sadistically sexually abuse their victims.

(e) The gender of the perpetrators who abused the women offenders when they were children

Most of the women who sexually abused children were sexually abused by male perpetrators. Two of the women who were sexually abused by women in their childhood said they had specifically targeted girls to sexually abuse to recreate that relationship.

CASE EXAMPLE 3.16

Rosie was sexually abused by a teacher from age 12 to 16. She became a social worker and she herself sexually abused a young woman. Many of the aspects of the abuse re-enacted the abuse she had experienced. Both 'relationships' started by the abuser targeting a vulnerable child, and forming a 'special relationship' with the child that was known to other staff. In both, the abuser took on a substitute mother role, and in both, the child was made to feel that she was the instigator of the sexual relationship.

(f) Sexual acts engaged in with other children during childhood

(i) Mutual sexual exploration with peers or siblings
Interestingly, a greater percentage of women in the comparison group (61%) as compared to women in the groups of offenders (19%) described mutual sexual exploration (reciprocal and non-abusive sexual contact) with other children, both siblings and peers, during their childhood years. The behaviours at all ages mostly involved mutual viewing and touching of genitalia.

(ii) Sexual acts imposed as children on other children
Three women who initially targeted young children and one initially coerced woman offender said they had imposed sexual acts on children when they themselves were children. Three of these four women were initially forced to perpetrate sexual acts on other children by their abusers. None of the women in the comparison group admitted to such behaviour.

CASE EXAMPLE 3.17

Pat's teenage stepbrother started sexually abusing her when she was four. After three or four years he started involving her younger brother and sister and then got other small children to come and 'play' with them. His greatest pleasure seemed to be to get the younger children to watch him raping and beating Pat. She said she believed that by 'allowing him' to do this she was protecting 'the little ones'. Her brother then began to force Pat to sexually abuse the little boys. Pat says when she refused he beat her and cut her with a knife. She talked of how relieved she was it was not her being abused but also 'the thrill' she got in both sexually abusing and hurting the children. When her stepbrother left home she began to abuse the children alone.

CASE EXAMPLE 3.18

A woman who was sexually abused by her brother was coerced by him into carrying out sexual acts with other children who lived in the same street. He would also make her do it to the same children when alone and then tell him about what she had done while masturbating him. When he left home, her abusive behaviour stopped completely until she met her second husband. (Paula)

REFLECTION AND COMMENT

All the women who acted as sole perpetrators of the sexual abuse of children were themselves initially sexually traumatised at developmentally crucial stages in the formation of sexual identity, that is infancy and adolescence. Consequently it would be highly likely that their sexual arousal was conditioned to images associated with these periods of development (Laws & Marshall, 1990). Many, but not all, of the women who were coerced into sexually abusing children had also been sexually abused. More importantly, almost all the women in this group had blurred sexual and generational boundaries with their primary attachment figure, their father.

In each case where a woman initiated the abuse as a sole perpetrator, the sexual abuse she perpetrated was in some way a reflection of the trauma that she experienced. This supports the idea that part of a woman's motivation to sexually abuse is re-enactment of trauma. For women in all the groups of offenders, the less a woman had cognitively and emotionally processed her childhood sexual abuse, and the less that she had recognised the experience as abusive, the more likely she was to replicate, in precise detail, the actual abuse that she experienced.

Most important, in terms of understanding the behaviour and thus facilitating treatment, are the thinking errors that the women internalised as a consequence of their own experience of abuse (Eldridge, 1992) Through her experiences as a child, each woman internalised specific beliefs about herself and her abuser/s that she then used, as conscious or unconscious rationalisations, to facilitate her sexually abusing children. This is reflected in the finding that the women tend to employ very similar cognitive distortions to those they themselves experienced from their abusers, to groom their targets and justify the abuse they perpetrate.

One particular thinking error each woman internalised as a child was that she herself was innately bad and thus responsible in some way for the abuse she experienced. This was confirmed by each woman's belief that other key adults in her life knew of the abuse and did not prevent it occurring. Thus there was either something about her that meant she deserved to be abused, or what she was experiencing was acceptable. Although these women may not have been totally accurate in their assessment of the situation, these were their beliefs and as such, would be internalised and inform their future behaviour. It is proposed that they may well have internalised the belief, on a deep level of consciousness, that to sexually abuse certain children is somehow permissible.

One hypothesis to explain the finding that more women in the comparison group reported engaging in mutual sexual exploration than did women offenders, may be that the women who became abusers rarely had friends, or indeed, any free social contact with other children. They also mostly felt different and isolated even from their siblings. Six of the seven women in the groups of female offenders who did engage in mutual sexual exploration, did so with their siblings. Another hypothesis is that the sexual abuse that many of the women in the offender groups were experiencing, inhibited developmentally 'appropriate' sexual exploration. In addition, it may also be that the women offenders were reluctant to disclose further sexual contact with children. Although the women in the groups of offenders were generally very open about the abuses that had already been recognised, they may not have wanted to disclose earlier sexual behaviours that may then have been construed as further examples of their abusing behaviour.

3. Emotional Abuse

Emotional abuse is extremely difficult to operationalise and measure in a meaningful way. Garbarino (1986) describes patterns of psychological maltreatment that attack a child's development of self and social competence, which recognise both cultural and developmental variables:

REJECTING, ISOLATING, TERRORIZING, IGNORING, CORRUPTING

(see Appendix 3). Each woman was asked to rate her experience of this form of treatment during four stages of her childhood. In addition, the

Table 3.4: Mean rating by the women in each group of their experience of emotional abuse within their home during childhood

	GROUP A (n=14)	GROUP B (n=10)	GROUP C (n=12)	GROUP D (n=36)
TOTALS max = 60	54.4	45.0	42.5	17.9

women were asked about their experiences of receiving human comfort as children; who they felt close to as a child, who comforted them when they were distressed, and from whom they received non-sexual physical touch.

FINDINGS

(a) Results based on Garbarino's definitions

One of the most compelling differences between the women in the comparison group and the offender groups was the degree of emotional deprivation and abuse experienced by the women offenders as children (Table 3.4). More than one-third of all the female offenders spontaneously stated that their mothers had not wanted them and/or wished that they had never been born. Importantly, the aspects of abuse most consistently reported by the women offenders in all three groups were rejection and ignoring. These are both active and passive forms of denial of the worth of the child. Only five women in the comparison group rated the emotional abuse experienced at a similar level to women offenders. The ratings were, however, not so consistently high across all factors and during all stages of development. These five women also differed from the women offenders in that each felt she did have positive emotional experience from people other than within her family.

CASE EXAMPLE 3.19

'My mother said I was a mistake. She wanted an abortion . . . she tried gin . . . hot baths . . . Epsom salts . . . throwing herself down stairs . . . she wished I'd never been born. . . she worshipped my brother . . . he was like a little God . . . she was always fussing him . . . She didn't like my dad either . . . he was frightened of her. I hit my head on the hearth . . . it was bleeding . . . my dad went to pick me up . . . my mum went mad, she screeched at him to leave me alone . . . he never touched me again . . . It was my job to do the housework and if it wern't done, she'd rant and rave at me and threaten to throw me out . . . she'd keep me off school if I was needed to do 'ought at home, she said school were a waste of time for me, I was thick, I'd always be thick . . . I got a certificate for swimming and she tore it up. I had no friends . . . she wouldn't have them in the house or let me out . . . she saw him [her brother, four years older] doing it to me, two or three times and never said a word to him but called me a slag . . . I told her what was happening, she laughed . . . said it were no less than I deserved . . .' Statements made by Tina (male-coerced offender) indicating the emotional climate in which she lived.

(b) Experiences of human comfort in childhood

Women who initially target young children and women who initially target adolescents (Groups A and B). It is significant that none of these women offenders *remembers* ever having experienced being cuddled, held or physically comforted by, or felt special to, anyone who did not also sexually abuse her. This is not to say it never occurred but that the women do not have any memories of this experience. None of these women remembered feeling emotionally close to anyone or having any adult to go to when she felt distressed.

Women who are initially coerced into offending. Only four of the women who were initially coerced by men into sexually abusing children, remember non-sexual touch, all saying it came from their fathers. A further three women said they believed their father would have cuddled and hugged them but their mothers prevented them from doing so. Each of the women in this group described 'feeling close to her father' but most added the caveat that it was not as close as it could/should have been. Only two women said they felt able as children to seek comfort when they were distressed. For both these women this was from her father.

The comparison group (Group D). All the women in the comparison group, even those who rated their level of emotional abuse to be in some ways similar to that of the offenders, remembered experiencing non-sexual touch from someone in their childhood. Each of the women in the comparison group could also name at least one adult to whom she felt emotionally close who did not sexually abuse her.

REFLECTION AND COMMENT

One of the greatest differences between the women in the comparison group and the women perpetrators was the degree of emotional abuse and emotional isolation in their childhood. The degree of emotional abuse experienced by all the women offenders would result in these women feeling powerful negative emotions that they were unable to express: isolation, humiliation, worthlessness, hopelessness, and rage. These feelings, exacerbated by being denied any source of human comfort and closeness, would have to be suppressed for the child's emotional survival. This would result in a well of anger and emotional pain that unless recognised and expressed would make the grown woman deaf and blind to any needs and desires of a child. In fact any behaviour that would tap these feelings may result in an unleashing of that suppressed rage.

RELATIONSHIPS WITH SIBLINGS

Siblings can be a very important part of the socialisation of children; they act as attachment figures, as well as a natural 'comparison group' through which a child can assess and evaluate her own experiences (Dunn, 1988). Those women who had siblings were asked to describe their relationship with each of them. Comparisons were also made in how the women construed themselves and their siblings on the Repertory Grid.

FINDINGS

Most of the women perpetrators described feeling very separate from their brothers and sisters. Very few felt that as a child they had positive relationships with their siblings. Every woman perpetrator who had siblings, believed she was the child that was loved the least, treated the most harshly, and hurt the most. Those women in the comparison group who had been badly hurt within their families, were more likely than the women in the clinical groups to recognise that their siblings may also have suffered equally from similar experiences (see Table 3.5).

Table 3.5: Comments made by the women about their siblings

Group A	The boys were as bad as my father, if they wern't hurting me in some way, they ignored me
	We lived together in the same house but I didn't know her
	I never felt like I was the same as any of them
Group B	I was the family slave, for my mum and my brothers
	He had a great life, he could do no wrong. Even if he did do something, she'd ignore him and take it out on me
	I really wanted a little brother and was so happy when he was born but when I realised that my dad wanted a boy so much, I began to really hate him
Group C	My brother was the favourite, he could do no wrong
	I hated my sister, especially when my dad gave her any attention at all, she was on my mum's side
	We got on alright but we had nothing in common
	My sister and I played a lot together as children but we just drifted apart
Group D	It was awful for all of us
	We fought like cat and dog but if the chips were down, he'd always be there for me
	When my mum was really stressed my sister would take over, she was like another mum to me
	I used to feel really sorry for my sister, she seemed to always be the one in trouble

REFLECTION AND COMMENT

The woman offender's belief that as a child she was treated more detrimentally than her siblings would further depress the developing child's sense of worth and self-esteem. This perception would also reinforce the woman's developing belief that there was something specific to, and intrinsic within, her that induced people to treat her badly.

RELATIONSHIPS WITH PEERS

Good peer relationships can offer an alternative model to that experienced within the family. However, children who have experienced difficult familial relationships are vulnerable to forming negative peer relationships (e.g. Sroufe, 1983).

FINDINGS

A very clear difference between the women offenders and the comparison group was the degree of intimacy in their peer relationships. Many of the offenders described feeling isolated and different from their peer groups. One of the major problems the women offenders experienced as children was bullying at school and/or in the neighbourhood in which they lived.

Women who initially target young children (Group A). None of the women who sexually abused young children had ever had anyone that she could call a friend throughout her childhood. A few of the women did describe 'playing' or 'hanging-around' or 'truanting' with other children but not having a close reciprocal relationship. None had had a 'best-friend'.

Women who initially target adolescents (Group B). The friendships these women formed were shallow, often short-lived and rarely extended to 'out-of-school' relationships.

Women who were initially coerced offenders (Group C). Seven of these twelve women described having had at least one friend during their childhood and adolescence. Two of these women said they felt emotionally close to a friend.

The comparison group (Group D). None of these women went through their whole childhood and adolescence without having a friend.

REFLECTION AND COMMENT

When the women offenders as children came in contact with peers, they would have already developed a negative model of themselves and their interpersonal relationships. It is very difficult for such a child to develop a friendship which is characterised by empathy, reciprocity, trust, and mutual enjoyment when the formative models of relationships have been characterised by rejection, hostility, exploitation of trust, and distress. It is unlikely that children from such abusive families as the women perpetrators had would have any expectation that relationships could be a source of support, pleasure and amusement. Sroufe and Fleeson (1986) argue that children internalise both sides of a relationship, in these cases abuser and abused, in conjunction with the emotions associated with each role. This might account for the higher proportion of women in the offenders group than the comparison group who experienced bullying or themselves bullied within their peer groups. It is proposed that when entering peer relationships the strategies used are either attack so as not to be in the position of victim, or avoidance of all peer contact, which leaves the child vulnerable to further victimisation due to lack of alliances within a peer group. Both these strategies would result in reinforcing a negative view of self and also in the formation of negative working models of peer relationships. Through the experiences she did have with peers, each woman perpetrator as a child received further negative messages about the value of herself and of human social contact. Therefore she would tend to become even more isolated within her family unit and have fewer alternatives by which to assess more objectively her own personal experience. Having no intimate companion, the child has no outlet for expression of any of her feelings, consequently the repression becomes further entrenched. Hartup (1986) stresses the importance of peer relationships for healthy development, describing how poor peer relationships in middle childhood are predictive of mental health and psychosexual difficulties in adulthood.

SUMMARY

- None of the women who sexually abused children were given 'good-enough' care, affection and protection.
- They had complex and distorted relationships with their parents. Mothers were perceived as cold, distant, weak, demanding, dominating and non-protective. *Sole perpetrators* had models of their fathers and/or father figures as threatening rather than protective. *Initially coerced*

perpetrators tended to idealise their fathers.

- Almost all of the women perpetrators repressed and/or denied negative aspects of their parents and developed a model of themselves as innately bad to explain their treatment by them.
- The women in the comparison group who had similar experiences with their parents were less likely to engage in extreme denial and cognitive rationalisations.
- The women perpetrators' beliefs about the roles, abilities and intent of children will have been distorted by their experiences. The model would be of children having to meet adult needs.
- All the women who sexually abused children experienced profound abuse in their own childhood: physical, sexual and/or emotional.
- As children, the women offenders all appeared to receive powerful messages, usually from adults who 'knew', or through the preferential treatment of the abuser, that it was permissible for them to be treated in this way and/or that they caused their own abuse.
- Due to the many abuses these women experienced, especially the feelings of rejection and ignoring at an early age, the women are likely to have internalised the belief about themselves as being worthless.
- The emotional abuse that the women perpetrators experienced as children will result in them being unable to feel genuine empathy or to recognise the emotional needs and/or experience of children.
- Some of the women perpetrators as children developed a stronger bond with their abusers who at least showed interest in them, than with their parent/s whom they experienced as ignoring or blatantly rejecting them.
- The women perpetrators' negative self-image when children, combined with intermittent rewards and some positive affirmation for sexually inappropriate behaviour, may have conveyed an assumption that their only source of esteem was through sexual contact.
- Possibly when the woman as an adult felt the need for human connection, she engaged in abusive relationships but protected herself by doing so in the perpetrator role rather than risk victimisation.
- The women perpetrators were very isolated in their childhoods and therefore had no alternative models or peers through which to express their feelings or examine their experience.
- Crucially, the women perpetrators entered adolescence with very negative internal models of self but with no social arenas in which to challenge these models and individuate. Thus intergenerational continuity would be more likely to occur.

4

RELATIONSHIPS: WITH SELF AND OTHERS

- FROM CHILD TO WOMAN: ADOLESCENCE, THE FORMATION OF IDENTITY
- THE WOMEN'S IMAGE OF SELF
- CARE-ELICITING AND CARE-RECEIVING
- ADULT PEER RELATIONSHIPS
- RELATIONSHIPS WITH PARTNERS
- SUMMARY

FROM CHILD TO WOMAN: ADOLESCENCE, THE FORMATION OF IDENTITY

'Adolescence is the successor of childhood and the predecessor to adult life' (Obholzer, 1992). It is the period of development during which most young people achieve a degree of disengagement from their dependency on parents and begin to evolve a more separate identity. Most theorists concur that the major task of adolescence is the formation of a sense of identity: social, psychological, and physical (Erikson, 1950). Youngson (1989) summarises this developmental process in terms of an individual realising that 'I am', 'I am me', and 'I am a person'. This involves developing personal integration, 'an appreciation, understanding and acceptance of self', 'I AM'; developing 'a perception of self in relation to others', 'I AM ME'; and developing a perception of self 'within the wider society and culture' and a knowledge of one's ability to live independently within that society; 'I AM A PERSON'. This identity also includes the beginning of the formation of a sexual identity and sexuality.

Adolescence is the period of development during which the internal models of self, others, competencies and social processes formed within the childhood years are put to the test within a wider environment to be either confirmed or repudiated. For this to occur effectively in Western culture, Erikson (1968) stresses the need for the adolescent to be part of a peer group and most particularly to develop specific friends and confidants (Duck, 1973). The peer group acts as a transitional support network to facilitate the process of forming a separate identity by forming an alternative environment in which the values and ideas of the parent can be reworked, and where necessary challenged and re-evaluated. In doing so, there can be the chance of a possible reassessment of the models held, and therefore the young person's identity and sense of self has the possibility of differing from that developed by the interactions with significant others during childhood.

Research has also indicated that it is the quality of the interactions with peers that is of vital importance rather than mere frequency of contact. The distinct lack of any such close friends or peer network in the lives of the women offenders when they were adolescents would mean that the internal models of themselves, others and the world established during their childhood would go relatively unchallenged. Thus the lack of acceptance within a peer group and having no close friends may be of crucial importance in these young women's lives.

There is considerable evidence to indicate that interactions with peers are fundamentally important in the development of an individual's sexual attitudes and behaviours (Hartup, 1983). None of the women offenders had a peer group within which to share, observe, experiment and discuss her own feelings and experiences. By adolescence, all bar three of the women offenders had already been engaged in sexual behaviours inappropriate to their age and developmental stage. At least 75% of the women offenders experienced sexual abuse during this important period of development of sexual identity. Thus the process of normal sexual discovery and experimentation with peers was lacking and/or had been corrupted by prior events.

Those women who as adolescents did form contacts and connections outside the family tended to do so with older people rather than peers and/or withpeople who in some way reinforced the internal models developed within their childhood. Many achieved some form of separation from their families by becoming involved in very unhealthy sexual relationships, which often led to marriage, in order to precipitate what was perceived as necessary disengagement. Evidence to support this idea comes from the Repertory Grids. The women who sexually abused very young children and those who sexually abused adolescents construed themselves as children/adolescents/adults to be very similar. The women who were initially coerced into sexually abusing children by men perceived themselves as adolescents to be different from themselves as a woman when sexually abusing. They tended to construe their adolescent self more positively than their adult abusing self. The women in the comparison group mostly construed 'Self as adult' as somewhat, but not very, different from 'Self as a child/adolescent'. The differences tended to be mainly on the constructs of 'In control of my life', 'Can cope alone', 'Able to form close relationships', and 'Sexual'.

THE WOMEN'S IMAGE OF SELF

Perception of self, others and the quality of relationships between them are dynamically interdependent. Each aspect of every interaction, observation and instruction that a person experiences is processed and internalised to form models of self, others and relationships between them (Bretherton & Waters, 1985). These models act as internal guides which powerfully influence the person's choice of which, from a range of possible behaviours that could be engaged in any given situation, will be most likely to meet the person's needs. Women who sexually abuse children have made the choice to meet certain of their needs via the sexual abuse of a child. In order to gain an insight as to why this particular relationship was utilised to meet her needs, each woman's relationships with herself and others were explored. A person's sense of self is the set of attitudes and beliefs that is held about the self. The self is multidimensional. Argyle (1983) describes three aspects of self: *self-image*, how the woman consciously perceives herself; *self-esteem*, the extent to which the woman approves of herself; *ideal self*, the self that the woman would most like to be. None of these may be the same as the *presenting self*, the self shown to others. A person's sense of their own ability to deal effectively with their environment, their *self-efficacy* (Bandura, 1977), will be incorporated into the sense of self. All the aspects of self are inextricably linked. The closer a person's self-image is to their ideal-self, the higher their self-esteem will be. The more positive a person's self-esteem, the more likely a person is to have a presenting self that is consistent with the self-image. Self-efficacy and self-esteem are also linked. A person who feels they can deal more effectively with their environment is likely to have enhanced self-esteem, the reverse also being true. Thus each of the measures is representative of the woman's sense of self.

1. Self-esteem, Self-image and Ideal Self

Each woman was asked to fill in Rosenberg's Self-esteem Test twice; once in relation to the present and once in relation to how she felt at the age when she was sexually abusing children (each woman in the comparison group was asked to think of how she felt at the age when the woman she was matched with was sexually abusing children). In addition, the differences, on the Repertory Grid, as to how the woman construed herself and her ideal self were calculated.

FINDINGS

Results from Rosenberg's Self-esteem Test and the differences between the women's construing of self and ideal self from the Repertory Grid, indicate that each of the women who sexually abused children had a very negative sense of self (Table 4.1). Some women in the comparison group also had a poor sense of self; however, the differences between the scores of the groups of offenders and the comparison group on Rosenberg's Self-esteem Test were statistically highly significant. There was also a statistically significant difference between the groups of offenders.

Women who initially target adolescents (Group B). The women who initially targeted adolescents tended to score more highly than the women offenders in the other two groups. It was noted that they consistently scored more highly on items that asked about the woman's sense of competence over their environment, self-efficacy. This is likely to be a reflection of women in this group's experiences of as a child having to take on the carer role within the family. As children they had had to achieve competencies inappropriate to their stage of development, or risk the terror of abandonment by the parent. On items on the scale that looked at the woman's beliefs about her personal characteristics, each rated herself as poorly as the other women offenders rated themselves to be.

CASE EXAMPLE 4.1

'From when I was a very young child I looked after my father. Even before I went to school, I had to make his sandwich and cups of tea. I'd also been taught how to do his wounds. As I got older I would have to clean the house and help with the shopping and cooking. After my brother was born [she was eight], I'd look after him too. I'd make-up his bottles, feed and change him. If my dad was really bad, I'd have to stay off school to look after him and my brother and get a meal while my mum was at work. I'd also do the washing

Table 4.1: Measures of the women's sense of self

	GROUP A (n=14)	GROUP B (n=10)	GROUP C (n=12)	GROUP D (n=36)
Rosenberg's self-esteem score during time when offenders were sexually abusing children (MAXIMUM: 63)	mean 14.4 (range 9–21)	mean 31.4 (range 19–44)	mean 15.4 (range 8–24)	mean 42.8 (range 33–54)
Rosenberg's self-esteem score during time when not sexually abusing (MAXIMUM: 63)	mean 17.4 (range 9–26)	mean 31 (range 17–44)	mean 28.6 (range 14–36)	mean 43.5 (range 34–53)
Difference between self at times of abusing and ideal self (Repertory Grid) (MAXIMUM: 100)	mean 72.7 (range 59–82)	mean 54.5 (range 32–68)	mean 68.1 (range 49–84)	mean 30.2 (range 2–46)

and the ironing . . . if any of it got forgotten I'd get a real hiding. From being a young kid, I could run the house and care for the family . . . I suppose it was good for me really. Taught me a lot young.' Glenda suffered from psoriasis and eczema as an adult and also has a variety of symptoms that doctors perceived as either self-inflicted or psychosomatic. She expected her son to carry out all her personal care, including bathing her and sleeping with her in case she should need him in the night. (Glenda)

Women who are initially coerced offenders (Group C). There was a statistically significant difference between how the women who were coerced into sexually abusing children perceived themselves while with their co-perpetrators, and how they perceived themselves apart from their partners. Being in prison or otherwise away from their partners, was the first time for years, if ever, they had not received daily criticism, humiliation, and condemnation from those closest to them.

CASE EXAMPLE 4.2

'. . . my mum always told me I couldn't do anything right . . . whatever I did was wrong and then if I did it her way . . . that'd be wrong too . . . he'd throw his dinner at me . . . he was always saying I'd be a whore but I was too ugly for anyone to pay for me . . . he'd say I was stupid and ignorant and knew nothing . . . he was always hitting me for getting things wrong . . . he'd hold my head down the toilet and get the kids to flush it saying I was just a piece of shit.' (Phrases taken from Diane's transcript.)

2. The Women's Beliefs about Power and Control: an Indication of Self-efficacy

Human beings who believe that they have little sense of control over their lives, as the women who sexually abuse children do, experience aversive events more negatively and do not benefit as greatly from positive experiences as others do (e.g. Averill, 1973; Schulz, 1976). To function effectively, a person needs to have a sense of control over life and environment (e.g. Rotter, 1966; Bandura, 1979). Power, defined as 'the ability to influence others to do what one wants' (Harper, 1985) is also important in maintaining well-being. This lack of a sense of power and control leads the women perpetrators to experience various symptoms of emotional distress and pathological behaviour (Gilbert, 1989). Speltz, Matthews and Mathews (1989) report that the women in their study 'asserted very little power and influence over their own destinies and environments' (p.31). In this study each woman was asked to rate, on a seven-point scale, herself and other people in her life, as to the degree of control she believed that each had over his or her own life and the degree of power she believed that she had over others.

FINDINGS

There was a statistically significant difference between the ratings of the groups of women offenders and the women in the comparison group as to the estimated degree of control they believed they had over their own lives and the degree of power they believed they had over others (Table 4.2). The women who sexually abused children believed that they had far less control over their own lives than the women in the comparison group believed that they had over theirs. Each woman offender also believed that other adults, and even children, had more control over their own lives than she had over her life. An indication that these women would have liked more control over their lives was the finding that each woman in the offender groups rated her 'ideal self' as having much more control over her life than she perceived that she actually had. The women offenders also believed they were able to exert significantly less power over others than the comparison group women, and each woman offender believed that other adults and children had more power to influence others than she had (Table 4.3).

Although almost all the women offenders in this study described that they felt powerless and that they asserted little control over their own destiny, *this is the women's own perception of themselves.* Some of the women in this

Table 4.2: Relative levels of control the women perceive themselves and others to have over life (max. = 7, min. = 1)

	GROUP A	GROUP B	GROUP C	GROUP D
SELF	1.9	3.4	1.4	5.1
	(range 1–3)	(range 2–5)	(range 1–2)	(range 3–7)
ADULTS	5.4	5.9	6.2	5.4
	(range 5–7)	(range 5–7)	(range 5–7)	(range 3–7)
CHILDREN	3.9	5.6	3.1	4.1
	(range 2–6)	(range 4–7) victims 6–7)	(range 2–4)	(range 1–6)

Table 4.3: Relative levels of power the women perceive themselves and others to have (max. = 7, min. = 1)

	GROUP A	GROUP B	GROUP C	GROUP D
SELF	1.2	2.7	1.3	4.9
	(range 1–2)	(range 2–4)	(range 1–2)	(range 3–7)
ADULTS	5.6	5.7	5.4	5.0
	(range 5–7)	(range 5–7)	(range 5–7)	(range 4–7)
CHILDREN	3.4	5.1	3.6	4.8
	(range 3–5)	(range 4–7) (victims 6–7)	(range 2–5)	(range 3–7)

study were seen as very powerful and controlling, particularly by their victims, and also by other adults, including many of the professionals involved with them.

Women who initially target young children (Group A). Each of these women held the belief that she had, and importantly that she had always had, a minimal degree of power and control over her own life. Each felt that almost all her decisions, particularly major ones such as her living circumstances and her choice of partners, were either forced on her or, as one said, were 'slipped into'. Many women describe always feeling as if they were in someone else's power despite living alone, or with their children, and managing their own lives.

CASE EXAMPLE 4.3

'I've never had any control over any part of my life . . . I've always been in someone's power, first my father's . . . when he died, social services took control of me and put me with another bastard . . . worse than my father . . . [both sexually, physically and emotionally abused her]. I had to ask permission to move . . . I could do nothing without his say-so. When I got pregnant by him [aged 19] he called me a whore and threw me out on the street. Social services put me in a mother and baby home . . . then it was the baby's turn, he controlled me . . . worst than the rest . . . each cry, each whimper, made me feel that I was still in his grip [foster-father's], it was as if I could never escape him. Social services took the baby away and put me in a bed-sit place with three men. It felt as if they'd given me to them to be used just as they'd given me to my foster father when I was a kid. I couldn't say no to any of them . . . when I fell for my daughter, I didn't even know which one was the father.They moved me . . . but I had her [her daughter] then she took me over as well, and now they've taken her too.' (Doreen)

Women who initially target adolescents (Group B). The women who sexually abused adolescents tended to believe that they had somewhat more control over their lives than the women in the other two offender groups. Significantly, most women in this group rated their adolescent victims as having complete control over their own lives.

Women who are initially coerced offenders (Group C). Although the difference was not statistically significant, there was a trend for the women who were initially coerced into sexually abusing children by men to believe that they had even less control of their lives than the women in any of the other groups. Most women in this group attributed their lack of control over their lives to their abusive relationships with their male partners. The male partners used force and fear, and/or withdrawal of any good or positive aspect of the relationship to exert supreme control over their partners. Many of these women relied on the power they perceived their male partners to have to exert any influence over their situation.

CASE EXAMPLE 4.4

Tina is a bubbly, seemingly self-confident woman with good social skills. This is not, however, the image she portrays of herself during the 25 years that she was married to her husband. 'From the start of us going together Bob took control of everything. I thought it was because he wanted to really look after me. When he was jealous I thought that it meant he really had the hots for me. The trouble started after we were married. I became like a prisoner. I had no friends, he'd forbidden me to see them all . . . Bob controlled all the money. I went to work and he even took the money I'd earned. He knew what bus I caught back and if I missed it, or it was late, I'd get a beating. There was a lock on the phone and nobody could use it but him. I could only buy what he said and I had to give him the receipts and the change. He had the say on what the children did, what they watched on TV, even where we all sat. I had to clean what he said when he said; cook exactly what he wanted when he wanted it. He also controlled when I went to bed when I got up. If I wore something he didn't like, I'd get pulped. The thing was what he liked one day, he hated the next so you could never tell. If I went against him, he'd beat me or choose one of the children to beat in front of me, to turn the kids against me. They sided with him on everything . . . When he was violent to them or sexually abused them, he blamed me and they believed him.'

The comparison group (Group D). The women in the comparison group generally rated themselves as having similar control over their lives as other adults and more control than children.

3. Aggressiveness

No matter how it is consciously rationalised by the abuser, the sexual abuse of a child is an aggressive act towards a vulnerable individual for the relief of tension in the aggressor. It is important for therapeutic intervention, to see whether or not the women perceive themselves to be aggressive.

FINDINGS

There was no statistically significant difference between the groups of women in how aggressive they rated themselves as actually being. Women within all four groups varied greatly in how they rated themselves, on a seven-point scale, in terms of aggressiveness (Table 4.4). Many women in each of the groups struggled verbally to reach a decision. The struggle centred on the discrepancy between their feelings of aggression and the expression of these feelings. Several women talked of feeling very aggressive at times but 'holding' or 'swallowing' these feelings. Women in the comparison group were as likely to engage in this struggle as women in the offender groups. It is of interest that *the majority of women,* including women in the comparison group, when asked; 'If you were to direct your frustration, anger and aggression towards another human being who would that most likely be?' answered 'A child'.

Table 4.4: Mean rating of aggressive they felt themselves to be (max. = 7, min. = 1)

	GROUP A	GROUP B	GROUP C	GROUP D
AGGRESSIVE	3.7 (range 1–6)	1.9 (range 1–3)	3.1 (range 1–5)	3.4 (range 1–6)

CARE-ELICITING AND CARE-RECEIVING

Human beings are social animals. Affiliation and cooperation are essential for the survival of the human species and are basic bio-social goals of human beings (Gilbert, 1989). This section will report on the woman's perception of self in relation to others and attempt to look at her level of emotional connectedness to those in her social world.

1. Perception of Self in Relation to Others

In the little work that has been presented on women who have sexually abused children, comments have been made as to how these women experience a sense of aloneness, isolation, seperateness and apartness from others. McCarty (1986) found this was particularly true of the independent female offender. How the women construed themselves in relation to others on the Repertory Grid was used to gain insight into the women's feelings about how similarly they saw themselves to other people in their life.

FINDINGS

Every woman who sexually abused children construed herself as being different from all other adults in her life and most similar to the children whom she sexually abused. This indicates that the women offenders did perceive themselves as being somewhat different to, and separate from, other adults. Each woman in the comparison group construed herself as more similar to at least one other adult in her life than to any child.

2. Perceived Ability to Form Close Relationships

An individual's experience of emotional loneliness is one of increasingly being associated with the instigation of offensive behaviours towards

Table 4.5: The women's perceived ability to form close relationships with adults and with children (max. = 7, min. = 1)

	GROUP A	GROUP B	GROUP C	GROUP D
Can form close relationships with adults	1.2 (range 1–2)	3.4 (range 2–4)	1.4 (range 1–2)	5.0 (range 2–7)
Can form close relationships with children non-abused	1.7 (range 1–2)	3.8 (range 2–4)	1.7 (range 1—2)	4.8 (range 2–7)
Can form close relationships with children abused	1.7 (range 1–2)	6.4 (range 6–7)	1.5 (range 1–2)	

others (e.g. Check, Perlman & Malamuth, 1985). The quality of the women's relationships is therefore an important area of interest. Speltz, Matthews and Mathews (1989) reported that the women in their study felt 'no emotional attachment to other human beings' (p.31).

FINDINGS

The women in the comparison group perceived themselves to be far more able to form close relationships with others, both with adults and children, than did the women who had sexually abused children. There was a trend for women in the offender groups to believe that they could make better relationships with children than adults. However, the difference was not marked except for the women who sexually abused adolescent children (Table 4.5).

Women who initially target young children (Group A). The women who sexually abused very young children generally rated themselves as the least able to form close relationships with adults but a few believed they did have close relationships with children.

CASE EXAMPLE 4.5

(Mavis) 'I don't feel as if I know what a relationship is . . . if I think about it, it's as if, I'm here and they're there, I'm separate, sort of enclosed . . . like everyone uses me . . . as if I'm a machine without thoughts or feelings.'

Women who initially target adolescents (Group B). The women who abused adolescents each believed they could, and did, have closer relationships with these adolescents than with anyone else in their lives. Three women objected when they were asked to consider these adolescents as children. Four women recognised they were able to make many superficially 'close relationships' with adults, and to appear well-liked and socially adept, but found it very hard to achieve real emotional intimacy.

Women who are initially coerced offenders (Group C). Several of these women felt that their ability to form relationships with others had been destroyed by their partners. Diane and Tina each said it was as if her partner stood between her and other people.

The comparison group (Group D). Although some of the women in this group were very specific about who they could and/or would form close relationships with, almost all felt that they had some ability to do so. Five women did talk of difficulties in forming close relationships but despite this, all bar one of these women had a close relationship with someone.

3. Feeling Loved and Cared For

Groth (1982) proposed that the need for nurturance is prominent in the lives of women who sexually abuse children. Speltz, Matthews and Mathews (1989) report that the women in their study describe themselves as 'needing acceptance, attention, closeness' (p. 28). These statements imply that women who sexually abuse children are unlikely to feel either loved or cared for. Each woman was asked to rate every person on her Repertory Grid as to how much she believed that person 'loved her', and then, on how much she believed that the person 'cared for her'.

FINDINGS

The women in the comparison group believed that they had received more care and felt more loved than any of the groups of women offenders (Table 4.6). This difference reached statistical significance.

Women who initially target young children (Group A). Very few women in this group believed that they had ever been loved or cared for by anyone. None of the women rated anyone caring for her any higher than 3, or loving her more than 4, on a seven-point scale. Interestingly, almost every woman in this group rated a child as the person who cared for her and loved her most.

CASE EXAMPLE 4.6

'When you say "loved me" and "cared for me", I can't say . . . I don't know what that would mean or how it would feel. I thought my grandfather loved

Table 4.6: Mean rating of how loved and cared for the women believed that they were by significant others in their lives (max. = 7, min. = 1)

	GROUP A	GROUP B	GROUP C	GROUP D
Loved	1.6	3.7	2.4	5.4
	(range	(range	(range	(range
	1.3–2.2)	3.2–4.9)	2.0–3.5)	3.4–6.7)
Cared for	1.7	3.4	2.5	4.9
	(range	(range	(range	(range
	1.2–2.2)	3.0–4.2)	1.8–3.6)	3.2–5.5)

me, and he sexually abused me . . . my husband never loved or cared for me, he wanted me for sex and married me when I was pregnant to save family scandal. I did think that my daughter loved me but . . . after what I did to her . . . as a young child she seemed to care for me . . . she was always looking after me . . . I now realise the care I thought she was showing me, was to appease me . . . I wanted my mother to love me . . . but it never felt like she did . . . she and father were never there. I was looked after by nannies . . . ' (Sophia)

Women who initially target adolescents (Group B). There was a trend for the women who primarily targeted adolescents to have higher overall scores in these areas than the other women perpetrators. This difference was due to the fact that each of these women rated the child or children that she had sexually abused as both 'loving her' and 'caring for her' very highly. Significantly, several of these women also described the people who had formed abusive relationships with them in their adolescence as both loving and caring for them.

CASE EXAMPLE 4.7

Alice would target a vulnerable young woman she saw 'hanging around' and strike up a conversation. She would then follow her for several days and eventually at an expedient time, 'accidentally bump into her'. She would buy the girl things like burgers, chips and shakes, and eventually actually arrange to meet her. During 'the date' Alice would sexually assault the girl, attributing to the girl the motivation for the act because she agreed to meet her. Alice never pursued the girl again after the sexual assault. When Alice was asked to rate on a seven-point scale how much she believed these girls loved her and cared for her, she scored each of them at the maximum seven on each factor.

Women who are initially coerced offenders (Group C). Almost all the women in this group rated her father, or father figure, as being the person that she believed had loved her most in her life. They also rated him as the person from whom they had received most care. They gave these ratings despite the fact that many of these women had been expected to give a great deal of care to their fathers in very inappropriate ways and some had been sexually abused by their fathers. Several of the women had also each rated the partner who had coerced her into sexually abusing children as loving her and caring for her a great deal, again despite the fact that in all of these cases, he had actively abused her.

CASE EXAMPLE 4.8

'Well I think I would have to give him a six for caring for me. I mean I lived with him all those years. I know he did all those things to me but my mother was just such a bitch to him, so he couldn't help it.'

'I'd give him seven for loving me. He really really loved me.'
(Carrie rating her father on his love and care of her. She had been virtually a house slave since her mother left when she was very young. She had taken over all the household tasks and if she had not performed them to standard, her father would lock her in a room until she had. As soon as her mother left, he had taken her into his bed and made her fulfil all his sexual needs. She was rarely allowed out unless she was out with her father or at her part-time job. This was still the situation when she was arrested aged 27.)

The comparison group (Group D). The women in the comparison group demonstrated a more realistic view of what constituted being loved and cared for than many of the women in the offender groups. Even though some of the women in the comparison group felt uncared for, none of them relied primarily on the children in their lives *to provide them with* care and affection.

4. Loving and Caring for Others

The need to love and to nurture is also a fundamental human need (Fogel, Melson & Mistry, 1986) although the objects of nurturance, both animate and/or inanimate, as well as the manner of nurturance, are often culturally and socially based. Fogel, Melson and Mistry also note how various factors can distort an individual's capacity to nurture, such as stress, personal resources, poor social support. Each woman in this study was asked to rate herself on how 'loving and affectionate' she perceived herself to be and also on her ability 'to care for' (nurture) others.

Table 4.7: Mean rating of how loving and affectionate the women felt themselves to be (max. = 7, min. = 1)

	GROUP A	GROUP B	GROUP C	GROUP D
Affectionate and loving	3.8 (range 2–6)	4.4 (range 3–6)	3.9 (range 2–5)	5.1 (range 3–7)
Able to care for others	2.4 (range 1–3)	4.9 (range 4–6)	2.8 (range 1–5)	5.2 (range 3–7)

FINDINGS

Although there was a trend for women who sexually abused young children and those who were initially coerced into sexually abusing children by men to feel that they were less loving and affectionate than the other women perceived themselves to be, there was no statistically significant difference between any of the groups (Table 4.7). However, the women who sexually abused adolescents and those in the comparison groups were more likely to believe that they could care for other people than the women who initially targeted very young children and those who were initially coerced into sexually abusing by men.

ADULT PEER RELATIONSHIPS

Another basic human need for survival is cooperativeness. Gilbert (1989) identifies several aspects of a cooperative relationship: teaching, revealing, sharing, reciprocation, complementarity, alliance formation, and helping. People are chosen with whom an individual has particular affiliation and this manifests itself as liking, friendship and friendly love (Gilbert, 1989). Gilbert emphasises the importance of friendship relationships for support and the enhancement of self-esteem and also for the development of empathy and morality. The women were all asked about their friendships and whether each of these aspects of a relationship was part of those friendships.

FINDINGS

One of the most overwhelming differences between the women in the groups of offenders and those in the comparison groups is that at the time that they were sexually abusing children, not one woman offender could name a person who was a friend. Those women offenders who were able to name someone shared almost none of their life with that person and the relationship was clearly superficial. Almost all of the women in the comparison group could name several people who were friends and with whom they shared many aspects of themselves and their lives.

Women who initially target young children (Group A). These women seem the most isolated of all. Only two women said they had friends at the time of the abuse, both professionals: one a minister, one a mess officer. However, neither woman talked to these people about herself, her life or any real problems.

CASE EXAMPLE 4.9

Q. 'Can you tell me a friend that you had at that time?'
A. 'I was never much of a one for friends.'
Q. 'Not anyone on the base who you'd chat to or pop into for a cup of tea or just say hello to as you walked past?'
A. 'No, no one, if he were away I'd go weeks without talking to a soul . . . oh wait. I did have someone once. Bob [her partner] got us into terrible debt and this officer on the base . . . she helped me sort it out.'
Q. 'And you got friendly after that?'
A. 'I only saw her that once, I didn't meet her afterwards but she was nice to me . . . said that I could go back anytime, I never did though.'

Women who initially target adolescents (Group B). Three of the women in this group did state that they had friends but on further exploration these friendships revealed that the women were not at all emotionally involved with these friends, and in fact, they were little more than acquaintances.

Women who are initially coerced offenders (Group C). Many of the women who were coerced by men into sexually abusing children described at some stages in their lives having had friends but that their partners had ensured an end to any relationship other than the most shallow.

The comparison group (Group D). Even the most distressed and emotionally disturbed women in the comparison group, some of whom had had very difficult lives, each had friends with whom she had cooperative and emotionally connected relationships.

RELATIONSHIPS WITH PARTNERS

Emotional loneliness, isolation from a lack of a social network, can be ameliorated by good relationships with sexual partners.

Table 4.8: Women's relationships with adult partners

	GROUP A	GROUP B	GROUP C	GROUP D
MOST COMMONLY USED WORDS TO DESCRIBE PARTNERS	violent selfish abusive	selfish promiscuous violent could be charming	sick perverted controlling selfish could be very loving	loving caring warm dull wonderful immature selfish
DISTANCE BETWEEN MAIN PARTNER/S AND IDEAL PARTNER (MAX=100)	78 (range 62–91)	68 (range 56–79)	64 (range 42–89)	36 (range 9–61)

1. Number of Partners

Speltz, Matthews and Mathews (1989) and McCarty (1986) found approximately 40% of the independent female abusers were promiscuous. The female abusers interviewed for this study, however, showed no significant differences in the number of adult sexual relationships from the women in the comparison group. In fact, with notable exceptions, the women in the comparison group were more likely to have had a higher number of adult sexual partners than the women offenders.

2. The Quality of Relationships with Partners

'You ask if any man who I've been in a relationship with has ever abused me, I've never had a relationship with a man who hasn't abused me!'

All the women perpetrators said that they had been extensively physically, sexually and/or emotionally abused in their relationships with their adult partners. Some women in the comparison group also had extremely abusive partners but each of these women had had at least one more positive relationship with a partner. There was a tendency for the women in all the offender groups to marry or form long-term relationships, primarily to get away from their home situation (Table 4.8).

Women who initially targeted young children (Group A). None of these women have ever ended the relationship with a partner, no matter how abusive he was; it was the man who left. Of the women in this group 64% were hospitalised at least once due to their partner's violence. Two women in this group were never physically hit by their partners but were emotionally terrorised and sexually tortured.

CASE EXAMPLE 4.10

Jean met her husband, Hal, while she was at school. She says that she married him to get away from her father who had sexually abused her all her life. She moved into his mother's home with Hal and married him a few months later when she was pregnant. Hal was always complaining about everything she did. He called her a whore, swearing that the baby wasn't his. When she was six months pregnant, he beat her so badly she spontaneously aborted the baby and was in hospital for several days. On the day she came home he raped her four times. Jean describes him wanting 'sex on demand' and if she wasn't as responsive as he thought she should be, he'd become sexually sadistic to her. Hal went off with another woman when Jean was pregnant with their second child, telling Jean it was because she was such a wreck, fat and ugly and useless as a wife and a mother. Jean got a bar job and one night the landlord raped her and after that she was forced to have sex with him regularly. As well as physically forcing her to do so, he said that if she left he would tell the DHSS of her earnings. She tried to avoid him but he turned up at her house and forced her to have sex with him. He was the father of her third daughter.

CASE EXAMPLE 4.11

'He moved in a couple of weeks after I had the baby. I was glad of the company really. He wanted sex a lot but I was used to that, what with m'dad at me all the time. At times he were lovely, I think he may be a lovely person somewhere in him really but he was sick, really sick, in sex. The very worse was when he'd bring his mates in and they'd all watch each other do it to me and yell and shout each other on. His biggest kick was to try and get two of them to do it to me at once. Afterwards he'd go on and on, telling me I was a whore and a nympho and that I do anything for a fuck.' (Rebecca)

Women who initially target adolescents (Group B). Several of the women who abused adolescents describe themselves as forming longer term relationships with people they describe as having 'dual-personalities'—able to be both loving and charming and violent and vicious. These women talk about men who, at the start of relationships, were loving, charming and exciting but, as the relationship progressed, became extremely abusive. These women also found it difficult to leave their partners. The two women in the group who targeted young women had also had very sexually, physically and emotionally abusive relationships with men. In the relationships with adult women, each had felt very hurt, abused and lacking in any form of control in these relationships. Alice had had one relationship in which she describes feeling constantly inadequate and rejected due to her female partner having a series of other lovers during their relationship and eventually leaving her. Rosie had had two relationships with adult women and describes feeling very hurt and abused in both.

CASE EXAMPLE 4.12

Angela describes herself as 'always having had a high sex drive'. She says that her 'first partner' was her mother's live-in lover with whom *she had started a relationship* when she was eleven. She said that that lasted for three years and then it was 'one man after another', most of whom were several years older than her and most of whom she describes as hurting and/or humiliating her. During her years at university, she had a relationship with one of her lecturers who was violent and sexually humiliated her and coerced her into continuing the 'relationship' by threats as to failing her for her degree. She became a Christian after she left university. She felt that she had been 'evil' and wanted a 'fresh start'. She was befriended by an older couple who would visit her frequently. The man visited more and more frequently alone after that and each time insisted on sex with her while telling her how evil and corrupt she was, both during and after the sexual act. Angela eventually tried to kill herself by overdosing after slashing both her wrists and her breasts. She spent almost a year in a psychiatric hospital which she describes as the safest time of her adult life. Angela then started teachers' training and met and married within 3 months the deputy head of a school at which she had done teaching practice. She says that she believed that he was her 'ideal man', so loving and gentle. He was more than twenty years older than her, had never married, and was desperate for her to have a child. She describes him as becoming totally controlling and obsessed with whatever she did. He'd write her daily routines that she had to keep to or he would 'turn on her'. He was impotent at times and he would become very abusive to her, verbally and at times physically. She found homosexual pornography and realised why they were having such sexual difficulties. She suspected that he had felt the need to marry her and to have a child by her to give him a cover of heterosexuality. She said that she felt trapped there by him. She did become pregnant after which there was no more sexual contact.

Women who are initially coerced offenders (Group C). Those women who had been coerced into abusing children became engaged in abusive relationships in which the negative aspects of their partners were initially denied. Some women said that they felt when they first met their partners they were the most perfect of partners. Three women in this group were still so emotionally involved with their partners (co-perpetrators) at the time of the interview, they found objective knowledge of these men to be totally incompatible with their feelings. Two of these women found this so difficult, that each spontaneously suggested discussing the man she fell in love with and the abuser as separate people. It is significant that all the women in this group construed their 'partner' as similar to their fathers.

CASE EXAMPLE 4.13

Susan met her partner through a 'lonely hearts column'. Both her previous husbands had been extremely abusive to her. She found motherhood difficult, and had poor relationships with her daughters. Susan said that Ted was like a 'dream come true'. He was 'the perfect partner in every way', kind, considerate, and especially wonderful with her children. She was determined this marriage would work 'at all costs'. She said he was a fantastic lover and she had orgasm for the first time. She noticed he never had an orgasm but he said he didn't matter. (He masturbated just before sex with her to ensure this.) After only five weeks, she had given up her job and moved 90 miles to live with him. Once she was totally dependent on him, he began to demand more 'unusual sex' yet still was not orgasmic. He began to lose his temper, blaming her and sometimes hitting her, then crying and being apologetic. He arranged a weekend away in a caravan, then, with the children in the same sleeping area, he had orgasm. At home, he used this to pressurise her to have sex in the room with the children asleep, 'just for him'. He began to lose his temper at other times and Susan describes being terrified of these outbursts but the rest of the time he returned to being 'Mr Perfect'. When he suggested introducing her elder daughter into their sexual activities, 'to please him but also to make them closer as a family' she succumbed. Susan said that his moods oscillated so strongly she feared for all their lives. She believed him when he told her that her daughter seemed to be enjoying it and was less resistant when he involved her younger daughter too. Even while in prison, when it came to describing him and rating him, Susan constantly separated out the 'wonderful partner' and the 'other part of him' and every time she said anything negative about him, she found an excuse. After they were arrested, it was found that he had previously had a conviction for sexually abusing female children.

The comparison group (Group D). Many of the women in the comparison group had also experienced difficult relationships with men, many having experienced divorce or separation from their partners. Four women in this group had also been violently abused by their partners. One woman had been raped many times within her marriage and another had been hospitalised twice as a result of her husband's violence towards her. Generally, however, these women experienced less ubiquitously negative relationships with partners and, most importantly, appeared to feel that they had somewhat more control within these relationships. Most of the relationship breakdowns that occurred for the women in this group were more mutually agreed.

REFLECTION AND COMMENT

The lower self-esteem of the women offenders would be predictable as self-esteem is a reflection of the conceptual internal working model that a person has of the self. This model is based on interactions with others and with the environment (Gergen, 1987). In her formative years, each woman in the groups of offenders received a negative model of herself via almost all her interpersonal relationships: her parental figures, her siblings and her peers. In adolescence, the women offenders did not have alternative models in which to challenge this negative model of themselves developed in the formative years; thus they carried it into their adult life.

Another crucial source of self-image is the roles that people have. People associate themselves with the attributes of such roles, which contributes to the person's self-estimation. Each woman perpetrator, as a child, had many roles imposed on her that were inappropriate to her stage of emotional, social and cognitive development. The dissonance between the child's actual abilities and the expectations of her would have necessarily led to her feeling inadequate and incompetent, even if she did objectively carry out the tasks. The roles she was given in her adult life, particularly by her partners, were such that feelings of inadequacy and worthlessness would have been compounded.

Social comparison is also an important contributory factor to a person's sense of self. The women abusers compared themselves unfavourably to almost all other people in their lives. Additionally, a person's sense of self is also affected by the perceived value of the social groups of which that person feels a member. Membership is psychological and is dependent on personal identification with that group (Tajfel, 1972). Most of the women offenders did not have any positively valued social group with which to identify in order to ameliorate some of the other detrimental influences on their image of self.

Marshall (1989) describes evidence that links the degree of parental rejection, isolation and denial of the needs of the child such as the women offenders experienced, to an inability to form emotional intimacy in adulthood. This is evidenced from the poor number and quality of general human relationships that the women abusers were able to develop. The most likely relationships formed are those that are similar to others that have been known, especially those formed in the earliest years. No matter how difficult that relationship, as it is 'known', 'the self' in that relationship seems familiar and hence safe. Relationships that differ too greatly from the models currently held are perceived as a psychic threat and are thus more difficult to assimilate and often rejected.

Almost all the women offenders became involved with men whom they each construed to be similar to their fathers/father figures. Thus their partners treated them in much the same way as they were treated during their childhood. The women were trapped in these relationships which were often experienced as cruel, and at best, uncaring. The continuing abuse would have compounded their childhood experiences of powerlessness and lack of control and the belief that adult relationships were a source of distress and difficulty rather than reward.

The women who had been coerced into abusing children, at one time held the belief that they could form beneficial intimate emotional relationships, with men, usually men similar to their fathers. They ignored, minimised and/or denied any negative characteristics they perceived, just as they did as children in relation to their fathers. Some of these women grow to value this relationship with their male partner above all others, including those with their children. These men exploited the woman's dependency and set up the situation whereby she would do anything to maintain her relationship with him, including sexually abusing a child. Additionally, almost all of these men used various forms of coercion to reinforce the power they had over them. When some of these coerced women then began to act as sole perpetrators, it is suggested that their motivation for doing so was similar to those for other female sole perpetrators of child sexual abuse and met similar needs.

Women in all groups had difficulty in perceiving themselves as aggressive. In part this is undoubtedly cultural. Women in our society are discouraged, via both modelling and direct instruction, from either feeling or expressing aggression. In part, the denial of aggressive feelings is likely to be intuitively strategic. Aggression is an instinctive characteristic that is exhibited by all species as it is essential for survival; defending self and others and for competition for resources. All threats to self or survival generate anger. Anger is the motivating emotion associated with aggressive behaviour and when any situation arises in which anger is experienced, some form of tension reduction needs to occur in order to prevent frustration and hence, unhealthy displacement of that anger, towards self or others by inappropriate or pathological aggression.

Aggressive behaviour is not exhibited in isolation, without reference to the situation in which it occurs. Often if aggressive feelings are elicited, these have to be suppressed due to the evaluation that to express these feelings in the appropriate direction would be more hazardous than helpful. In many situations, such as when a child or adult endures abuse by a more powerful other (as each of these women did both as a child and as an adult), she learns to repress and suppress these angry feelings. Megargee (1966) describes how many extremely aggressive crimes are committed by those who repress their anger over a long period of time. The women who sexually abused children had many reasons to be angry but this anger had almost always had to be suppressed. Severe repression of these feelings can lead to depression, schizophrenia, paranoia and psychopathy (Storr, 1966). However, individuals may appear to be submissive and passive but a small trigger can lead to the aggression being unleashed. For example, it has been seen that people who perceive themselves to be of lower status and who have been angered by a higher status person will relieve the emotional tension aroused by direct aggression towards a person of lower status, such as a child. For the women offenders, as a result of their experiences of abuses both as children and as adults, personal anger would have been connected to sexual experience, both by classical conditioning and observation and by internalisation of the emotional experience of their abusers. Consequently, it is proposed that part of the motivation for a woman offender to sexually abuse children, may be that she is discharging some of the tension of the emotional arousal that she feels as a result of her own experiences of abuse, and at times, because of her own experiences, she chooses to do so in a sexual manner.

The women who sexually abused children tended to feel unloved throughout their lives. Although they feel the need to be affectionate and loving and to be loved and cared for, they believe they are unable to form relationships with adults in which this is possible. Consequently they may turn to children. Whenever these women experienced any form of attention, affection and care, it was usually at a price, most often their sexual exploitation. Therefore some of these women were very likely, as adults, to have associated any feelings of caring and being cared for as connected to sexual feelings. When feelings of love, affection and sexual arousal become enmeshed, their only relationships are with children, and since they themselves have been exploited in a similar way and that exploitation appears to have been condoned, they use the child to express these needs. For *some* of the women this may form part of their motivation for sexually abusing children.

SUMMARY

- The women who sexually abused children did not have the opportunities in adolescence to challenge the sense of themselves that they formed during their childhood years.
- The women who sexually abused children tended to have very poor self-image and self-esteem.
- They believe they have very little control over their own lives or the lives of others and little power to influence others.
- Others in contact with these women can perceive them as very powerful and controlling.
- The women who sexually abuse children construe themselves as being different from other adults and most like the children or adolescents whom they sexually abuse.
- The women who sexually abuse children are not confident in their ability to form close relationships with other adults, peers and/or partners.
- Those relationships that the women do form with partners tend to be emotionally destructive.
- Although the women feel a similar level of need to care and be cared for and to love and be loved as women in the comparison group, their experiences of relationships with both peers and partners preclude these as sources of meeting their needs.

5

STRESSES, SOCIAL SUPPORT AND COPING MECHANISMS

- THE WOMEN'S ESTIMATE OF THEIR LEVEL OF STRESS
- THE WOMEN'S ACCESS TO, AND USE OF, SOCIAL SUPPORT
- THE WOMEN'S MENTAL HEALTH HISTORIES
- THE WOMEN'S USE OF DRUGS AND ALCOHOL
- THE WOMEN'S RELIGIOUS BELIEFS
- SUMMARY

The sexual abuse of a child is an act which meets some need within the perpetrator which may or may not be essentially a sexual need. Even when it may appear to be a spontaneous act, it is in fact part of a learnt, dynamic and complex cycle of behaviour in which the sexual event results in the modulation of emotional arousal in the perpetrator. One of the major causes of emotional arousal is stress. Stress can be defined as the psychological reaction that a person endures in response to aversive environmental events. Those events appear to be those related to harm, loss, threat or challenge for the individual (Lazarus, Kanner & Folkman, 1980). Similar events, however, do not lead to similar levels of stress in different individuals. A person's response to stress is related to the appraisal by that individual of the event itself and the resources, both internal and external, available to respond to that event (Lazarus, 1966). Numerous studies have associated a perceived high level of stressful experiences in conjunction with a judgement of limited resources to deal with the stress, with the onset of various pathological symptoms, physical and psychological, including aggression towards others. The level of distress is exacerbated by limited social support. Hence, when considering

Table 5.1: Women's estimate of the degree of stress experienced in adult life

	GROUP A (n=14)	GROUP B (n=10)	GROUP C (n=12)	GROUP D (n=36)
Estimate of stress levels (max=40)	29.7 (range 23–37)	27.4 (range 19–32)	31 (range 24–38)	17.5 (range 9–23)

the degree of stress that women who sexually abused children perceived they experienced in their adult lives, it is also important to evaluate their perception of the social support networks available to them to help attenuate that stress.

THE WOMEN'S ESTIMATE OF THEIR LEVEL OF STRESS

An estimate of the level of stress that each woman perceived that she had experienced in her adult life was taken using the Dependency Grid. Each woman was asked to rate on a four-point scale the degree to which she believed that she had experienced stress from each of ten common problems: money, parents/family of origin, loneliness, anger, illness, depression, partner, children, neighbours/friends, feeling at the end of her tether.

FINDINGS

There were statistically significant differences between the women in the groups of offenders and the women in the comparison group with regard to the level of stress that they perceived that they had experienced in their adult lives (Table 5.1). There was, however, no statistically significant difference between the groups of women offenders although there was a slight tendency for the women initially coerced by men into sexually abusing children to believe that they experienced a greater level of stress.

CASE EXAMPLES 5.1

'It was all so much . . . I just used to let it all wash over me . . . the kids'd be screaming and whining, he'd be at me, bills'd be pouring in, the whole place'd be a tip and him next door'd would be having a go about the dog, the kids or both. In my head I'd be screaming and screaming like I'd never stop and I'd be lying there hoping when he laid into me, he'd kill me this time.'

'He was an up and coming doctor and wanted everything that went with it, perfect house, perfect dinner parties, perfect decor, . . . perfect wife and the child seen but not heard, . . . and me to do it . . . We'd always had a cook, a housekeeper, a nanny and other help. I never had to do anything at home nor had my mother . . . I'd not even seen how those things got done. I tried to learn but it was just a constant stress. He wouldn't even pay anyone to help me. Even though he had a good salary, there was never any money, he had control of it all . . . he was out with his pals, drinking, gambling and at clubs until all hours. When he was at home he had such a short fuse, he'd just go for me, verbally and physically . . . I was at the end of my tether all the time.
(Comments taken from two women's transcripts relating to stress)

THE WOMEN'S ACCESS TO, AND USE OF, SOCIAL SUPPORT

Many studies have indicated that when one is faced with stressful experiences, social supports can be vital in order to maintain good health (Cohen & Wills, 1985; Leavy, 1983). Kahn and Antonucci (1980) have defined social support as receiving from others within the social network:

affect—expressing care and emotional intimacy;
affirmation—reassurance and emotional support;
providing information and advice;
aid—the supply of practical interventions.

'The absence of social supports is associated with increased psychological distress' (Leavy,1983). It is clear that quality as well as quantity of support is important. In this study the quality and quantity of support was evaluated by use of the Dependency Grid. Each woman was asked to indicate whether she felt that she could ask for support from each person for each specific problem. She was then asked to estimate the level of support she believed that she would receive as either 1 (some support) or 2 (good support). Having an intimate friend or a confidante has also been discussed as a protective factor against psychological distress (e.g. Brown & Harris, 1978). Thus a measure was also taken of the number of people each of the women had in her life with whom she felt able to talk about any problem and difficulty.

Table 5.2: Women's estimate of the level of social support available

	GROUP A (n=14)	GROUP B (n=10)	GROUP C (n=12)	GROUP D (n=36)
Estimate of social support (max=200)	22.5 (range 11–34)	47.8 (range 32–62)	26.3 (range 14–41)	106.7 (range 76–162)
Without the children whom she sexually abused	–	27.6 (range 12–44)	–	–

FINDINGS

1. Level of Social Support Available

There was a very large statistically significant difference between the women who sexually abused children and the comparison group of women in both the quantity and quality of social support that they felt that they had at the time that they were sexually abusing children. There was also a statistically significant difference between the groups of women; the women who sexually abused adolescents believed that they had greater social resources than did the women in the other groups of offenders (Table 5.2).

Women who initially target adolescents (Group B). A further analysis of the results showed the difference was due to the belief each of these women held that she could have called on the child whom she had sexually abused for advice about, and help with, every difficulty, and that the help that she would receive would be useful and effective. If these children were excluded from the analysis there was no difference between the groups of women offenders.

CASE EXAMPLE 5.2

'I could rely on him for anything . . . He'd give me good advice . . . I'd never met another man I could talk to the way I could talk to him. We'd discuss everything . . . I was never lonely when he was around, we'd share everything together, we were so close . . . He'd look after me if I was feeling low . . . I could tell him anything . . . He'd do the shopping, help me out with the kids. When my husband comes to see the kids I'm glad that he's there . . . if my husband was to start on me again, I know he'd lay into him for me. He'd be there for me whatever.' (Statements taken from Liz's interview talking about the 13-year-old boy whom she had sexually abused.)

The support these women believed they could rely on from these children was similar to that the women in the comparison group would rely on from their adult partners or their parents.

2. Number of People With Whom Any Topic Could Be Discussed

There were conspicuous differences between the groups of offenders and the women in the comparison group with regard to the number of people the women felt close enough to be able to share all their problems with.

Women who initially target young children and those women initially coerced into offending (Groups A and C). Not one of the women in these groups believed that there was any person in her life with whom she was close enough to share all her problems.

Women who initially target adolescents (Group B). All bar one of the women in this group stated that the one person that she believed that there was in her life with whom she could share all her problems was an adolescent whom she had sexually abused. The one woman who did not do so had had only brief encounters with the young women whom she sexually abused. Regardless of the brevity of her contact with them, this woman felt that she shared more with, and got more help from, these young women than from any other person in her life.

The comparison group (Group D). All the women in the comparison group had *at least one person* with whom they felt that they could discuss any topic. This person was most likely to be a partner, a friend or, less frequently, a parent.

REFLECTION AND COMMENT

Chronic, unameliorated stress has been cited as a contributory socio-environmental factor to the circumstances in which the sexual abuse of a child occurs (Renshaw, 1982). Repeated stresses lead to emotional arousal which, if not effectively reduced, produces frustration which can, in turn, lead to aggressive acts (Berkowitz, 1969). The sexual abuse of a child, even if construed by the abuser as 'loving', is an act of aggression; obtaining power over a vulnerable individual.

Stressful experiences, such as these women have endured, reinforce feelings of low status, isolation and abandonment, and trigger a survival response (Gilbert, 1984). This specifically tends to occur when the woman makes a negative evaluation of her capacity to gain support, love and respect from other human beings, and thus to help relieve the distress caused. Several writers have commented that women who sexually abuse children tend to suffer from a sense of aloneness, isolation and separation from others (Groth, 1982; McCarty, 1986; Welldon, 1988; Chasnoff et al., 1986) The findings of this study are consistent with those observations. Gilbert argues that this isolation increases the feelings of low self-worth and abandonment and therefore the woman experiences a fundamental threat to survival. The consequences of such a threat are either a depressive state with the possibility of suicidal actions, or attempts to increase feelings of status and reduce feelings of isolation and abandonment via significant interactions with others. It is hypothesised therefore that the women who initiate sexual abuse against children have taken the latter course of action. The child is the one person with whom the woman has contact, that she perceives as being of similar status to herself. Aggression is rarely directed at those perceived to be of higher status (Montagu, 1976). In fact, in many cases the child is the woman's sole relationship. By targeting a child to sexually abuse, she meets both her needs for power and control and her needs for a significant interaction with another human being. She thus reduces her feelings of threat to her survival and ameliorates her emotional arousal and distress.

Repeated stress has been found to bring about neurochemical changes (e.g. Anisman, 1978). One such change is a depletion of the neurochemical serotonin. Low levels of serotonin increase both aggressive behaviour (Brown & Goodwin, 1984) and impulsivity (e.g. Linnoila et al., 1983). In this context impulsivity refers to a reduction in internal inhibitions to an act. To sexually abuse a child, even the most prolific abuser has to overcome her internal resistances. A woman experiencing repeated stress, in conjunction with the social isolation which prevents any amelioration of the stress, tends to be in a state of intense emotional arousal. This can lead to an increase in aggressive behaviour and 'impulsivity' which acts to disinhibit the woman's use of sexual acts to regulate her emotional state. (Gilbert, 1984, provides the theoretical basis for this hypothesis.)

THE WOMEN'S MENTAL HEALTH HISTORIES

Stressful life events and social isolation such as these women experienced are closely associated with various forms of psychological distress (e.g. Paykel, 1974; Brown, Andrews, Harris et al., 1986; Brewin, 1988). The life experiences of the women offenders, in particular those who experienced extensive abuse from a very young age, are also predictive of psychological difficulties in adulthood (e.g. Finkelhor, 1986; Wyatt & Powell, 1988). Several authors have in fact commented that the women they have reported on who have sexually abused children, either have severe psychological disturbances or are mentally ill (Wahl, 1960; Mayer, 1983; McCarty, 1986 (50%); Kramer, 1980; Meiselman, 1978; Holubinskyj & Foley, 1986). The women in this study were therefore asked about their experiences of depression, including pre-menstrual tension and post-natal depression, anxiety, eating disorders, suicidal feelings, self-mutilation, and the primary symptoms of schizophrenia.

FINDINGS

During the time when the women were actively sexually abusing children, few women who initiated the sexual abuse of children (Groups A and B), described experiencing any of the severe symptoms predictable on the basis of their life experience. Five of the twelve women interviewed who were coerced by men into perpetrating (Group C), said they had experienced depression, anxiety and suicidal feelings during the period they were involved in the sexual abuse of children. None of the women had suffered from anorexia or bulimia. Five women—three who had sexually abused very young children and two male-coerced perpetrators—were very overweight and talked about using food to relieve stress, as did other women offenders and women in the comparison group.

When the women were not sexually abusing children, either prior to that abuse and/or after the abuse had stopped, many of the women offenders in all three groups suffered with severe symptoms of psychological distress. These included misuse of alcohol, promiscuity, self-mutilation, suicide attempts, severe depression and anxiety disorders. Some women also had increased disturbing, vivid, visual 'flashbacks' associated with their own experiences of abuse and very painful physical 'body memories'.

CASE EXAMPLE 5.3

Throughout her childhood, Vera suffered severe physical, emotional and sexual abuse. Her father sexually abused her even after she left home, including raping her on her wedding day. The relationship between Vera and her husband was poor, he was often away from home. Vera sexually abused each of her five children. She says that prior to the acts of abusing them the only emotions she remembers feeling are tension and anger, the rest of the time she felt numb. Vera carried on sexually abusing her youngest son until his first ejaculation after which she said that she felt repulsed by him. Vera said from that time she became increasingly tense and suffered from panic and depression. She self-harmed and a year later made her first suicide attempt. She spent several years in psychiatric hospitals.

CASE EXAMPLE 5.4

'I was always depressed until I met Tony [the 13-year-old boy whom she sexually abused]. I felt hopeless, worthless, somedays I couldn't even get out of bed. I'd been treated like a piece of dirt all my life and that's just what I felt like . . . Tony was different, I could tell from the start . . . for the first time in my life . . . I felt really happy . . . it was lovely to be so in love with someone who really loved me.' (Rather than love, Tony talks of repulsion and distress and how dirty, and guilty he felt.)

CASE EXAMPLE 5.5

Paula was very depressed when she met her second husband, her co-accused, at a single parents' group meeting. She described him as *initially* seeming like the 'ideal husband', caring in every way even though she found some of his sexual interests 'a bit odd'. He loved taking photographs of her and him naked in various sexual poses. He had always taken photographs of her daughters naked which she thought was fine but then began to involve them in photographs with him and her in sexual poses which involved increasingly more sexual interaction between the adults and children. Her husband made many veiled and then overt threats if she did not comply with his 'needs'. Paula says she began getting 'flashbacks' of her brother's abuse of her. She described experiencing anxiety and tension, tantamount to panic attacks but also feeling sexually aroused. She describes that the only way she knew to reduce that arousal and stop the bodily feelings that she was going to die, was to be sexual with one of her daughters. Abusing her daughters made her feel powerful, in control, elated and loved, not by them but by her husband or brother. It was as if by abusing her children, she had pleased these men and she felt more secure in their love for her. She said if she did not sexually abuse her daughters, she had feelings of overwhelming devastation, loss, fear and depression, just as when her brother left. She then became terrified her husband would also leave her.

Two women interviewed had been diagnosed as having a severe mental illness. As these women appeared to be floridly psychotic *at the time that the sexual abuse occurred* they will be discussed in the 'atypical perpetrators' chapter.

The comparison group (Group D). All the women in the comparison group who had endured severe difficulties throughout their lives, had suffered the type of psychological distress that would be consistent with these experiences: anxiety disorders, depression, and feelings of worthlessness and of self-harm. Two women in this group had overdosed and one had had a brief period of hospitalisation during an episode of psychosis.

THE WOMEN'S USE OF DRUGS AND ALCOHOL

Other means by which people alleviate excessive stress are mind-altering substances. Several authors have noted that the women who sexually abused children were likely to be heavy users of psychotropic drugs and/or alcohol (Groth, 1982; McCarty, 1986 (46%); Speltz, Matthews and Mathews, 1989; Allen, 1962; Faller, 1987 (57%); Chasnoff et al., 1986; Wahl, 1960).

FINDINGS

There was no difference between the levels of alcohol use or the use of other psychotropic drugs between the women in the offender groups and the women in the comparison group. *None* of the women who sexually abused children did so solely when she was in an altered psychological state. There was in fact a tendency for more women in the comparison group to be heavier users of these substances than the women offenders.

1. Alcohol

Several women offenders in all groups stated that in *some* instances the sexual abuse of the child occurred when they were intoxicated but none of the women said the abuse occurred only at those times. The women who sexually abused adolescents were the most likely to use alcohol as a disinhibitor for both perpetrator and victim. Some men who coerced women into sexually abusing used alcohol as a disinhibitor when initially coercing the women into sexual acts with children.

2. Drugs

None of the women who sexually abused children were, at the time that the abuse occurred, regular users of psychotropic drugs, either legal or illegal.

Many of the women in the offender groups stated clear objections to the use of drugs of any sort including minor pain killers. Interestingly, the women in the comparison group were much more likely to have tried and to have been regular users of both legal and illegal psychotropic drugs, especially anti-depressants, anxiolytics and cannabis. Only one woman of all the 72 interviewed had used any of the 'harder drugs'. As a young adult, she had used heroin several times. It is possible that women who sexually abuse children may have a particular fear of the consequences for them of a drug-induced state of disinhibition (Wilson, 1994).

REFLECTION AND COMMENT

Rather than exhibiting overt symptoms of mental illness during the periods in which the abuse was taking place, the women who sexually abused children were curiously less symptomatic than would have been predicted, given knowledge of their life events and emotional experiences. Nor did these women appear to 'cope with' their symptoms by resource to heavy use of psychotropic substances. The lack of such problems, and/or the intermittence of their presentation, could be accounted for if the sexual abuse of the child in some way allayed their distress. It is hypothesised that this is indeed the case and that the sexual abuse of the child, particularly for sole women abusers, but also for some of the women coerced into sexually abusing children, becomes a means of 'self-medication' to alleviate stress and distress. It is proposed that, by sexually abusing a child, a person, be it a man or a woman, engages in a sexual activity in which he or she feels in control. Any sexual experience in which an individual feels in control, especially one in which orgasm occurs, is intrinsically rewarding. The person experiences the 'reward' as an internal feeling of well-being. This is caused by the release of endogenous opioids which also act as a 'cerebral analgesic'. (See Chapter 10 for a full discussion.)

When the woman is not able to abuse the child then the feelings of distress and tension are experienced and 'dealt with' in self-harming ways which also precipitate the release of endogenous opioids. For example, women who self-mutilate describe the act of self-mutilation as a means by which they reduce intense feelings of physiological arousal and return to a 'normal state' (Fisher, 1994). The women who were coerced into sexually abusing children who never experience the abuse that they perpetrate as them being in control, do not experience this 'internal reward' and hence are likely to continually experience on-going symptoms of psychological distress. Those women who are initially coerced into sexually abusing a child but who then experience the sexual abuse of that child as being powerful and with them in control are less likely to suffer from symptoms of distress and are also more likely to initiate sexually abusive acts when the male partner is not present. Hence it is proposed that the sexual abuse of a child may be seen as a 'coping strategy' used by some women to alleviate distress (Figure 5.1).

THE WOMEN'S RELIGIOUS BELIEFS

An important finding was how many of the women who had sexually abused children became 'christians' after the abuse was discovered (Table 5.3). Some women had rejoined churches to which they had been connected, however nebulously, as a child. Many women, however, were attracted to, and became involved with 'charismatic' groups with a tendency to 'heavy shepherding'. Heavy shepherding involves a very active ministry and conversion programme; strong eldership, almost exclusively male; a pre-ordained system of behaviour; and a professed network of support with a proclivity for controlling the individual in the ways of the church. Several of the women were converted when they were in prison. Although some of the women kept their past and their offences secret from almost everyone in the church, most did not. Four of these women went through forgiveness ceremonies for their offences.

CASE EXAMPLE 5.6

Amanda was converted to Christianity in prison by a prison visitor. Several members of the church became regular visitors to her and when she was released she went to live with a church elder. At a special service of renewal, Amanda stood in front of the congregation and confessed the sexual abuse of her daughter. Interestingly, she also 'confessed' her own experience of sexual abuse as a child, talking about her victim experience in an equivalent way to her perpetrating behaviour. Amanda was forgiven, then took off her gown and went naked through a full immersion to come out the other side and be gowned in a white robe for purity and new life.

REFLECTION AND COMMENT

For the women who sexually abuse children, adopting a Christian way of life can appear to be an instant route to a new life, solve many problems related to being a known offender, and alleviate many stresses. The most important function of such a religion for these women is that it provides a

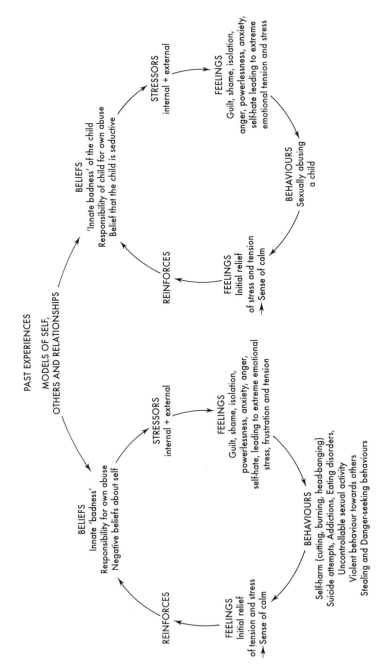

Figure 5.1: The use of behaviours to alleviate stress

Table 5.3: Women's religious beliefs

	GROUP A	GROUP B	GROUP C	GROUP D[a]
Strong religious beliefs prior to the discovery of the abuse	1 7%	1 10%	1 8%	7 19%
Strong religious beliefs after the discovery of the abuse	10 71%	5 50%	7 58%	8 22%
Of which were charismatic groups	4 28%	2 20%	3 25%	2 5%

[a]The time-scale was taken as being that of the woman with whom the Group D participant was matched.

way of life that appears diametrically opposed to their previous existence but in which *they have to change very little*. Some churches do provide good care, support and role models for such women while they work on their problems. Other churches, as described here, directly work against the woman's addressing her offending behaviour.

The most attractive features for all offenders are the tenets of forgiveness, rebirth and acceptance. By asking for forgiveness, the woman can attribute her sexual abuse of children to 'a sinful self', now rejected via her 'rebirth' as a Christian. When offending she used cognitive distortions to attribute the blame for her actions onto the child, her partner, or some other outside agency. Now she attributes these acts to the past 'sinful self'. Therefore the woman has not owned her behaviour and taken full responsibility for it.

The woman's feelings of inability to have power and control over her own life are reinforced because the church—mostly the men in the church—takes all power and control from her. In some groups, the elders even dictate where the woman will live, who she will be befriended by, and who she will marry. The church also provides a behavioural code which prevents the woman having to reassess her own values and make her own decisions. She does not have to earn respect and trust. By wearing the mantle of Christianity the woman cloaks herself in trust, morality, acceptability and self-esteem. Her inner feelings of being untrustworthy, immoral, and unacceptable are not addressed.

A church provides the prospect of 'good parents'. A prospect of older people who will provide parental care and guidance to those in the congregation perceived as needy and vulnerable. The church also provides a ready-made social network of people who will accept the woman unquestioningly, and to whom she can turn for many of her needs to be met. The woman does not have to make any effort in forming these relationships as they are based on the person's perceived Christianity rather than who she is. The real woman is never seen, only the part that acts as the acceptable Christian. In most cases therefore, the woman never forms a truly intimate relationship, or obtains the benefits of a genuinely close connection with another human being.

Thus almost all the characteristics that make a woman vulnerable to sexually abusing a child remain unchanged but are concealed by her 'new identity' and consequently can be denied. Some of the more extreme churches collude with this denial, by preaching that counselling by anyone not within the church is wrong. Any symptoms the woman experiences will either have to be hidden or else seen as evidence of her incomplete repentance. One woman who became very depressed and self-harmed was considered to be carrying a demon which had prevented her from her full repentance. She therefore was made to endure an exorcism by a church counsellor which left her feeling even more humiliated, depressed and guilty than before.

With no means of even owning her feelings, the woman needs some way of dissipating them. Having repented, been forgiven, and reborn into the church, full acceptance means full trust. It would be unthinkable for any church member to doubt a woman's sincerity or the completeness of her 'healing'. Therefore even the most prolific offender will be trusted with the care of children! Thus the means of release are readily available, and should the trigger feelings or situations occur, the woman is liable to reoffend.

SUMMARY

- The women who sexually abused children perceived themselves as experiencing significantly more stress than the women in the comparison group.
- The women in the comparison group perceived themselves as having more resources, internal and external, to cope with stress.
- All the women offenders were socially isolated and none had an adult confidante.
- During the period in which they were sexually abusing children, the women offenders suffered few severe symptoms of psychic distress. At other times the women experienced an escalation in mental health problems.
- Although none of the women who sexually abused children were addicted to alcohol or drugs at the time that they were sexually abusing

children, several experienced an increase in their use of psychotropic substances after the abuse stopped.

- Some women also used alcohol as a disinhibitor both for themselves and/or the children they sexually abused, but none did so on every occasion.
- It is hypothesised that the women use sexual acts with a child to reduce their feelings of emotional arousal and bring about a brief sense of calm.
- After the abuse has been discovered many women offenders become Christians. Membership of some churches can act against a woman undertaking a programme to bring about genuine change, thus she is vulnerable to reoffending.

6

THE CHILDREN WHOM THE WOMEN TARGET TO SEXUALLY ABUSE

- DIFFERENCES BETWEEN THE WOMEN'S PERCEPTIONS OF CHILDREN THEY DO AND DO NOT SEXUALLY ABUSE
- MOTHERS WHO SEXUALLY ABUSE: THEIR EXPERIENCE AS MOTHERS
- ACTS OF MURDER AND ATTEMPTED MURDER
- SUMMARY

With few notable exceptions, women who sexually abuse children do not target every child with whom they are in intimate contact. When women act as sole perpetrators they tend to target specific children. Looking for characteristics within the children that predisposed the women to target these particular children proved futile. The results of this study clearly indicated that the key factors leading a woman to target particular children were her own perceptions and beliefs about these children. Her perceptions and beliefs were a construction of the woman's psychopathology which, initially at least, bore little concurrence with the actual attributes of the child. Understanding the abusers' perception of, and beliefs about, target children and the factors that lead to the choice of a particular child is vital. Through this knowledge we can gain further insight into the woman abuser's motivations and justifications for the offending behaviour and thus facilitate therapeutic intervention with both the offender and her victim/s. The beliefs and perceptions of the child held by the abuser have a crucial role to play in a victim's construction of self, particularly when the abuser is the sole, or primary, carer as is often the case with a female perpetrator. The victim's construction of self will be rooted in the abuser's construction of the victim. Hence, knowledge of the perpetrator's perceptions and beliefs about the target child is indispensable in therapeutic work with survivors.

The presentation of this set of data has proved complex as although all the women offenders have sexually abused children, some of the women (albeit in this study the majority of the women) are also the children's mothers. It was therefore important to consider whether there were any factors in their experience as mothers that would predispose them to sexually abuse their own children.

Since this is a retrospective study only the women's perceptions of the children *after* the sexual abuse has occurred can be considered. Thus it will be distorted by the women's cognitive construction as a result of the abuse that they have perpetrated.

DIFFERENCES BETWEEN THE WOMEN'S PERCEPTIONS OF CHILDREN THEY DO AND DO NOT SEXUALLY ABUSE

Aspects of the women's perception of children—target children and other children—were accessed in various ways:

Repertory Grid: similarity of child to ideal child;
  similarity of child to other people in her life.
Characteristics of the child: the women were asked to provide three characteristics of each child and to rate the child on those characteristics and also on seven provided characteristics. For each characteristic, the women were asked to judge each characteristic as positive or negative.
Structured Interview: accessed various aspects of the women's attitudes and beliefs towards children.

FINDINGS

1. How Positively the Women Perceived the Children Whom They Sexually Abused

There were large statistically significant differences between the groups of women in the way they perceived the children they sexually abused. There were also statistically significant differences between the way the women perceived the children they sexually abused and those that they did not. The women offenders tended to be more extreme either positively or

Table 6.1: How favourably the women perceive the children

	GROUP A		GROUP B		GROUP C		GROUP D
	Target	Non-target	Target	Non-target	Target	Non-target	
DIFFERENCES BETWEEN CHILD AND IDEAL CHILD (MAX=100)	58 Mean (range 29–83)	19 Mean (range 5–32)	5.8 Mean (range 0–9)	13.5 Mean (range 11–26)	53 Mean (range 17–79)	16.6 Mean (range 7–30)	17.4 Mean (range 4–29)
CHARACTERISTICS OF THE CHILD (MAX=60)[a]	22.5 Mean (range 17–30)	39.4 Mean (range 27–56)	54.5 Mean (range 51–59)	42 Mean (range 34–48)	25.8 Mean (range 19–38)	42.5 Mean (range 31–52)	42.4 Mean (range 33–58)

[a]The higher the score the most positive.

negatively in their attributions towards children, whereas the women in the comparison group tended to be more balanced in their appraisal of the children (Table 6.1).

Women who initially target young children (Group A). The women who initially targeted very young children generally negatively perceived the children they sexually abused. Although few were overtly critical when speaking about the children, all rated the children they sexually abused very differently from their ideal child. They also tended to rate these children negatively on the Characteristics of the Child questionnaire. The characteristics chosen to add to those provided were generally negative. Many of the negative attributions were manifestly projections onto the child, or were related to behaviours incongruous with the age or developmental stage of that child. Some women perceived many developmentally normal behaviours of these children as personal 'attacks'.

CASE EXAMPLE 6.1

'I hated him . . . he'd do anything to get at me . . . always crying, crying, crying . . . I'd tell him to "Shut up" and he wouldn't . . . he does it to wind me up . . . he'd be . . . always wanting something . . . he'd not give up . . . he'd look at me with that look. [Q. What look?] weak, pitiful . . . pathetic . . . he makes me want to really hurt him . . .' (Connie talking about her son who she had sexually abused since soon after he was born until the abuse was discovered when the child was four and half. The abuse she perpetrated was extremely sadistic.)

Even if the sexual acts perpetrated are construed by the women as being 'loving' in character, they still tend to perceive the children in a negative manner. Several of the women who originally targeted young children made extremely contradictory statements about the children they sexually abused; at times exalting them in a romanticised and idealistic way and at others, making extremely detrimental statements about the child.

CASE EXAMPLE 6.2

Karen initially described her daughter as 'wonderful', 'perfect' and 'beautiful'. She was effusive describing how she loved her daughter. Yet when rating her on the Repertory Grid she construed her as very different from her ideal child and also rated her negatively on the Characteristics of the Child questionnaire. Further exploration led to Karen saying how at times she would feel angry and hurt as the child was not responding to her how she wanted, thus she felt rejected by the child. Karen said she felt 'abandoned' by the child and then 'needed' to be sexual with her to feel connection with her.

The children in the lives of these women who were not sexually abused by them were perceived far more positively than their target children.

SPECIAL CASE EXAMPLE 6.3

Mary was an extremely prolific sexual offender. She tried to target any child she came into contact with. She preferred toddlers, but could and did sexually abuse children of all ages. She could not describe any characteristics of the children she sexually abused. To her, who the child was was less important than the fact it was a child. Her abusive behaviour would consist of 'accidentally' touching the child's genitalia and later masturbating to thoughts of the touch. Her motivations included feelings of exceptional envy and anger towards children especially when she sees them 'having fun'. She says she then feels like she wants to hurt them 'just like she was hurt'. The closer the relationship and the more time she had with the children, the more extensive the sexual acts she perpetrated would be. Mary was also 'in a sexual relationship' with two 14-year-old boys. She construed these boys positively and saw herself as their peer. Her responses to these children were similar to those of women who primarily targeted adolescents.

Women who initially target adolescents (Group B). The women who initially targeted adolescent children construed the children whom they sexually abused as very similar to their ideal child. The characteristics they chose for the children to add to the list of those provided were very positive. Again these chosen characteristics were clearly projections onto the child and incongruous with the age or developmental stage of that child. There was almost always inconsistency between the women's description of these adolescents and their actual behaviour. The women tended to idealise these children, rating them at the most positive end of any scale. In order to be able to do so, the women denied any negative characteristics and/or created elaborate justifications for such characteristics. The women did not extend this idealisation to children they did not sexually abuse. They tended to perceive these children less favourably than those they did sexually abuse.

Only one woman negatively described an adolescent whom she had sexually abused. This woman had 'begun a relationship with' a 12-year-old boy. She had befriended him but as soon as she became sexual with him, he left and never came back to the house. She was very angry and perceived the boy as 'leading her on' and then 'rejecting' her. Other women who had had 'previous relationships' with adolescents persisted in idealising these children.

Some of the adolescents individually described their abusers as being very threatening and punishing, particularly if they did not conform to the behaviours the women expected of them. The women themselves did recognise that they behaved in this way.

CASE EXAMPLE 6.4

Glenda had sexually abused her son throughout his adolescence. He first physically assaulted her when he was ten years old. During the next five years he did so on many occasions; she sustained severe bruising, broken ribs, was hospitalised twice, once with concussion, and twice he strangled her to the point of unconsciousness. Glenda was asked to rate her son on the construct of aggressiveness, using a seven-point scale with seven being the most aggressive and one being least. She rated him at two, saying her son was not really aggressive, 'not really within himself, that's just his father in him'.

Women initially coerced to offend (Group C). The women who were initially coerced into sexually abusing children tended to rate the children they sexually abused very negatively. They construed these children to be unlike their ideal children. This was most true of the women who went on to sexually abuse the children as sole perpetrators. These women also perceived those children they did not sexually abuse more positively than those they did.

Three women in this group did perceive the children in a more positive manner. None of these women sexually abused children when not coerced to do so. Two of these women were those who found some way of stopping the abuse and protecting their children.

The comparison group (Group D). The women in the comparison group were inclined to have a more balanced view of each child which was consistent throughout the interview. They tended to construe the children as reasonably similar to their ideal children.

2. How Similar the Women Perceived Themselves To Be to Their Target Children, Other Children, and Adults

From the Repertory Grids it was found that the women who sexually abused children construed themselves as very similar to their target children. The women perceived both themselves and their target children to be different from children they did not sexually abuse as well as different from other people.

Women who initially target young children (Group A). These women who initially targeted very young children construed their target children to be very similar to themselves. Three women in this group also perceived their target child/ren to be similar to their primary childhood abuser/s. This tended to be, *although certainly not exclusively,* gender specific; boy children being more likely to be perceived as similar to the abuser/s. A woman who was sexually abused by her mother saw her female victim as being more similar to herself than her mother.

CASE EXAMPLE 6.5

Vera's father had sexually abused her most of her childhood and into her adulthood. He was the father of her two eldest sons. Vera describes seeing her father in the faces of these two sons and wanting to hurt and control them. She also describes becoming tense and angry if any characteristic of her sons reminded her of him. Vera construes these children as being more similar to her father and her brother who also sexually abused her, than herself. Vera also had two daughters and a younger son. These children she construed as being very similar to herself. Through therapy she began to realise she sexually abused them when she felt most self-hatred, guilt and anger.

Women who initially target adolescents (Group B). The women who primarily targeted adolescents construed the adolescent/s they sexually abused to be very similar to themselves. The differences were due to the women rating these children more positively than they rated themselves. The people in the women's lives they perceived to be most like themselves and their target adolescents were other adolescents they had not sexually abused.

Women initially coerced to offend (Group C). The women who were initially coerced into sexually abusing children by men tended to construe the children that they sexually abused as being most similar to themselves when abusing. There were three women who did not do so. They saw the children they were coerced into sexually abusing as different from themselves. None of these three women sexually abused as sole perpetrators.

The comparison group (Group D). All the women in the comparison group construed themselves as adults to be most like other adults in their lives. However, some women did also construe their children to be similar to themselves as a child.

SPECIAL CASE EXAMPLE 6.6

Cathy, who was initially coerced into sexually abusing their four children by her partner, went on to target two of those children, to sexually abuse as a sole perpetrator. The girl was her daughter and the abuse she perpetrated on her was very sadistic. Her perception of this young woman was very negative. She construed her on the Repertory Grid as very unlike her ideal child but as being very similar to herself. This woman also independently sexually abused her stepson. She believed they had 'a special relationship' and treated him in a very similar manner to the women who acted as sole perpetrators with adolescent targets. She construed him very positively; very similar to her ideal child, her ideal lover and to 'herself as an adolescent'. Thus although initially a coerced offender Cathy subsequently abused independently in similar ways to women in the other two groups but towards different children.

3. How Similar the Women Perceive Target Children To Be to Their Ideal Partner

The women who targeted adolescents construed these children to be very similar to their ideal partner, whereas the women perpetrators in the other two groups construed the children as very different from their ideal partner.

Women who initially target adolescents (Group B). The women who targeted adolescents idealised the relationship with their target children in a manner that often bore little resemblance to the child's perception of that relationship. The women in this group perceived the child to be their 'lover'; an equal relationship freely chosen by the child.

CASE EXAMPLE 6.7

Nancy had not seen the adolescent boy she had begun to sexually abuse when he was 12 years of age for three years. She had served a prison sentence for that abuse and there was an injunction on Nancy to stay away from the boy. She was convinced, however, that when he was 18 years of age he would find her and they would be married. She rigidly held the belief that the relationship was a 'mutual love affair'. In contrast, the adolescent described 'hating' Nancy, 'fearing' her and never wanting to see her again.

Even in cases when the woman was predatory and/or sadistic with the adolescent, she still perceived the relationship as mutually ideal and loving.

Table 6.2: Similarity between child and ideal partner

	GROUP A	GROUP B	GROUP C
DIFFERENCE BETWEEN	52.8	4.2	48.6
CHILD AND IDEAL	Mean	Mean	Mean
PARTNER (MAX. = 100)	(range	(range	(range
	40–68)	0–9)	36–72)

CASE EXAMPLE 6.8

Angela targeted a neighbour's child who did paid jobs for her around the house. He felt trapped as his parents were very close friends of Angela's husband and were also keen for him to earn his own pocket money. Initially the sexual acts she perpetrated against him were seductive but at times became extremely sexually sadistic. It culminated in her arranging with his parents for him to stay for the weekend when her husband was away. During this time she perpetrated terrible sadistic acts on him. The next day he ran away from home. Angela says 'he was the love of my life, I was devastated when he left, I cried for days'. When asked why she thought he'd left she replied: 'It must have been something dreadful at home or school or with his mates. It must have been very serious for him to just leave me like that when we were so in love.'

The degree of unconsidered idealisation of the women who target adolescents can be seen in the way they perceive these children to be similar both to their ideal child and their to ideal partner (Table 6.2).

REFLECTION AND COMMENT

These data seem to support the suggestion that the relationship between a female perpetrator and the child whom she sexually abuses is, in many cases, symbiotic (Kramer, 1980; Welldon, 1988). Kramer (1980), commenting on three women who initially targeted very young children, proposes that although symbiotic, the relationship is also unsatisfying and unrewarding even from birth. This proposition is supported by the data as many of the women who initially targeted young children perceive those children very negatively. This is also true for many of the women who are initially coerced into sexually abusing children by men, in particular those who go on to initiate sexual abuse as sole perpetrators. One hypothesis is that these women appear to project negative aspects of themselves onto the children they then target to sexually abuse. They identify strongly with these children and hurt them, almost as if they were attacking part of themselves. Some women who see 'self when abusing', 'their primary abuser' and their 'target child' as similar, may be acting-out, attacking and taking control over 'the abuser' by sexually assaulting the child.

The women who target adolescents also seem to form symbiotic relationships with them. The women's expectations of these children mirrored the expectations made of them when they themselves were adolescents. It is suggested these women perceive the children they sexually abuse as extensions of 'themselves as adolescents' but in idealised form. The women perceive these children as having all the characteristics they want in a partner. The women then constructed a relationship with the image they projected. These women tended to minimise the abusiveness of their own sexual experiences in adolescence and were often supported in this belief by what they perceived to be the 'acceptance' of others of those relationships (see Chapter 3). Many of the women in this group also perceived their own abusers as the one person who showed them care and affection. Thus they were more able to construe the abuse that they themselves perpetrated as 'caring' and 'affectionate' even when some of the acts were blatantly sadistic, as were those they experienced. The women who were initially coerced into sexually abusing by men also tended to identify very powerfully with the children they sexually abused. It is proposed that these women personally identified with the child; both being victims, therefore perceiving themselves and the children as equivalent. Many stopped seeing the children as separate individuals but objectified them in order to carry out the abuse. Some women displaced the guilt and the anger that they felt against themselves and their partners onto the children and attacked the child to release the feelings. At other times, it may be that the women are making a connection to these children in the only way they know how to have a close human connection: via a sexual act.

In almost all aspects of the interviews which related to the children they sexually abused, the sole perpetrators seemed to be oblivious to the child as an individual person, separate from their abuser. The perceptions these women had of the target children were based on their personal projections, which thus precluded any real knowledge of, or empathy with, the actual experience of the child. The women offenders used ostensibly innocuous characteristics of the children as evidence upon which to construct the 'personality' of the child. In this way a woman projected onto the children the images of who she wanted the child to be in order for her to resolve some need within herself. For some women, the child represents the woman herself or some aspect of the woman. Some women perceived the child they sexually abused as their abuser. For some women the child represented both aspects of the self and her ideal partner. These projections onto the children are not mutually exclusive. Due to the distortions the woman is able to make in relation to the child, at different times the child can represent different 'personalities' and fulfil different functions, depending on the needs of the woman.

The attributes the woman projects onto the child act as the basis of the cognitive distortions she uses to facilitate her sexual abuse of the child. The total lack of ability of the women perpetrators to genuinely empathise with the children whom they sexually abuse is ubiquitous across the groups.

In interviews with some of the target children of these women, each independently described personal struggles in asserting an individuality or separation from the woman who was sexually abusing them. Several recounted difficulties related to not feeling as if they existed as a person at all. Both Kramer (1980) and Welldon (1988) observed that the mothers who sexually abused their children seemed unable to allow the child to individuate and/or separate from them. If a woman is projecting personalities onto her target children in the manner described here, the children cannot be allowed to be individual, separate people as this would challenge the woman's personal construction of the world and leave her without resources to meet her needs.

The women each give many examples of how they interpreted any aspect possible of the child's behaviour to validate the perception of the child they had constructed. Then they used this as a justification and rationalisation to facilitate their acts of abuse. These behaviours of the women offenders can be seen as a defence against threats to their personal constructions of the world. Abandonment of a person's construction of the world can lead to cognitive and emotional chaos. In order to prevent this, there is a tendency to become 'hostile'. 'Hostility' in these terms means the determined effort to find evidence, however meagre, in order to preserve the existing constructs and prevent psychological chaos. A woman will thus act to prevent the child from separating from her and never acknowledge the child's individual identity. She will also have to accommodate any action of behaviour that does not fit in with her constructions and consequently exacerbates her cognitive distortions in relation to the child. This results in the degradation or idealisation the women engage in in relation to these children.

Although women do target specific children, if for any reason these children become unavailable to them there is no reason to believe the women will not create a similar construction of perceptions and beliefs around another child in order to perpetuate their abusing behaviour.

Table 6.3:: Mothers who sexually abused their own children

	GROUP A (n=14)	GROUP B (n=10)	GROUP C (n=12)
Sexually abused at least one of her own children	13	3	10
Had other children whom she did not sexually abuse	7	2	5

MOTHERS WHO SEXUALLY ABUSE: THEIR EXPERIENCE AS MOTHERS

As discussed previously, the children the women perpetrators were most likely to sexually abuse were their own children, the children most closely related to them, or children to whom they were in a caretaking/parental role. It was therefore of interest to consider whether there was any specific aspect of these women's mothering experience of the particular children they targeted, compared to those they did not, that would increase the vulnerability of the sexually abused child (Table 6.3).

1. Experiences of Pregnancy, Birth and Early Relationship With the Child

Women who initially target young children (Group A). Most mothers who initially targeted their infant children conceived these children in difficult circumstances. Almost all the women initially perceived the children they sexually abused to be 'unwanted'. Nine of the children, the offspring of five of the mothers, were the product of incest. The children they did not sexually abuse were more likely to be wanted and planned for. Two women did 'plan' to have the child that was sexually abused; one got pregnant to escape her abusive living situation and one (Karen) desperately wanted a daughter to 'recreate' an incestuous relationship with her mother (Case Example 3.10). She was the *only* woman who said she felt the infant was truly connected to her in the early days after giving birth. The women gave various reasons for this: the circumstances in which they became pregnant; the reaction of their partner to the child; the child being in an incubator for some time after the birth; the woman initially not being the primary carer of the child; and the child not being the 'right sex'. The women did not describe these feelings around the births of the children whom they did not sexually abuse.

CASE EXAMPLE 6.9

Connie married a man she'd met while prostituting. She had two sons by him whom she loved and cared for relatively well. She says she was 'reasonably happy if you compare it to the rest of my life'. She described her husband's physical, sexual and emotional abuse of her as 'the price I was used to paying for a roof over my head'. She said 'it wasn't that frequent or bad compared to my childhood'. When she became pregnant with her third child, her husband said it 'was her problem'. He refused to believe it was his, raped her and left her. Soon after her son was born, Connie started sexually abusing him in a sadistic manner. In therapy, Connie recognised how her husband's abandonment of her triggered feelings of her mother abandoning her to her father's abuse. She describes 'releasing' these feelings by sadistically abusing her son.

CASE EXAMPLE 6.10

Amanda was initially angry at being pregnant just after she had 'got free from' her sexually abusive grandfather. Her soldier husband seemed delighted at the prospect of having a son; he talked of nothing else. He was present at the birth but when the baby was a girl, he punched Amanda in the face saying not another 'split-arse'. He walked out on her and did not come back.

The women who initially target very young children tend to infantalise these children and resist their growing independence. Conversely, at other times they expect the children to behave in a pseudo-adult manner, fulfilling the mother's needs. Several of the women in this group recounted incidents of playing with and relating to their children as if they themselves were a peer of the child rather than an adult.

Women who initially target adolescents (Group B). None of the three women who sexually abused their adolescent sons described any difficulties around the pregnancies or the births. On the contrary, like all other aspects of these women's accounts of their relationships with the adolescents they sexually abused, there was a tendency to idealisation. Each of the children was described as very wanted, even though one of the women had become pregnant by her childhood abuser.

All three women who sexually abused their adolescent sons were inappropriately emotionally enmeshed with them. For example, each of these women talked of experiencing great jealousy about her child's relationships with others. Their own relationships with their children appeared peer-like rather than parental. These children, from a young age, were each treated as pseudo-adults. Although two of these women had a husband who lived with them at the time of the abuse, the child was seen by the woman as her principal intimate relationship. The women began to behave towards the child in ways more appropriate to an adult partner and eventually began a sexual relationship with the child. The two women who had children other than their target child, did not refer to these children in this way.

CASE EXAMPLE 6.11

Sandra had been sexually abused from the age of 11 by the one person in her childhood who she felt had ever shown her any attention or affection: a male teacher who was 26 years older than her. She became pregnant by him when 15 and he refused to have any further contact with her. Sandra did not see the sexual relationship with him as abusive. She believed it was sex that 'bound her to him'. However, she did experience *his rejection of her as very abusive.* Sandra's mother made her leave home and she gave birth to her son in a hostel for the homeless. She said she decided, 'This child would never stop loving her or leave her'. She describes her son as 'the most beautiful baby ever born'. She says 'he was perfect'. Sandra became involved in further abusive relationships with older men but she then 'gave up men' and 'stuck-to' her son. She 'told him everything': how she felt, money problems, domestic issues. When he was 10, she forbade him to go to a girl at the school's 'disco-party' because Sandra felt she was 'left-out' and she was 'worried he would meet someone'. She said that it was soon after that the sexual contact with him began. The sexual abuse eventually involved intercourse. She said that she saw it as 'an extension of our love for each other'. 'It satisfied both our needs'; 'We didn't need anyone else for anything.' The abuse stopped when he was arrested for assaulting a woman in the street when he was 15.

Women initially coerced to offend (Group C). There was no consistent pattern in the pregnancies, birth situations or early relationships with their children of the women who were initially coerced into sexually abusing them. However, there was a tendency for these mothers, like the other mothers who had sexually abused their children, to describe the relationships with their children as 'peer-like' rather than 'parental'. There was also a propensity for the woman's relationship with her partner to take precedence over the relationship with her child/ren. This may have been due either to the manipulation of partners and/or the women's personal disposition. Several women described incidents between themselves and their children, tantamount to sibling rivalry.

CASE EXAMPLE 6.12

Just as Carol had always shared her parents' bed, her daughter Lyn had also never slept in a separate bed. Carol had an ambivalent relationship with her husband, Pete. On one hand he was sexually and physically abusive to her but he could also be very loving and caring. Carol describes enjoying some sexual acts but not others and before Lyn was born he would make her endure these. When Lyn was physically able, Pete would engage in these with her. Carol describes this being a relief but it also made her feel very jealous that Lyn could bring him so much pleasure. Pete used this to promote rivalry between Carol and Lyn to his own advantage. Carol describes feeling that she had to compete with Lyn. They had 'petty rows'. She said that Pete would often have to intervene and 'scold us both'. Carol describes the only time that she felt any real control over Lyn was when she was sexually abusing her alone. Carol appeared to be an adequate mother to her two sons, she did not argue or compete with them in this way and there is no evidence either she or Pete had sexually assaulted them. The aspects of the interview that relate to them are consistent with those of the mothers in the comparison groups.

REFLECTION AND COMMENT

The narratives of the mothers who were *sole* perpetrators point to the differences in their perceptions of their target children beginning very early, in many cases pre-birth. Shengold (1980) proposed the idea that the target children were 'unwanted'. This was supported by the descriptions of many of the women who initially targeted their very young children. Conversely the women who targeted adolescents, and in addition a small number of the women who initially targeted very young children, appeared to target very much wanted children. However, these children appeared to be 'wanted' to fulfil specific and preconceived roles. The children as individuals were rarely considered.

It may be significant that almost all of the mothers who sexually abused their very young children initially felt in some way disconnected from these children. These women then seem to take the reverse position, identify very strongly with the children and become unable to separate from the child or to allow the child to separate from them. This initial disconnection from the children, both emotional and/or physical, may facilitate the women in projecting onto the child the womens' own model of who they need the child to be. Studies on other forms of child abuse by mothers indicate that parents who are predisposed to maltreatment are more likely to perpetrate abuse if they have experienced early separation from their babies (e.g. Vietze, Falsey, Sandler et al., 1980).

For *all the women* who sexually abused children, the generational boundaries between parents and children were blurred, probably because of the model they held of their relationships with their own parents. In some cases this was amplified by the father of the child the woman sexually abused being the woman's own father, stepfather, or grandfather. All the mothers who sexually abused their children, including those initially coerced into sexually abusing, related to the children more as peers than parents. This mode of interaction was exacerbated by the women's partners who made little distinction between how they related to the women and/or the children.

2. The Mothers' Expectations of their Children

From the women's answers to the questions on the structured interview relating to child care beliefs and practices, it was evident that the mothers who sexually abused children had far greater distortions in their understanding of appropriate developmental behaviour of children than the mothers in the comparison groups. It was noticeable that, although these distortions were more pronounced and exaggerated in relation to their target children, these mothers held similar distortions in their beliefs about all children. In almost all cases the mothers projected onto their children, particularly those they sexually abused, a greater level of understanding and competence in all aspects of their behaviour than was developmentally appropriate. In particular, many of the mothers believed that children had an age-inappropriate ability to recognise and meet their mothers' physical and emotional needs. Ironically, although attributing to these children a greater level of competence than they could possibly have at their stage of development, almost all of the perpetrators wanted their children to have less independence and separation from them than was developmentally appropriate.

CASE EXAMPLE 6.13

Jenny refused to let her 4-year old daughter Zoe go to a nursery, saying she was 'too young to be away from her mother'. Jenny dressed her daughter completely, bathed her and would not allow her to play with other children. Zoe still wore a nappy at night, had a bottle and a dummy and slept in her mother's bed. At the same time, Jenny believed that 4-year old Zoe should be making cups of tea for her, going to the local shop, notice when jobs needed doing around the house and do them: clearing the table, hoovering, tidying, and feeding the cat. Jenny also believed Zoe should be able to recognise when she was feeling low and comfort her. She expected the child to listen to her problems and difficulties, especially in relation to 'her partner', a violent, sexually abusive man who turned up from time to time. Jenny lost her temper with her daughter when she did not behave how she expected her to and frequently hit her for not doing 'what she should'.

3. Discipline and Control of the Children

Very few of the mothers who sexually abused their children felt they could effectively control or discipline these children. The problems the women seemed to find the greatest source of difficulty were attempts on the part of the child for separation and independence. Mothers in all three groups of perpetrators described at times using sexual acts with the child as a way of regaining power and control (see Chapter 7).

Women who initially target young children (Group A). Many of the women who initially targeted very young children perceived the children's inability to respond how they expected them to, as disobedience or deliberate malice. The women would then be very angry with the children. Both the child who cannot respond as expected, and the woman who cannot make the child do so, experience feelings of intense helplessness. This also exacerbates the woman's belief that she has little control over the child and intensifies her anger and negativity towards the child. The child responds by being more testing and exacting which then intensifies the mother's reaction. This negative dynamic between the mother and child spirals unabated.

Women who initially target adolescents (Group B). A similar scenario is applicable to mothers who target the adolescents. They also hold distorted beliefs that the children are far more capable than they are developmentally able to be. Because of there idealisation of the adolescewnt, if at any time a woman perceives the adolescent is not behaving congruently with these beliefs, she construes it as her inability to make him or her do so rather than any inability within the adolescent to respond. Consequently the woman feels the adolescent has more control than she has and uses whatever means she can to manipulate his or her behaviour.

Women initially coerced to offend (Group C). Many, but not all, of the mothers who were coerced into sexually abusing by men also had very inappropriate expectations of the children they sexually abused. The powerful negative attitudes expressed by these mothers were again based on age-inappropriate expectations of the children's capabilities. The women in this group also frequently used the power and threat of the male perpetrator to control the children, hence inflating his authority and control.

REFLECTION AND COMMENT

The women perpetrators' lack of understanding of appropriate developmental behaviours undoubtedly reflected the lack of appropriate parenting that they received throughout their own childhoods, in conjunction with the lack of alternative models available to them. Having never been mothered in an adequate way or even having observed appropriate mothering, the women could not be 'good-enough' mothers. Throughout their childhoods the women perpetrators had been treated in ways inappropriate to their age and stage of development. The beliefs and expectations that were held in relation to them, they held in relation to their own children. These beliefs and understanding of children were not related to the women's intellectual or educational level. Even very intelligent women who had been highly educated held surprisingly distorted beliefs about what children of all ages and stages were capable of.

Having as children internalised both sides of the relationships they had experienced (Sroufe & Fleeson, 1986), as adults they related to their children as they had experienced being related to by adults when they themselves were children. During childhood sexual contact was experienced by many of these mothers as the main source of human connection. They also experienced it as making them feel powerless and controlled. The children's behaviours being inconsistent with their mothers' expectations of them elicits feelings of anger and rejection in the women. The mothers' response will be to feel the need to both control the children and to 'make a human contact' with them. Thus part of the mothers' motivation for the sexual abuse of their children may be the use of sexual contact as a means by which to gain power and control over them. It may also be the only way they know to make a human contact and meet their affiliation needs. Adrienne Rich suggests that motherhood is full of responsibility but no real authority. Mothers who sexually abuse their children have both responsibility and authority secured by exploitation.

The women did not appear to know the difference between children and adults. They needed the children to act like adults in order that their needs could be met but wanted them to be as dependent as children so they could maintain some control over them and thus ensure their needs were met (Youngson, 1994).

ACTS OF MURDER AND ATTEMPTED MURDER

Murder of children who have been sexually abused by women is rare but it does happen. If the child dies, the woman is most likely to be charged with infanticide, manslaughter or murder. The prior sexual assault of the child is rarely recognised, or if it is, it is ignored.

Acts of attempted or 'pseudo' murder of a child who has been sexually abused are not as rare as murder. Four of the fourteen women who targeted young children, and two of the twelve women initially coerced into abusing admitted to perpetrating such acts. The women described attempting to suffocate, strangle or drown the children they had sexually abused, but stopping as the child slipped into unconsciousness or just prior to that point. When the child 'becomes silent' the women report feeling a sense of relief and being able to stop. The women describe these acts of violence as being precipitated by becoming so angry with the children they 'want to kill' them. One woman described this anger as 'enormous but not explosive, eating away at me until I can no longer bear it and the child seems to personify the whole cause of that feeling'. Two of the women who targeted adolescents engaged them in sadistic sexual acts that included suffocation. Both denied aggressive intent but described the behaviour as ways of heightening sexual excitement of themselves and the adolescent.

From discussions with the women who did admit to trying to kill the children, it appears there are two main aetiologies for this anger which are not mutually exclusive:

1. The women recognise (often unconsciously) the 'victimised' aspect of themselves in the child and are infuriated by the 'weakness' and 'vulnerability' which they perceive as associated with their own victimisation.
2. The women project all the shame and self-hatred for the acts they have perpetrated onto the child. One woman said of her daughter 'her just walking around seemed to just throw in my face what I'd done'. The child becomes a living symbol of all that is negative and the women want to 'wipe the children out'.

CASE EXAMPLE 6.14

Paula describes often having felt like she wanted to kill her children. On several occasions she had tried to do so. She had held pillows over their heads and had held their heads under water when they were in the bath. Once she had locked them in the car in the garage and turned the engine on but went out and rescued them in time. 'It was as if something just clicked and when I looked at them all I could see was . . . not them as them . . . they just seemed to summarise everything terrible in my life, everything I loathed. When I looked at them all I could see was what I had done to them, and what my brother did to me, it was as if they were the weak part of me, the dirty part . . . the feelings were dreadful, . . . uncontrollable, it was as if they were overtaking me, and I just wanted to wipe the children out.'

SPECIAL CASE EXAMPLE 6.15

Sally was imprisoned for sexual assault and attempt to endanger the life of an 11-year-old boy. Sally is part of a large, ostensibly cohesive family with many 'unwritten rules'. Any family member who 'breaks the rules' is disowned and vilified by all other members of the family until they return to the fold, resubmitting themselves to the family's jurisdiction. On the day of her offence, she had just had an argument with her older brother Michael. Sally went out and met an 11-year-old boy who, although she was in her twenties, she saw as 'a mate'. He did something that 'got on her nerves' and she said she felt as if she really wanted to hurt him. She bought some alcohol which they shared and then Sally sexually assaulted him in a sadistic manner after which she attempted to drown him in the local pond, leaving him unconscious and face down. He was rescued by a passer-by. Initially, Sally said they 'had sex' and she was just trying to 'sober him up' before he went home. She then tried to blame the boy, saying he had been drunk and was making-up stories because of a feud between their families. Nevertheless, Sally was arrested, convicted and served her sentence. In prison Sally disclosed for the first time she had a long history of sexual abuse by various perpetrators, extra- and intra- familial. Of all her abusers, Sally was most able to express her anger with her brother, Michael, whom she had argued with just prior to the sexual assault.

COMMENT
Sally construed the child she sexually assaulted and then tried to drown, to be most similar to Michael, the brother who had sexually abused her for most of her life. Her argument with her brother that day triggered a vast well of rage she had never even been allowed to show, partly because of fear of him and partly because of the family rules for harmony. Sally wanted to retaliate but feeling constrained by her powerlessness against her brother, she projected characteristics of her brother onto her 'mate' and directed her anger to him. She sexually abused him in the sadistic and brutal way she had frequently experienced when being sexually abused by her brother. Sally said she was not initially sexually aroused but became so as the assault progressed, connecting increasing feelings of power with increasing feelings of sexual arousal. After the sexual assault she said she felt 'so ashamed' she kept 'trying to pretend it had never happened'. She wanted nothing to remind her of it. To try and remove, physically and psychologically, most importantly from one's self, all evidence of any behaviour one is ashamed of is common human need. In addition, it is possible that the state the child was in after she had sexually assaulted him reminded Sally of herself in a similar situation. Thus leading to intolerable feelings of identification which she would want to block out. She said she 'just wanted him to stop snivelling . . . it made her feel sick'. Another motivation was to minimise the possibility of her behaviour coming to public,

and more particularly, her family's attention. Sally describes being more worried about 'exposing' her family than the legal consequences.

SUMMARY

- The factors that lead a woman to target a specific child are related to projections the woman makes onto the child.
- Thus target children are perceived by the women offenders to be different from other children. These differences are primarily the construction of the woman offender. Non-target children tend to be perceived similarly to other peoples' perception of those children.
- If a woman no longer has access to her chosen targets, the woman may project these constructions onto another child to enable her to continue abusing.
- For mothers who sexually abuse children, the negative projections onto target children are facilitated by the circumstances around the birth or conception of the child.
- The women who sexually abuse children find it difficult to perceive the children whom they sexually abuse as individuals, separate from themselves.
- The women who initially target very young children tend to denigrate those children.
- The women who initially target adolescents idealise these children, both as children and as partners.
- Neither the women who initially target very young children nor those who are initially coerced into sexually abusing children by men perceive their target children as ideal children or ideal partners.
- The women who are initially coerced into sexually abusing children by men, are likely to denigrate the children that they sexually abuse.
- The mothers who sexually abused their children all primarily related to the children as a peer rather than a parent. They tended to infantilise the child or treat the child as a pseudo-adult. Some women did both simultaneously.
- When a child did not respond to the women in the way that they expected, they construed it either as the child being deliberately pernicious or that they themselves had no control over the child.
- Most women were unable to allow children they sexually abused to separate or become independent from them and were threatened by any behaviour of a child to do so.
- Therefore they frequently felt angry with the children and a need to regain power and control over them. From experience in their own childhood they knew this could be achieved by means of sexual contact.

- For some women the target child personifies negative feelings to such an extent, they try to obliterate them by attempting to obliterate the child. They can attack the child, sometimes to the point of unconsciousness, which can lead to the murder of the child.

7

THE WOMEN'S EXPERIENCE OF SEX: LOOKING AT MOTIVATIONS TO OFFEND

- THE WOMEN'S PERCEPTION OF THEIR SEXUALITY IN RELATION TO THAT OF OTHER PEOPLE
- THE WOMEN'S EXPERIENCE OF SEXUAL ACTS
- THE WOMEN'S USE OF SEXUAL FANTASY
- SUMMARY

(Human beings) are not gentle creatures who want to be loved ... on the contrary, creatures among whose instinctual endowments is to be reckoned a powerful share of aggressiveness. ... their neighbour is for them not only a potential helper or sexual object, but also someone who tempts them to satisfy their aggressiveness on him ... to use him sexually without his consent, to seize his possessions, to humiliate him, to cause him pain, to torture him and to kill him. (Sigmund Freud, Civilization and its Discontents)

THE WOMEN'S PERCEPTION OF THEIR SEXUALITY IN RELATION TO THAT OF OTHER PEOPLE

There have been those who have suggested that women who sexually abuse children are extremely highly sexed and promiscuous or have a history of indiscriminate or compulsive sexual activity (e.g. Wahl, 1960; Groth, 1982; Meiselman, 1978; Mzarek & Kempe, 1987; Allen, 1991). Several writers have hypothesised that as a consequence of poor relationships with adult partners the women seek substitute gratification with the child (Wahl, 1960; Margolis, 1975; Shengold, 1980; Mayer, 1983; McCarty, 1986; Krug, 1989). Very few of the women offenders in this study could have been considered to have been promiscuous with adult partners (see Chapter 4), however this does not mean they do not experience themselves as having a high sex drive.

In order to explore this issue, each woman was asked to rate herself and others on the Repertory Grid on the construct of sexuality (7–1). This is a complex construct, related to sexual drive, sexual desire and sexual activity. Some time was spent with each woman discussing this construct in order that a shared understanding was reached. Using these ratings, it will also be possible to consider the women's beliefs about how sexual they perceive the children they sexually abuse to be.

FINDINGS

The women who sexually abused adolescents (Group B) rated themselves on the construct 'sexual' similarly to the women in the comparison group. The women who targeted very young children (Group A) and those who were initially coerced into sexually abusing by male partners (Group C) tended to rate themselves as having a lower sexual drive than the women in the other groups.

With few exceptions, the women who sexually abused children rated the children they sexually abused as having either the same or higher sexual drive than they perceived themselves to have. Interestingly, these women rated those children in their lives whom they did not sexually abuse in a more age-appropriate manner, that is similarly to the women in the comparison group (Table 7.1).

Women who initially target young children (Group A). Although these women describe having frequent, some daily, sexual contact with the children they abuse, they tend to rate themselves low on the construct 'sexual'. On further exploration it was clear that these women were not able to identify the feelings they had as sexual feelings. Regardless of the children being less than five years old when they were initially targeted, all bar one of these women rated the children higher on the construct of 'sexual' than she rated herself. The women interpreted the children's behaviours as meaning they wanted sexual contact (Case Examples 7.1). The one woman who did not rate the children she sexually abused as more sexual than herself wanted to hurt the children by her behaviour (Case Example 7.2).

Table 7.1: Women's ratings of their own sexual drive and that of other people[a]

RATINGS max–min 7–1	SELF	CHILDREN ABUSED AGED 0–10	CHILDREN NOT ABUSED AGED 0–10	CHILDREN ABUSED AGED 11–16	CHILDREN NOT ABUSED AGED 11–16	ABUSERS
GROUP A (n=14)	2.3 (range 1–5)	3.6 (range 1–7)	1.04 (range 1–2)	4.2 (range 4–5)	4.1 (range 3–4)	6.3 (range 5–7)
GROUP B (n=10)	4.9 (range 4–6)	—	1.0 (range 1)	5.4 (range 4–6)	4.5 (range 4–5)	5.8 (range 5–7)
GROUP C (n=12)	2.6 (range 1–5)	2.8 (range 1–6)	1.0 (range 1)	4.5 (range 2–6)	3.6 (range 2–4)	5.9 (range 5–7)
GROUP D (n=36)	4.4 (range 1–6)	—	1.03 (range 1–2)	—	3.1 (range 2–4)	6.8 (range 6–7)

[a]The number of children in each cell will vary.

CASE EXAMPLES 7.1

Mavis, seeing her two-year-old son playing with his penis, said she thought 'Men, men, men, sex, sex, sex, that's all they want' and sexually abused him.

Sarah, who had sexually abused her son from birth to his teenage years, said 'I knew he wanted sex because he always had an erection, if he didn't want it, he wouldn't have had one would he?' This statement reflects Sarah's own experience. She had been sexually abused by her grandfather and knew when he wanted sex because he would open his trouser fly and show her his erection.

CASE EXAMPLE 7.2

Mary was a very prolific abuser who targeted any child. She was herself extensively abused by many perpetrators, both as an adult and as a child. She would go quickly from wanting to abuse a child to abusing. She said she knew the child did not feel sexual. She said 'I want to ruin his or her childhood as mine was ruined'. (She rated all children as 1.) Mary also had sexual contact with two 14-year-old boys. She perceived them to be abusing her. She rated these boys as more sexual (6) than herself (5).

Women who initially target adolescents (Group B). The women who sexually abused adolescents used the fact that these adolescents were older and ostensibly independent to attribute the sexual desire to them. They said things such as: 'if he did not want the sex he could have walked away', 'you know what boys are, sex on the brain', 'she made the date with me, then cried rape'. They manipulated and coerced the adolescents into behaving in specific ways and then interpreted their compliance as sexual desire.

CASE EXAMPLE 7.3

Pam began grooming her son sexually when he was 8 and began actual sexual acts with him when he was 11. This continued until he had a psychotic breakdown in his mid-teens. She rated herself as 5 on the construct of sexual and her son as 6. Her belief that he had sexual desire was based on her interpretation of her son wanting her to hold him and cuddle him and him wanting to sit on her knee. When he did she would sexually touch him. The fact that she bought him his favourite comics each week and made him sit on her knee and be touched by her before he was allowed to have them was ignored in her assessment of his sexual desire. Other evidence Pam gave of her son's desire to have sexual contact with her was his going upstairs to the toilet in the evening. The only toilet in the house was in the bathroom. When he went to the bathroom in the evening she would attribute it to him 'teasing her' and she would bath him. She would masturbate him to the point of ejaculation saying to clean him 'from the inside out'. She bought him a ring and would punish him if he did not wear it. If he did wear it she would attribute this to 'testimony to their love for each other' and his desire of her.

Women who are initially coerced offenders (Group C). The women who were initially coerced into sexually offending by men made similar types of distortions to the other women offenders. The most common basis of these women's thinking errors was to interpret the children's compliance in response to the man's manipulations as sexual desire. The men also groomed many of these women very well in order to ensure this was what they believed, thus also securing the women's compliance.

Interestingly, it tended to be the women who were not sexually abused themselves as children, or were very clear that the sexual abuse perpetrated against them as children was abuse, who were able to recognise that the children they sexually abused did not have a high sexual drive. Two such women were responsible for disclosing the abuse and eventually protecting the child. However, one woman who was initially coerced into sexually abusing children by a man said that she had not been sexually abused in her childhood but she became a very active and sadistic sole perpetrator. She rated the children she abused as having high sexual drives.

CASE EXAMPLE 7.4

Penny, who had not been sexually abused, was a single parent with no social support. When her daughter was five, they were targeted by a Schedule 1 Offender who told Penny he was a photographer and was attracted to her 'unusual beauty'. He took many photos of her, some of which were erotic in nature. At times he had included her daughter in the photographs and then began to also include her in the more erotic poses. Penny said that it was so gradual and natural she did not really realise what they had become involved with. By then they had moved in with him and were financially dependent on him. She initially thought nothing of it as her daughter enjoyed posing and looked relaxed. Penny also knew how sexually aroused he was by these sessions and wanted to please him. Nevertheless, Penny felt increasingly uncomfortable as the poses became more pornographic. She also recognised that although the child appeared to be enjoying herself, what they were doing was actual sexual acts. Penny said she was horrified when she recognised this, like she 'just woke up'. Penny left, took her daughter to a woman's refuge, and told the police.

REFLECTION AND COMMENT

With the exception of some of the women who sexually abused adolescents, the women offenders' ratings of their sexual drive are at variance with their sexual behaviour. This may be because the abuse of adolescents by older women, in particular of adolescent boys, is often socially sanctioned and therefore it is easier for them to accept the feelings as sexual. For women in the other groups whose targets are not socially sanctioned, it is more difficult to accept their behaviour is sexual, even to themselves. This difficulty is intensified by the woman's confusion related to the appropriate identification of any of her own feelings, and thus in turn, those of the child. This denial and/or confusion on the part of the woman in identifying her own feelings seems to be related both to her learning experiences in her childhood and to her psychological defence.

The women misinterpreted the children's normal needs, childhood explorations and behaviours, and reactions to being sexually abused, as sexual acts and desires. Facilitating this belief system, is the woman's internal models of children and adults who abuse them, gained from her own childhood experience and/or, in the case of the male-coerced perpetrators, via orchestration of the situation by her partner. Just as the women as children were made to carry the responsibility and hence guilt for acts perpetrated against them by their abusers, by rating the children they have sexually abused as 'more sexual' than themselves, the women have, in turn, projected responsibility onto their child victims for their victimisation. Using this psychological defence mechanism, the woman relieves the burden of guilt she has for meeting her own needs via the sexual abuse of a child.

THE WOMEN'S EXPERIENCE OF SEXUAL ACTS

No sexual act, including the sexual abuse of a child, is purely about sexual gratification, there are always non-sexual motivations involved: comfort, affiliation needs, power, etc. However, the abuse the women perpetrated was sexual. It was therefore important to explore the possible meaning of sex for these women that might motivate them to sexually abuse children. As there was no test or questionnaire readily available, one was constructed for this study. It produced some interesting qualitative data but this was a naïvely constructed tool and was not standardised or tested for reliability or validity. The results should therefore be considered in the light of the method by which they were collected.

1. The Women's Experiences of Sexual Acts with Adults

Each woman was asked to fill in the 'What Sex Means' Questionnaire in relation to her most common feelings during sex with her significant adult partners.

FINDINGS

The major difference between the women in the comparison group and the women who sexually abused children was that all the women offenders ticked at least one negative statement when describing their personal experience during sex with their adult partners, male and/or female. Two women in the comparison group described their experience of sex with adult partners as almost completely negative. One of these women had experienced extensive sexual abuse in her childhood and the other had had poor personal as well as sexual relationships with male partners (Table 7.2)

Women who initially target young children (Group A). These women describe sex with adult partners as generally a very negative experience but one from which they obtain some positive physical feelings. All the women in this group ticked at least three negative statements about their experience of sex with each adult partner. The most commonly ticked statements were 'It makes me feel humiliated' and 'It makes me feel used'. Eleven of the fourteen women ticked statements relating to positive physical feelings: most commonly—'It fulfils a physical need in me'. Only four women picked any other category: 'It's a bonding with someone' (2); 'It makes me feel loved' (4).

CASE EXAMPLES 7.5

Jean said she felt her partner used her 'like a toilet in which to deposit bodily products and to relieve himself'. At the same time, regardless of how 'humiliated and dirty' she felt, she said having sex, 'somehow calmed my body'.

'I don't really understand it. I hated and loathed having sex with him yet, . . . it still made me feel like I was loved. But . . . I knew I wasn't.' (Doreen)

Women who initially target adolescents (Group B). The pattern of responses made by this group of women was similar to that of women in the comparison group. The major difference was that the offenders much more generally experienced sex with adults as also often being a negative

Table 7.2: Women's subjective experience of sex with adult partners[a]

	WARMTH	BONDING	GIVE PLEASURE	OWN PLEASURE	POSITIVE PHYSICAL FEELINGS	POWER AND CONTROL	NEGATIVE
GROUP A	0.3	0.15	0.0	0.0	1.8	0.0	3.75
GROUP B	0.8	1.1	1.1	0.4	0.4	0.0	2.2
GROUP C	0.8	0.4	0.5	0.3	0.4	0.0	3.6
GROUP D	1.8	1.3	0.8	0.8	0.7	0.15	0.45

[a]Because the numbers in each group were very different, as the women each had various numbers of partners and victims, the results in each category were averaged overall. Total per individual woman = 6 units.

experience. Additionally, they were more likely to feel sex was about giving pleasure and bonding with partners. The women in this group were the least likely to acknowledge the physical aspects of a sexual contact.

CASE EXAMPLE 7.6

Fiona married a man who was twenty years older than her. She believed that it was her duty to please him sexually if he was to stay with her. She asked if she could tick the statement 'It means absolutely nothing to me' twice because it was just how she felt. She also ticked 'It makes me feel used'. She said she thought she might get something out of sex 'like in the movies' if only she could 'find the right man'. Fiona masturbated in front of her stepson. In the interview several years later she rationalised this by saying she felt that if she could 'train a man from when he was young' she might be able 'to get some satisfaction from a sexual relationship'.

Women who are initially coerced offenders (Group C). These women generally had a negative experience of sexual acts with adult partners. Most were made to endure extremely humiliating sexual experiences by their partners. All the women in this group ticked at least three negative statements for each of their sexual partners. Seven of the twelve women, however, described how *initially* their sexual experiences with the men who coerced them into sexually abusing children were the best that they had ever had. For three of these women this was their experience throughout their relationship. They completely separated out sex when abusing children and sex when not. Most of the other women said that once the abuse of children had started the sexual acts became solely for the gratification of their male partner.

CASE EXAMPLE 7.7

Joan said until she met Lionel she had never enjoyed sex but he was different. But he used a great deal of hard core pornography, which he said was to 'help him find other ways to please her' and would then use the magazines to suggest they try what Joan described as 'bizarre things'. Her pleasure became less and less important. He talked about how sexy the models were and Joan was very jealous. He brought her daughter a camera and suggested she could take photographs of their sexual activity 'instead of using the magazines'. Joan readily agreed. It was not until they had separated that Joan said she could allow herself to see clearly what she had really felt about the sex even from the start. On the 'What Sex Means' Questionnaire Joan ticked one statement about giving him pleasure, one about bonding, one about positive physical feelings and three negative statements.

REFLECTION AND COMMENT

All the women offenders in this study describe their sexual experiences with adult partners as being overwhelmingly negative but also fulfilling some need in them. These results are consistent with the work of Speltz, Matthews and Mathews (1989) who also described the women in their study as having a generally negative experience of sex with adult partners. One hypothesis could be that women target children to sexually abuse so as to gain the positive experiences of sexual acts with men without the negative effects of the relationship: both sexual and general.

2. The Women's Experience of Sex with Children

It would be expected that a woman's experience of sex with children would be different in some way to her experience of sex with adults, thus motivating her to target a child. The women were asked to fill in the 'What Sex Means' Questionnaire specifically with regard to how they felt *during* the actual sexual behaviour with the child (not *about* their sexual abuse of the child).

FINDINGS

With the exception of two of the women who were coerced into sexually abusing children, all the women ticked at least one statement relating to power and control in their feelings during sexual interactions with children. Most of the women ticked more than one statement in this category (Table 7.3).

Women who initially target young children (Group A). All these women described experiencing positive physical feelings during sexual interactions with children. The most commonly ticked statement was that 'It gives me a release of tension and makes me feel calm'. Several women in this group described a build up of physical tension and knowing it could only be released by a sexual interaction with a child. All the women ticked power and control statements and nine women in the group ticked the statement 'It gives me a way to hurt someone, get my own back'. 'Hurting the child' was a very common theme with this group of women. Some women were explicit about their use of sex as a method of punishing and hurting the child. Some women recognised they had a need to 'lash-out' and hurt. Although the feeling was not necessarily generated by the child, the child was the only possible non-threatening recipient of these feelings.

Table 7.3: Women's subjective experience of sex with children[a]

	WARMTH	BONDING	GIVE PLEASURE	OWN PLEASURE	POSITIVE PHYSICAL FEELINGS	POWER AND CONTROL	NEGATIVE
GROUP A	0.8	0.75	0.1	0.0	2.1	2.25	0.0
GROUP B	1.1	1.4	1.1	0.4	0.5	1.5	0.0
GROUP C	0.25	0.25	0.5	0.0	1.4	2.0	1.6

[a]Because the numbers in each group were very different, as the women each had various numbers of partners and victims, the results in each category were averaged overall. Total per individual woman = 6 units.

Some women also recognised their affiliation needs were met at times through sex. 'It makes me feel loved' (8), 'It makes me feel very close to someone' (2) 'Being sexual means a complete union with someone' (8).

CASE EXAMPLE 7.8

'There were different reasons at different times. No one was going to take this baby from me. My foster father used to say sex made me really his and it was as if I'd put my mark on her. . . she was still part of me. If I'd feel her slipping away, I'd need to be sexual with her. At other times I was just so angry I wanted to hurt someone, anyone, so I hurt her; sexually. Other times, I'd get worked up inside and I'd masturbate myself and her at the same time It . . . made me feel so calm and as if she truly loved me.' (Doreen)

REFLECTION AND COMMENT

The sexual abuse these women perpetrate against very young children seems to be for physical gratification and an attempt to feel power and control over the situation. In addition many of the women in this group experience the sexual act between themselves and a child as somehow being symbolic of the emotional feelings and the relationship bond between them. It may be the only way these women have experienced any feelings of attachment to another human being through sexual acts. Thus it is via sexual acts the woman makes these connections with her child. For almost all the women in this group from their earliest years sexual activity has been a prominent feature of their lives. Because of this experience, there may have been physiological changes associated with psychological changes which mean the woman uses the sexual act as a modulator of both psychological and physiological arousal (see Chapter 10). The prominence of positive physical feelings in the responses of these women to sexual acts with both adults and children supports this proposal. Sexual acts with children would be more rewarding than those with adults, as with children the women also experience the positive feelings of power and control, as well as meeting at least some of their affiliation needs.

Women who initially target adolescents (Group B). The women who sexually abused adolescents have a very similar profile in their feelings during a sexual interaction with adolescents to that of the women in the comparison group in their sexual interactions with adult partners. The main differences were that the women who sexually abused adolescents felt that they gained a greater sense of power and control from these interactions. These women also held the belief that the sexual acts they were perpetrating were giving pleasure to the adolescents. None of the women in this group of perpetrators ticked the statement, 'It gives me a way to hurt someone, get my own back', whereas many women in the other two groups of perpetrators did. Some of these women's victims, however, described feeling that the woman was trying to hurt them at times. Two victims described the women who abused them as overtly sadistic. The women described these same sadistic acts in terms of a 'fun' part of a sexual relationship.

REFLECTION AND COMMENT

These women tended to 'romanticise' their feelings during sex with the children. The motivation for the women seemed to be to have a 'normal' sexual relationship with a partner, but choosing an adolescent to target in order to gain power and control over the situation. All the women in this group had themselves been sexually abused during their adolescence but most perceived themselves to have been 'equal partners'. Although they projected this same distortion onto their victims, equality is of course inconsistent with the women's stated feelings of power and control during the sexual acts with these children.

Women who are initially coerced offenders (Group C). The women who were initially coerced into sexually abusing by men tended to find it more difficult than the other women offenders to define how they felt during the sexual acts with children in which they were active participants. They tended to find it difficult to disentangle their feelings towards their partners and those towards the child.

Five women in this group said they felt negative feelings *during* the sexual acts with children. Their most commonly ticked statement was 'It's an ordeal that I go though to keep my relationship'. Six women ticked statements related to 'giving pleasure', warmth and/or 'bonding'. They described these feelings as relating to the relationship with their partner. They perceived the sexual acts with children as an extension of this relationship. The most common statement ticked by this group of women was, 'It's how you show someone you really love them'.

All bar two women ticked statements relating to power and control and/or positive physical feelings. Interestingly, these two women were both women involved in pornographic photography with children rather than actual sexual acts. These feelings related to power and control are of interest as the women would say the men had all the power and control in these situations. However, several women who were initially coerced into sexually abusing children were able to talk about how their sexual arousal had become conditioned to sexual acts with children, and how they eventually began to feel much more sexually aroused and powerful in this scenario than they did having sex with their adult partner alone. The seven women who acted at times as sole perpetrators ticked almost all the statements in the categories of power and control and positive physical feelings. A subgroup of women, predominantly those who went on to offend independently, ticked the statement 'It gives me a way to hurt someone, get my own back'. In a similar way to the women who targeted young children, these women described using sex as a punishment, to hurt, and to discharge angry feelings, even if the anger was not initially generated by that child.

CASE EXAMPLE 7.9

Tina's husband would bring other women home and expect Tina to have sex with him and them. Sometimes he would force her into having sex with them for money and then beat her for doing so. He began including adolescent children in their sexual acts. These tended to be 'runaways' and underage prostitutes. Tina said 'to my shame I felt highly sexually aroused ... particularly to the sex with the children'. Sometimes the children stayed in the house and Tina said that she began to sexually abuse them when her partner was not there. She said, 'It felt so good to be able to do something sexually I actually chose to do, to have my sexual needs met as I wanted them to be'. She describes feelings of power and control and physical release. Tina recounts a particularly sadistic feeling when sexually abusing one teenage girl whom she perceived as being all the things that she was no longer: attractive, free, happy, independent. She said she 'desperately wanted to hurt her'.

Four of the women described sexually abusing the child to protect him or her from 'worse sexual abuse' by their male partner. Although this can be seen as a post hoc justification, it is also a belief implanted by some male perpetrators as part of the initial coercion.

REFLECTION AND COMMENT

For all these women the *initial* motivation to sexually abuse children was connected to the motivations of their partners. For some women this behaviour personally remains a totally negative experience, for others, as a result of modelling and conditioning, their sexual arousal becomes associated with acts with children. The woman will internalise both the victim experience of the child, and the arousal and reward experienced by the perpetrator. Repeated exposure to such behaviours will facilitate the woman to become sexually aroused by abusing children and taking the role of the perpetrator, thus avoiding and/or alleviating the aversive experience of victimisation. Via these same processes, some of the women come to associate sexual acts with children with strong feelings of power and control. These feelings generated by sexually abusing a child will go some way to counteract the lack of power and control they feel in all other aspects of their lives. Consistent with this is the finding that power and control and positive physical feelings were the most prominent experience of all seven women who subsequently acted as independent perpetrators.

THE WOMEN'S USE OF SEXUAL FANTASY

Sexual fantasy, the mental rehearsal of a sexual scene accompanied by sexual arousal and masturbation, has been found to play a considerable role in the offending behaviour of many male offenders. In their discussion of male offenders, Laws and Marshall (1990) propose that the use of deviant fantasy during masturbation may be the most influential learning process to becoming sexually aroused by deviant stimuli. Fantasies can be along the continuum from seductive to sadistic; sexual offenders can engage in both. Sometimes sexual fantasy can stem from 'flashbacks' or re-enactment of a person's own experience of being abused but with the self in the perpetrator role. These fantasies then become modified and amplified. Fantasy can also act as a rehearsal of behaviour and can desensitise an individual to committing those acts. Offenders can also use fantasy to project onto their victim the responses they most desire. This in turn adds to the cognitive distortions offenders hold about their victims. Fantasy can lead to escalation in behaviour as 'new acts' and 'new victims' can be 'tried out' in the fantasies. It was therefore very important to investigate whether sexual fantasy also played a role in women's sexual offending behaviour. Therefore all the women involved in the study were asked about their masturbation practices, their fantasies while masturbating, and also sexual thoughts that occurred to them at other times.

FINDINGS

In general, all of the women who took part, whether an offender or in the comparison group, were more reluctant to talk about masturbation and sexual fantasy than any other area of the interview. Masturbation to deviant sexual fantasy did not appear to be prevalent among the women who sexually abused children. However, many of the women offenders did describe having 'sexual thoughts' and preoccupations about children.

The comparison group (Group D). Of the women in the comparison group, 75% percent (27/36) said they masturbated and 80% (29/36) said that they used sexual fantasy either during love-making and/or during masturbation. None of the women in the comparison group said they fantasised sexual acts with children. One woman, however, who had a history of extensive sexual abuse, did describe 'intrusive thoughts' about sexual acts with children while she was sexually aroused. She found these thoughts totally repellent and when she had them, her sexual arousal immediately diminished.

Women who initially target young children (Group A). All of the women in this group had repeated images and thoughts of sexual acts with children. These thoughts could be seductive and/or sadistic in nature. In association with these thoughts the women frequently experienced arousal. Few of the women were able to specifically identify this as being sexual arousal. Most of the women in this group seemed unable to identify any emotional states. Many appeared not to have a language that enabled them to do so and described feelings in terms of bodily sensations.

Only five of the fourteen women (35%) who sexually abused very young children said they had masturbated to sexual fantasies when not actually engaged in sexual activity with children. These fantasies could be both seductive and/or sadistic. Only four of these five women masturbated to sexual fantasies of acts that involved children. One of these women described using masturbation to sexual images of her abusing her son at times when she was trying *not* to sexually abuse her child. Two other women also described masturbating to sexual fantasies involving children more frequently at times when they had less or no access to their target child/ren. The fifth woman, Karen (Case Example 3.10) remembers that after the sexual abuse by her mother stopped, she comforted herself by masturbating to fantasies in which her mother was sexually abusing her. This behaviour continued even after as an adult she begun sexually abusing her own daughter.

CASE EXAMPLE 7.10

Mary describes her fantasies as 'blue' and 'red' fantasies: loving and angry. She had no access to her own children but describes almost constant sexual arousal partly due to the use of fantasy. Mary would sexually touch a child, then use that touch as the basis of fantasies to which she would masturbate. She would then escalate the fantasies and masturbate to them until she could touch another child.

Three other women in this group said that in order to have an orgasm while engaged in sexual activities with adult partners they had to have sexual fantasies of children. One woman said she could only have an orgasm with an adult male partner if she fantasised sadistic sexual acts with children.

REFLECTION AND COMMENT

Many of the women in this group were severely sexually abused themselves as children, and the fact that they did not masturbate may be due to an inhibition to doing so as a consequence of their own sexually abusive experience (Eldridge, 1994). It may also be that as the children they sexually abused were so readily available to them, they could engage in sexual activity whenever they wanted to, therefore rarely needed to masturbate.

Women who initially target adolescents (Group B). Almost all these women describe having frequent sexual thoughts about their victims that were associated with feelings of well-being, but to which they did not masturbate. Some of the thoughts were instantaneous and some were described as tantamount to complex 'daydreaming'. These 'daydreams' could be romantic and/or erotic during which the women saw the children as equal partners. In these fantasies, the women saw both themselves and their victims as equivalent in every way, often seeing their victims as instigators of sexual activities. The women also perceived their victims as being both willing and very eager participants.

Of the women who sexually abused adolescents 80% (8/10) described having masturbated to sexual fantasies involving the children they sexually abused. All the fantasies they *described* were seductive in nature, in which the women totally idealised the relationship between themselves and the children. The two women who said they had never masturbated to fantasies of sexually abusing their victims or other children, were both women who had sexually abused their own sons. One of these women perpetrated subtle sexual abuse by crossing many sexual boundaries with her son in demanding that he physically care for her (Case Example 1.5). She denies any sexual intention in this behaviour; however, this woman's description of her feelings during these 'acts of physical care', accessed via the 'What Sex Means' Questionnaire, were similar to how the other women in this group describe their feelings during sexual acts with their victims.

REFLECTION AND COMMENT

The women who sexually abused adolescents tended to use their masturbatory sexual fantasies and 'daydreams' to normalise their behaviour. It is hypothesised that the women in this group used both masturbatory fantasy and sexual 'daydreaming' to facilitate the idealisation of what they perceived to be the relationship between themselves and the children they abused. In the fantasies the child held all the characteristics the woman ideally would like him or her to hold, and the activities were as she would have wanted them to be. Her cognitive distortions were hence reinforced.

Women who are initially coerced offenders (Group C). Similarly to the other women offenders, many of the women in this group also described regularly experiencing sexual images and thoughts about children to which they did not masturbate. Only one of the women said she had had such thoughts before being coerced into sexually abusing children by her partner. This woman was sexually abused by both her parents. As soon as her daughter was born she had sexual thoughts about the child but says that she did not act on them and tried to push them away, until her partner encouraged and coerced her into actually sexually abusing the child. She eventually also became an independent perpetrator against her daughter. Three women who were coerced into offending said they found the sexual thoughts of children intrusive and repugnant. The other nine women described arousal or neutral feelings accompanying these thoughts.

Four of the twelve women who were initially coerced into sexually abusing children said they had masturbated to fantasies of sexual acts with children. None of the women said they had ever done so before being coerced into sexual activities with children by their partners. Interestingly, all four of these women went on to sexually abuse children independently.

REFLECTION AND COMMENT

Those women who masturbated to sexual fantasies of children and those who felt aroused in some way to images and thoughts of sexual acts with children had associated sexual arousal to the sexual acts with children. Importantly, it was two of the women who were not themselves sexually abused as children, who found sexual thoughts about children repugnant and who were eventually able to stop the abuse of their children. It is hypothesised that those women who experienced the thoughts of sexually abusing children as 'neutral' were very likely to have cut-off from their feelings in a similar way when actually engaged in the sexual acts with children. This method of 'emotionally cutting-off' is also likely to be the way in which they dealt with their own experience of being sexually abused.

SUMMARY

- The women sexual offenders rate themselves as having low sexual interest/activity which is contrary to their overt sexual behaviour.
- The women's experiences have meant that they have learnt to behave sexually in response to a variety of stimuli including anger, anxiety, and powerful affiliation needs.
- Women in all groups of offenders tended to have negative experiences in their sexual interactions with adult partners; however, sexual activity also produces some positive feelings that seem to be unavailable to them in other areas of their lives.
- The women who sexually abuse children find that these needs can be met by sexual contact with children while the women maintain power and control.
- Those women who are initially coerced into sexually offending who report experiencing feelings of power and control during the abuse are the most likely to subsequently sexually abuse children as sole perpetrators.
- The women who sexually abused younger children and those who were originally coerced into sexually abusing by men, were more likely to recognise that some of the abuse was sadistic. Those women who sexually abused adolescents were the least likely to adjudge the abuse they perpetrated as sadistic.
- The women's use of sexual fantasy appears to be less extensive and universal than that of the men who sexually abuse children.
- Sexual 'daydreaming', however, does seem to play a similar role to masturbatory fantasies. This 'daydreaming' allows the woman to normalise her behaviour in her own mind and manipulate the reaction of the child so that the woman can project onto the child whatever response she desires.

8

'TYPICAL' AND 'ATYPICAL' FEMALE PERPETRATORS OF CHILD SEXUAL ABUSE

- GENERAL CHARACTERISTICS OF 'TYPICAL' FEMALE PERPETRATORS
- 'ATYPICAL' FEMALE PERPETRATORS*
- THE 'MISSING' FEMALE PERPETRATORS?
- SUMMARY

It is both academically and clinically useful to find that there are enough factors within groups of women who sexually abuse children to produce typical profiles. These profiles are presented with the caution that they should be considered as heuristic rather than categorical: 'basic sets of directions' rather than 'definitive fully annotated maps'.

GENERAL CHARACTERISTICS OF 'TYPICAL' FEMALE PERPETRATORS

Women who sexually abuse children can be of any age, social class, intellectual ability, and marital status, and can be involved in any type of employment. They can perpetrate any form of sexual act and can behave seductively or sadistically towards their victims. Some women behave

---

* This section was written with much consultation and discussion with Mimi Howett, Probation Officer, Wilmslow Probation Office, for which I owe her much thanks.

Table 8.1: Typical features of female perpetrators of child sexual abuse—childhood

	WOMEN WHO INITIALLY TARGET YOUNG CHILDREN	WOMEN WHO INITIALLY TARGET ADOLESCENTS	WOMEN WHO ARE INITIALLY COERCED BY MEN
Relationship with mother/maternal figure	Mainly distant, can be idealised thus inconsistent	More peer-like than parental	Less positive than with father, often hostile
Relationship with father/paternal figure	Very negative, likely to be abused by him	Mostly absent, but if there, likely to be negative	Often idealised, thus present inconsistent model
Relationships with siblings	Poor—feel most badly treated	Poor—often act as parent to peer	Mostly poor
Relationships with peers	Poor, tend to be very isolated	Tend to be superficial	Some reasonable, most superficial
Sexual abuse in childhood	Highly likely. Began at a young age, usually intrafamilial Experienced it as abusive but believed people knew and sanctioned it	Highly likely. Began in adolescence. Often extrafamilial Tended to deny the abusiveness as believed people knew and sanctioned it	Likely. Intra- or extrafamilial Some experienced it as abusive some not. Most denied abusive behaviour by father
Physical abuse	Likely	Possible	Possible
Emotional abuse	Likely to be severe, particularly to feel rejected and emotionally isolated	Likely to be quite severe, particularly to feel rejected and emotionally isolated	Likely to be quite severe, particularly to feel rejected and emotionally isolated
Self-esteem	Very low	Relatively low	Very low
Relationships with partners	Tend to have few but very abusive relationships. Can be promiscuous. Unable to end relationships	Tend to have had several/many relationships, most/all abusive See a partner as very important	Tend to deny negative aspects of relationships if there are *any* good aspects
Experience of sex with adult partners	Mainly negative but positive physical feelings	Similar to comparison group but more negative. No power + control	Mostly negative but include all other aspects but no power + control

Table 8.1: (*continued*)

	WOMEN WHO INITIALLY TARGET YOUNG CHILDREN	WOMEN WHO INITIALLY TARGET ADOLESCENTS	WOMEN WHO ARE INITIALLY COERCED BY MEN
Relationships with peers	Very poor, rarely had a real friend	Tend to make superficial friendships	May have friends but been isolated by the partners
Experience of stress and social support	High levels of stress and no social support	High levels of stress; main source of support their target adolescents	High levels of stress and no social support
Grooming for compliance	Rarely needed as target children very young	Similar methods as were used on them, i.e. thinking errors coercion, etc.	Target children groomed by men
Grooming for secrecy	Mainly fear; using aggression, social disbelief	As above plus threats	Often use threat of the man's anger and aggression
Perception of children they sexually abuse	Tend to identify strongly with the children and to perceive them	Tend to idealise the children and see them as perfect	Tend to identify with the child and take on the man's perception of that child
Perception of sex with the child	Positive physical feelings, some affiliation needs, high levels of power and control	Similar range to comparison group but with high levels of power and control	Can be negative, can be to please men, can be high levels of positive physical feelings and power and control

both seductively and sadistically. Although a woman may initially target a child or children within a specific age range, she may not continue to exclusively target children in this age range (Table 8.1).

'ATYPICAL' FEMALE PERPETRATORS

The large majority of the women interviewed could be classified into these three categories. However, some of the women could not be. Although at present these women are described as 'atypical', it is suggested that as more is found out about women who sexually abuse children, this may not be the case.

1. Women Who Sexually Abuse As Equal Partners with Men (*n*=2)

When men and women sexually abuse children together it is almost always assumed that the male coerced the woman into the perpetrating behaviour. Two women were interviewed who were not coerced but from the start were equal co-perpetrators, both of whom appeared to seek out men with whom they could sexually abuse children.

CASE EXAMPLE—A WOMAN CO-PERPETRATOR

Kim was serving a prison sentence for the sexual abuse of her two sons and a daughter. Kim, her husband and a male friend had been jointly charged. Each child had made compelling disclosures stating Kim had sexually abused them and often initiated the sexual abuse. All three children had mild learning disabilities which seemed to improve once taken away from their abusive home situation. Kim steadfastly denied the abuse for the whole of her prison sentence.

On the first meeting with Kim, she cried, at times deeply sobbing about the death of her father. She said he was 'caring, loving, affectionate, kind'. She said he 'adored' her and took her 'everywhere with him'. She believed 'he'd have given me the world if he could' and said 'I miss him dearly . . . when I die and I can be with my dad again'. She went on to say how she looked for men who were like her father. It appeared to be a very recent bereavement but she said her father had died when she was six; 22 years ago.

Kim said she had always wished it had been her mum who had died. She had not spoken to her mother or sister for years because 'they told terrible lies' about her father. They said her father had been a vicious and violent man who had beaten all three of them and had sexually abused both Kim and her sister. Kim does remember often being in casualty but she puts this down to accidents.

Kim's emotional confusion was illustrated in her description of her mother. 'I love my mum . . . but I don't want to talk to her because she tells so many lies about my dad. She's jealous, my sister's jealous too [about] how my dad and I felt about each other. She's been a good mum, well to my sister anyway, . . . I never lived with her . . . after my dad died.' After her father's death, Kim remembers constantly crying for daddy. She refused to eat so her mother sent her to live with her paternal grandparents. She felt her grandmother 'didn't really care about her' but she adored her grandad. She said he was 'almost like dad . . . big, strong and powerful'. He would treat her as 'special' and buy her gifts and sweets. He was sexual with her but she did not see it as abuse or herself as a victim. When her grandad died Kim says she 'couldn't cope at all'. Kim had no friends at school, saying she didn't like girls: 'I never have, no disrespect but I really can't stand women'. The words Kim used to describe her mother were pathetic, a liar, and weak. She gave very similar descriptions of her sister and her grandmother. Kim had never had a female friend or any positive connections with women at all.

Kim's school days were apparently 'made worse with more lies'. She says, 'people are always telling lies . . . Me and one of the lads had been larking around, you know, and this younger kid comes up and catches us and she wanted to join in . . . She then went and said I'd made her do it. It was all lies.'

Kim met her husband when she was '14ish'. He was eight years older and in the army. Kim said she was drawn to her husband because 'He could be really rough . . . that really turned me on'. She became pregnant and had her first baby just before she was 16. Kim said *she knew when she married him that he had a sexual interest in children* but she 'didn't think it was unusual'. Kim said her husband 'would beat-up on me, really bad' and had raped her. At these times she described him as 'a real nasty pig, selfish, violent, like living with a time-bomb'. Regardless of these negative views in Kim's Repertory Grid she saw her husband, father, grandfather, her ideal partner, a person who sexually abuses children and herself, as virtually identical. This group were very different from everyone else on the grid. It is of particular interest, considering her verbal descriptions of her father, that she rated him low on affection (2/7) and high on both aggressive (7/7) and sexual (7/7) constructs.

Kim divorced her husband, 'because of all the lies he was telling about her sexually abusing the children'. Kim became a prison pen-pal targeting men who were imprisoned for sexually abusing children. Kim wrote to these men with great passion, physical and emotional, declaring her 'absolute' love for them and promising to marry them. She would reject any men she perceived to be weak or vulnerable in any way. The prison authorities had a considerable task, keeping track of her 'lonely hearts club' for paedophiles.

REFLECTION AND COMMENT

It is hypothesised that through her early experience Kim recognised perpetrators had power and victims got hurt. Consequently she tried to align herself with the perpetrator rather than the victim. She made herself feel somewhat safer by believing she had a very strong alliance with the main perpetrator: her father. In order to do this, she would have to deny, even to herself, she had ever been his victim. She would also have to

maintain separation between herself and females whom she saw as
potential victims: particularly females within her own family. She could
maintain this illusion of an alliance with the perpetrator by denying the
negative aspects of his behaviour and constructing his 'faults'—violence
and aggressive sexual behaviour—as 'virtues'. This is indicated both by
the kind of men with whom Kim forms relationships and also by the
characteristics she indicates as being desirable in an ideal father and an
ideal partner. When Kim was asked to rate her ideal father and her ideal
partner, in terms of how aggressive and how sexual she would like them
to be, she rated them both at the maximum possible score for each
characteristic. Kim looks for alliances with such men and then behaves as
they do. In doing so she is able to maintain a sense of power and control in
her life. To further facilitate this alliance and her sense of power, she
vilifies women, particularly women who have been victimised. Kim feels
she needs to be in an alliance with 'a strong man', as without it she could
be vulnerable to the aversive experience of victimisation. When Kim was
not connected to a man, she described herself as weak, vulnerable,
unloving, not able to trust anyone, not in control of her life, asexual,
isolated and uncared for. She also rated herself as having low self-esteem.
However, when she was connected to a man her image of herself was the
antithesis of this. For Kim, only when she was attached to specific kinds of
men, men like her father and ex-husband, did she feel a whole person, or
as she put it, 'more herself'.

Kim did agree to fill in the 'What Sex Means' Questionnaire in relation to
her sexual experience with men and what she believed she would feel like
if she did have sexual contact with children. In her sexual relationships
with men, Kim commonly experienced negative feelings with some
positive physical feelings. She also sees sex as a way to 'become attached
to a man'. Kim 'imagined' if she were to have sexual contact with children
it would bring her feelings of power and control, positive physical
feelings and bonding. Although denying sexual fantasies involving
children, those she did reveal involved Kim as initiating overtly sexually
sadistic acts and controlling the sexual activity of a group of people.
Interestingly this is very similar to an actual scenario of their abuse
described by her children.

2. Women Who Coerce Men to Sexually Abuse Children (*n*=1)

One woman who was interviewed had been imprisoned for her part in the
sexual assault by her husband on a 13-year-old girl. Although the woman

did not sexually touch the girl, she had coerced the man into carrying out the act. It is predicted this is likely to be the least common form of sexual abuse by a woman.

CASE EXAMPLE—A WOMAN WHO COERCED A MAN TO SEXUALLY ABUSE A CHILD

Stephanie was the oldest of three daughters. Her parents were strict and each child was expected to obey them unquestioningly. Stephanie describes the family as 'centred around her father'. She saw her mother as a cold and distant woman who really took very little notice of her daughters. She says her mother was 'my father's handmaiden . . . there to ensure he was happy at all times'. Academic success was the only criteria for which the girls were valued. Stephanie was not as bright as her younger sisters and felt there was something intrinsically wrong with her. At times, her father seemed more indulgent with her, and she would get more 'privileges and treats' than her sisters. They would say she was 'Daddy's favourite' and Stephanie felt her sisters resented her. Her relationship with them became distant. Not being allowed to have any other friends, she became increasingly isolated.

In her early teens her father began to kiss and touch her sexually, and eventually had full sexual intercourse with her. Stephanie told her mother who said she must have misunderstood and her father would not harm her and he had the right to total respect and obedience from his daughter. Stephanie never tried to tell again and said she felt more angry about her mother's collusion than about the sexual abuse by her father. She tried to leave home but her parents said it was 'improper' for her to live away from home unless she was married. She had no friends and the only person she really developed any relationship with was her husband, who she met through her work. She said she had few feelings for this man, but used him to get away from home. Her father sexually abused Stephanie until the night before her wedding, when she was 23.

Stephanie became obsessed with how her mother must have felt knowing that her father had sexually abused her. She would mentally put herself into her mother's position and imagine it being her husband. Jill was a young girl who lived nearby who baby-sat for them. Stephanie said she believed Jill to be extremely sexually precocious for a girl of 14. She began to fantasise her husband having sex with her and to suggest to her husband the idea that he wanted to have sex with Jill. She tried telling him how promiscuous Jill was, and how he would be just an addition to her list. Stephanie says she pressurised him so much that she eventually made him feel that he had no choice but to do it.

He did have sexual intercourse with Jill and Stephanie watched. Stephanie describes her feelings as intolerable; as having no physical sensation in her own body, as if paralysed from the neck down, yet her mind was in emotional turmoil. She could not speak and she said she felt just how she did when she was being sexually abused herself. Soon after the incident, the young girl told her parents that she had been raped by Stephanie's husband.

REFLECTION AND COMMENT

On her Repertory Grid, Stephanie construed herself as a teenager, to be very similar to the young woman she coerced her husband into sexually abusing. Interestingly, she also construed her husband when he was sexually abusing the young woman as identical to her father. At other times, she perceived her husband as very different from her father, although not at all like her ideal husband. Stephanie found it very hard to construe herself at the time the offence was occurring. She said it was as if there were two parts to her, the one that wanted it to happen and the one that wanted it to stop, so she rated each part separately. Interestingly, the part that wanted the abuse to continue was virtually identical to Stephanie's perception of her mother. Stephanie described the part that wanted it to stop as 'the person she hid after her mother colluded with her father's abuse of her'; vulnerable, helpless, totally lacking in trust, meek, emotionally distant, self-hating and isolated.

The offence Stephanie committed was a re-enactment of her own experience of sexual abuse. Stephanie was trying to re-enact the abuse she felt her mother perpetrated against her by her collusion with her father. In spite of this, rather than experiencing the emotions her mother felt, Stephanie actually triggered off the feelings associated with being victimised.

3. The Psychotic Offender (*n*=3)

A psychotic state is one in which thought and emotion are so impaired that the person appears unable to perceive reality. Although psychosis can occur in any of the psychiatric disorders, it is most likely to be associated with a diagnosis of schizophrenia. The misconception that if a woman sexually abuses a child she is most likely to be psychotic, is being slowly rectified. Nevertheless, there are women who sexually abuse children when they are psychotic and these women also need to be understood if effective help is to be provided.

CASE EXAMPLE—A WOMAN WHO SEXUALLY ABUSES A CHILD WHEN PSYCHOTIC

June spent much of her adult life in hospital having been given a diagnosis of paranoid schizophrenia, and medicated accordingly. Her symptoms were terrifying hallucinations of her father. She believed his presence to be absolutely real, regardless of the fact he had been dead for years. His voice controlled her, telling her she would never get away from him, he had spies everywhere and would know everything. When she was having visual hallucinations, her terror was visible. She would cower in a corner, recoiling from the place where she believed her father was standing, and once jumped from a first-floor window. She was also suffered severe prolonged panic states.

Soon after the birth of their second child, her husband walked in and found June in the process of sexually abusing the baby. He immediately had her admitted to hospital and the psychiatrist asked for a psychological assessment of her. June began to talk, very hesitantly at first, both about her actual experiences and about the content of her hallucinations. Even at this stage, her ability to accept that her father was dead was somewhat tenuous.

June's father forced her mother to leave as she could not have any more children when June was three years old. He immediately moved another woman in, with whom he eventually had eight children. June was sexually, physically and emotionally tortured by her father from infancy. Using her, he sexually abused all his other children while they were babies. Her father was 'very into black magic' but does not appear to have been actively involved in any groups. He called June 'the devil's daughter' and told her her task was to 'anoint babies for the devil'. This involved penetrating each of the babies in all their orifices. While she did this, he sexually stimulated her and after sexually assaulted her in each of her orifices. When he had no more babies of his own, he insisted June took up baby-sitting. He would always 'turn up' and force her to carry out 'an anointing'. Thus whenever June saw a baby, she became highly sexually aroused and felt a desperation to sexually penetrate the infant. She says she often did so whether her father was with her or not. Her father died when she was 17. He told her he would have a place of glory in hell and would follow her and see her everywhere she went. A year after he died, June was diagnosed as being psychotic due to her images of her father.

It took several years to stabilise June on medication. During a calm period, June met and married Dan who recognised her vulnerability and wanted to care for her. They were happy together for a few years and June was very stable until, by accident, she became pregnant. She immediately began to hear her father's voice and see him telling her 'to anoint' the child. June could not tolerate the voices and the flashbacks and tried to kill herself by slashing her wrists. Her husband found her and she was hospitalised. She was unable to tell anyone what was disturbing her, only that her father was there. Dan gave up work in order to care for June and the child. When her first daughter was three, she became pregnant again and a similar scenario occurred. One day, he walked in to the bathroom and saw June sexually abusing their new baby.

REFLECTION AND COMMENT

June admits to being sexually aroused to children whether or not she is in a psychotic state. When she actually sexually touches the child, she describes her father always being 'present'.

June had sexually abused many infants she had had access to. She describes feeling a compulsion to do this to babies and the immediate feelings of release and relief after she has done so. In addition, June gets flashbacks of what she had done to the infants, which are accompanied by extreme sexual arousal. She describes the only relief that she can get at this point is to masturbate to these fantasies, thus reinforcing the images and the behaviour. However, June also describes this as leading to mounting feelings of intense despair and self-hatred, culminating, over time, in some form of self-harm, particularly self-mutilation.

June was clear that she knew that the babies neither wanted nor enjoyed the sexual acts. Rather than projecting the desire for the sexual contact onto the child she was abusing, it is proposed that the main way June allayed some of the shame and the guilt was by attributing responsibility to her father's 'presence'. It is not suggested that June *consciously* used this to justify her sexual abuse of children and there is also no doubting the actuality of her 'psychotic' experiences. It is suggested that June's father's 'presence' is a cognitive defence borne out of the internal struggle between June's feelings of sexual arousal leading to the drive to be sexual with a child, and her simultaneous feelings of inhibition about doing so. In addition, like many survivors, June had vivid and terrifying flashbacks of her own sexual abuse by her father. The flashbacks were reinforced by her father's assertion that he would be everywhere, even after death. Thus the sense June made of these flashbacks, which to her felt so real, was to interpret them as her father actually being present. In these flashbacks/hallucinations, her father would be telling her in graphic detail how he was going to torture her, physically and sexually, exactly as he had when she was a child. These flashbacks caused her terror and hysteria. June's flashbacks included body-memories during which she had the actual physical feelings she had when her father was sexually abusing her.

Throughout all her difficulties, Dan had loved and cared for his wife even after he found out about the extent of her abusive behaviour. Unlike other women who had sexually abused children, June had not been further physically or sexually abused in reality, in her adult life. However, the vividness of her 'hallucinations' was tantamount to ongoing abuse.

It is not suggested that all women diagnosed as psychotic who sexually abuse children are experiencing the same kind of psychosis as this woman. However, the widely accepted stress-diathesis model of psychiatric illness indicates that predisposing biological factors interact with psychological stress to produce a disorder. It is highly likely that part of the stress experienced by a psychotic woman who sexually abuses children, will include her own sexual abuse as a child. It is also suggested that some aspects of the psychotic thinking may be partially functional in order to facilitate the woman to sexually abuse the child.

4. Abuse of a Child While in a Dissociative State (*n*=2)

A dissociative state is one in which there is 'a sudden and temporary alteration in the normal integrative functions of consciousness, identity or motor behaviour'. (DSM-III, p.253)

While in a dissociative state, the person's usual identity is temporarily submerged and there is accompanying memory loss for events that occur during that time. Dissociation occurs as a response to a traumatic event that is perceived by the individual as intolerable (Putnam, 1985). Consequently repression occurs, resulting in the event being eradicated from conscious knowledge. Some people who have experienced dissociation as a response to trauma suffer subsequent dissociation and thus develop a dissociative disorder. Subsequent dissociation following the initial trauma is usually precipitated by specific emotional states associated with the primary trauma. These emotional states can themselves be triggered by events, images or even thoughts associated with that trauma. Such a dissociative state can last for a few minutes, several hours, days and even months.

In extreme cases of dissociation, the person can develop multiple personality disorder (DSM-III) in which consciousness in the dissociative state becomes completely split off and a separate identity is established for the split part of the self. Some theorists have hypothesised that the alter-personality/ies can 'express affects and impulses unacceptable to the primary personality such as anger, depression or sexuality' (Coons, 1986, p.456).

CASE EXAMPLE—A WOMAN WHO SEXUALLY ABUSED WHEN DISSOCIATED

Sylvia presented as a quiet, articulate, well-spoken woman who appeared to be genuinely shocked at her daughters' disclosures of her sexual and physical abuse of them. Although admitting to smacking the children, Sylvia totally denied having sexually or physically abused them. Both girls, however, made clear and consistent disclosures and there were also physical and behavioural indicators that physical and sexual abuse had occurred.

Sylvia appeared to be very open with the child protection team. During these sessions it emerged that Sylvia 'lost' periods of time. This piece of information was arrived at fortuitously, as Sylvia did not realise that it 'wasn't normal' as it had been her experience all of her life. Sylvia, an only child, had sketchy memories of her childhood and none at all of her early life. Those memories she did have seemed to be centred on school, 'playing-out' and the several times she had been in hospital. She believed she had had very good parents and a happy childhood. Other information about her life was pieced together for her by her excellent social worker from Sylvia's medical records, social work records, school reports and files.

Sylvia had come to the attention of the local authority herself as a child, when she was seven years old. A nurse at a local hospital became concerned on seeing Sylvia in casualty for the third time in five weeks. Each time her parents said she had had 'an accident' which on all three occasions was serious enough to require hospital admission. There was a child abuse investigation, and Sylvia was allocated a social worker and was considered to be 'at risk'. Reports were written but it was eventually decided there was not enough evidence to substantiate any further action and to quote from the file 'Sylvia is adamant that she has no memory of how the injuries had occurred'. Sylvia's parents were assessed as concerned, articulate, professional people who cooperated in every way with the investigation and had 'credible accounts of how the many injuries were sustained'. There was a report from her school class teacher indicating she had noted Sylvia seemed to have had a number of 'accidents', but she added Sylvia was 'a very clumsy child'. This report also highlights other aspects of Sylvia's behaviour, such as 'precocious sexual behaviour' which must have been fairly marked to warrant comment in 1973. The report also describes Sylvia as having done several explicit drawings of her father, uncle and small children, which included details of genitalia. The teacher writes, 'Sylvia was told that this was not nice and in future she must put clothes on all the people in her drawings'. It was also reported that Sylvia was 'an unpredictable child' who could be difficult and disobedient, and who at times would blatantly lie. Sylvia would insist that she did not know about, do or remember certain events when the teacher 'knew full well that she did'. The teacher also indicates that Sylvia was an 'unpopular child, with no friends'. In the report she also commented on what nice people Sylvia's parents were and how caring and distressed they always were about 'their daughter's misbehaviour'.

There was also an interesting entry in Sylvia's medical notes with regard to a consultation when Sylvia was four years old. She had been taken to the doctor by her mother because of repeated 'tummy aches'. The doctor asked her to climb up on the table so that he could feel her 'tummy'. He describes Sylvia having quickly taken off her underpants, climbed onto the table and opened her legs wide exposing her genitals. As he went to examine her, Sylvia appeared to have fainted. He noted in his observation that her genitals looked sore. The doctor also noted the mother's comment that her daughter was always touching and rubbing herself there and still occasionally 'wet herself'. The doctor was concerned enough to detail this incident in his notes.

Sylvia has no clear memory of being sexually abused as a child, or of how she sustained many of her more serious physical injuries. She does, however, remember other children she did not know being brought to stay and her having 'very strange feelings, almost memories' of sexual acts which involved these children and her father and uncle.

Sylvia managed to get several jobs but she could never keep them mainly due to her 'losing time'. Her parents were killed in a car crash when she was 19 and she inherited the house and a considerable sum of money on which she has lived ever since. Sylvia had no friends but had many bad relationships with men. She says she finds it impossible to refuse any man, whatever he asks. Even if she thinks of refusing, she says she becomes racked with feelings of total fear and panic. Sylvia knows she has had sex with many men but has no memory of the physical acts. Sylvia describes being somewhere and then 'waking-up', sometimes in a different place, with a man she hardly knew, with no idea of what had taken place during the time lapse. As an adult, Sylvia also recounts having twice found herself in hospital having been beaten up but having no idea of what had happened or who had attacked her.

REFLECTION AND COMMENT

Although nothing can be concluded with any certainty, the reports of Sylvia's behaviour are consistent with her having been both physically and sexually abused from a very young age. The lack of memories for these events are consistent with her use of dissociation as a psychic coping strategy for dealing with severe trauma. The 'fainting' has been found to be a reaction of some sexually abused children to being physically examined (Hanks, 1989) and the 'memory gaps' are congruous with the use of dissociation throughout her life. It is hypothesised that Sylvia dissociates when events trigger a similar emotional reaction to that she experienced during her own abuse as a child. Thus she has few memories of any sexual acts or physically abusive experiences occurring in her adult life. The dissociative states Sylvia experiences may be different in character: one the passive victim enduring abuse, the other carrying the anger which re-enacts the trauma she experienced in the role of perpetrator. McKeller (1989) describes several cases of such dissociative states in which previously occurring traumatic events were re-enacted, 'in a spontaneously occurring altered mental state' (p. 76). He goes on to describe how some children respond to insufferable abuse in their childhood by repression of 'defensive rage'. This rage builds up, and with appropriate triggers explodes into expression of that rage within an alternative state of consciousness, which itself is then repressed.

5. Breaching Sexual Boundaries (*n*=3)

Three women have now been interviewed who had no intention at all of sexually abusing their children but who all violated the children's sexual boundaries. All three women were survivors of childhood sexual abuse and were intent that this should *not* happen to their children. Thus they constantly examined and washed the children's genitals. As the children became old enough the women frequently questioned the children as to whether they had been touched or hurt by anyone. This sometimes extended to involving doctors in carrying out physical investigations of the child's genitalia, and even to making allegations to social services of suspected perpetrators. While trying to protect the children, these behaviours were in themselves abusive.

REFLECTION AND COMMENT

In many ways these 'atypical' women are very similar to those in the other groups of offenders. They have had difficult distressing childhoods, in which they have experienced multiple abuse. They continued to experience various forms of abuse into their adulthood. They were generally socially isolated both as children and as adults, and had low self-esteem. They perceived they experienced a great deal of stress in their adult lives and had few external resources to help them deal with this. They also facilitated the abuse they perpetrated by projecting onto others, usually the children, characteristics that would justify their actions, if only to themselves. These women all re-enacted some aspect of their own victimisation. As with all the other women who perpetrated sexual assaults against children, the trauma they suffered generated feelings of powerlessness which, when triggered in later life led them to retaliate, in whichever way was most applicable to them, in order to regain some sense of control over their lives. These 'atypical' women sexual offenders are very important as they remind us that no matter how many aspects female perpetrators have in common, each has individual triggers and motivations, specific to each woman.

THE 'MISSING' FEMALE PERPETRATORS?

There are still certain behaviours common among male perpetrators that have been difficult to investigate in women. This may be because women are less likely to behave in this way or, more likely, because there has been less access to such women.

1. Women Who Specifically Target Children of Mid-childhood Years

No sole woman perpetrator has been interviewed who specifically initially chooses to target children in the six- to ten-year-old age range. Several such women were known of; for example, a ballet teacher who gave 'special help' at her home to the girls she targeted, and an 'akela' who was suspected of sexually abusing boys, but there was not enough evidence for convictions.

One factor in the under-detection of such women may be that children initially targeted at that age, particularly by a woman, are even less likely than younger or older children to tell, or to draw attention to their experiences by exhibiting distress behaviour.

Interestingly, some studies such as Finkelhor (1988) and Faller (1987) show that when males and females had access to similar age children females targeted younger children. This may also be an issue of dominance; the least dominant children, that is the youngest children, are the most likely to be targeted.

If women have the desire to sexually abuse a child, as a consequence of society's roles for women they tend to have access to children from a younger age than men. As well as ease of access, women have a greater ease of breaking through the child's defence. Children in the pre-five age range are sensual, tactile and require a great deal of physical contact. In adolescence, young people are more sexually aware and active. In both these periods of development, it would be far easier for a woman to use the developmentally appropriate behaviour of the child as a basis for imposing the cognitive distortions that she uses to facilitate her abusing behaviour (Smith, 1994). Children aged between six and ten years old are in the period of development which Freud called 'latency'. During this time sexual forces are considered to be dormant. At this stage of development children develop their sense of competence about the world (Erikson, 1968). They are relatively independent and have an intact sense of their own body and ego boundaries. Initial sexual assaults on children at this stage of development need to be all the more predatory as it would be far harder to groom these children or to misconstrue a child's normal behaviour as consistent with an abuser's cognitive distortions.

2. All-Female Paedophile Groups

The work of researchers into sexual abuse in day care centres, such as that described by Finkelhor (1988) in *Nursery Crimes*, shows that women can and do act in conjunction with each other to sexually abuse children. Women can also be very active and self-motivated members of mixed paedophile groups and do sexually abuse children in female groups which are associated with these larger groups. In spite of this, there has been no evidence of any *all-female* paedophile rings or of networks solely of female sexual offenders.

SUMMARY

• Although the idea of typologies of women who sexually abuse children is very useful in terms of understanding the women and their behaviour, this does not preclude the emergence of women who do not fit precisely into these typologies but who also sexually abuse children.
• In each of these 'atypical' cases, however, there are great similarities to the other women who sexually abuse children: the connections between the offending behaviours and the re-enactment of past experiences, impoverished emotional environments both in childhood and throughout their adult lives; poor non-abusing social contacts; and internalised models of self and others that predispose to the abusing behaviour.

- Whether a woman 'fits' into a typology or not, it is of vital importance that each aspect of her offending behaviour, the meaning of her behaviours, and her own individual experience are closely investigated if an accurate risk assessment and effective intervention plan are to be carried out.

9

WOMEN INVOLVED AS PERPETRATORS IN THE RITUAL ABUSE OF CHILDREN*

- THE PERPETRATORS WHO FORM THE FOCUS OF THIS CHAPTER
- THE WOMEN'S DESCRIPTION OF RITUAL ABUSE
- THE ROLE OF WOMEN
- THE LIVES OF THE WOMEN
- PERSONAL COMMENT

The cognitive structures required for vision are the anticipatory schemata that prepare the receiver to accept certain kinds of information rather than others, and thus control the activity of looking. Because we can only see what we know how to look for, it is these schemata (together with information actually available) that will determine what will be perceived. Perception is indeed a constructive process ... at each moment the perceiver is constructing anticipations of certain kinds of information, that enable him to accept it as it becomes available ... Information already acquired determines what will be picked up. (Neisser, 1976)

Another arena in which severe sexual, emotional and physical abuse of children occurs is that of ritual abuse. Knowledge about, descriptions of, and attempts to define ritual abuse have appeared relatively recently in clinical research and academic literature (e.g. Finkelhor, 1988; McFadyen, Hanks & James, 1993; LaFontaine, 1993; Sinason, 1994). The Los Angeles County Commission for Women describes ritual abuse as:

---

* I should particularly like to acknowledge the help given to me by Sheila Youngson in the preparation of this chapter.

A brutal form of abuse of children, adolescents and adults, consisting of physical, sexual, and psychological abuse and involving the use of rituals. Ritual does not necessarily mean satanic ... Ritual abuse rarely consists of a single episode. It usually involves repeated abuse over an extended period of time. (Los Angeles County Commission for Women, 1989)

A discussion of this form of child abuse is of particular importance in a book about women who sexually abuse children, as in almost all cases of ritual abuse that have come to public attention women have been specified as being among the perpetrators. Ritual abuse has now been reported in several countries, for example the United States (Kelley, 1993; Finkelhor, 1988), Great Britain (Dawson & Johnson, 1989; Tate, 1994), Holland (Jonker & Jonker-Bakker, 1991), Australia, South Africa, Italy and France (Boyd, 1991), and Sweden (Sinason & Svensson, 1994). Yet there are few cases in which enough 'concrete evidence', physical and forensic, has been presented to allow the possibility of prosecution. Even when there is evidence of gross, multiple and multifaceted abusive behaviour, a decision is often made to prosecute only on the grounds of sexual abuse. This decision is most frequently justified by fear of 'causing more confusion and disbelief' by including 'bizarre material' and hence forfeiting the case (cited in Sinason, 1994). Those prosecutions that have been successful (over a dozen in the UK) have mostly involved an individual, or a small group, carrying out ritually abusive practices.

It is true to say that, in the early 1990s, there is much controversy surrounding ritual abuse: its definition, the practices involved, the underlying belief systems, indeed on occasion its very existence. The focus of this chapter is the experience of four women who have struggled to tell of their involvement as perpetrators in ritual abuse despite their fear and pain, and their doubts that they would be believed. The latter part of the chapter will consider some of the controversies that have grown up around this form of abuse.

THE PERPETRATORS WHO FORM THE FOCUS OF THIS CHAPTER

Four women were interviewed who claim to have been perpetrators in groups involved in ritual abuse. Each of these women maintains that the underlying belief system of these groups was the idolisation of Satan. Three of the women were sentenced, but although the prison authorities, probation officers, social services and the police were made aware of the women's further disclosures of ritual abuse no further prosecutions resulted. The fourth woman had recently made detailed disclosures to the police about the group in which she had had involvement, several years previously. The police forensic psychologist who assessed this woman and the investigating police officers accepted the substance and content of her disclosures as likely to be accurate and true. Two of the women claim to have been born into families involved in ritual abuse and two described becoming involved during their adolescence. All four women were geographically separate and had no knowledge of or connection with each other.

THE WOMEN'S DESCRIPTION OF RITUAL ABUSE

If absolutely everything these patients tell us is false, we have stumbled onto a clinical phenomenon most worthy of study and we are honoured to study it; if anything these patients tell us is true, we have stumbled onto a phenomenon most horrible and are obliged to study it (Young, 1990, p.10)

The types of behaviour involved in ritual abuse have been described by various authors (Finkelhor, 1988; Kelley, 1989, 1993; Snow & Sorenson, 1990; Waterman, Kelly, Oliveri & McCord, 1993; Youngson, 1994). The personal descriptions given by the four women interviewed for *this* study describe markedly similar activities. For example:

1. 'Ceremonies' or 'parties' on regular occasions throughout the year, dates frequently corresponding to the 'Satanic calendar'. Also 'celebrations' of important individual days, e.g. birthdays.
2. The use of various locations: cellars; houses, rich and poor, large and small; barns; graveyards; woods; churches.
3. The wearing of robes, costumes, and masks. An atmosphere of spiritualism and magic intensified by way of chants and dances.
4. Sexual activity of all types and forms: anal, oral, vaginal; heterosexual and homosexual; between adults, between adults and children; between children. Animals are also used, as well as penetration with a variety of objects.
5. Torturous activities: cuts and burns in significant configurations; near drowning; suspension by ropes and chains; electric shocks; the children put in cages or coffins and terrorised with spiders, worms and snakes.
6. Descriptions of the consumption of blood, urine, faeces, and the smearing of bodies with the same.
7. Ritual sacrifices of animals, using designated knives, collection of blood and flesh in specific bowls or goblets. All four women described human sacrifice and cannibalism, including foetuses. Bodies were burnt, buried or fed to animals.

8. The use of video cameras to record activities; the films sold as pornography and/or as a threat to disclosure.

THE ROLE OF WOMEN

The pleasure in the complete domination over another person is the essence of the sadistic drive. (Deitz, Hazelwood & Warren, 1990)

I just can't explain the feeling it gave me ... You couldn't understand, nothing compares to the high, nothing, not drink, drugs nothing. It's power I think, I feel really strong, powerful and important nothing and no one can hurt me. The high is incredible. There's nothing, there just aren't words to describe it. (Female perpetrator involved in ritual abuse)

Within ritual abuse, the roles that are constructed for, and enacted by, women seem to endow them with great power. However, when the women have left the groups, some recognise the power they held was illusionary, held only by the sanction of men. In the groups in which these four perpetrators were involved, women appeared to take major roles, some seeming to have equal status to the men. All four women explicitly described feelings of importance within the groups that they had experienced in no other aspects of their lives. When they described this aspect of their experiences, in every case the women's demeanour changed to being more upright, commanding, in posture and attitude, and their tone became more animated, bordering on excited. Table 9.1 presents these four women's self-esteem scores when sexually abusing children, as compared to the women perpetrators in the other groups.

Each of these four women described how they were involved in introducing children into the activities of the groups. They describe physically, sexually and emotionally stimulating (abusing) their own children and other children associated with the group to prepare them for these acts. Each of them also described how they made children perform abusive acts on each other. The children were highly praised for their abusive behaviours, being told that they chose to do it, enjoyed doing it, and were very good at it. During all torturous acts the pain of the children was laughed at, ridiculed and denigrated. One woman described someone within the group whose specific role was to laugh when a child was hurt. Thus the children learn to hide and eventually repress and deny their (appropriate to us) emotions and instead learn to show and ultimately to feel pleasure in experiencing, witnessing, and inflicting pain, fear and horror. Sometimes the children were told that they were evil and that they belonged to the devil or Satan.

Table 9.1: The women's self-esteem scores both when they were and when they were not sexually abusing children (max. = 63)

	DURING THE TIME WHEN SEXUALLY ABUSING CHILDREN	DURING PERIODS WHEN NOT SEXUALLY ABUSING CHILDREN
Perpetrators (n=4) ritual abuse	Mean 55.5 (range (52–60)	Mean 20 (range 10–28)
Perpetrators (n=14) (young children)	Mean 14.4 (range 9–21)	Mean 17.4 (range 9–26)
Perpetrators (n=10) (adolescents)	Mean 31.4 (range 19–44)	Mean 31 (range 17–44)
Perpetrators (n=12) (male-coerced)	Mean 15.4 (range 8–24)	Mean 28.6 (range 14–40)
Control group (n=36)	—	Mean 43.5 (range 34–53)

CASE EXAMPLE 9.1

'I became an abuser when I was three years old . . . we were all made to do it by my mum and my dad . . . in sort of parties . . . sometimes other people too, friends of the family . . . me dad said if you tell anyone I'll kill you . . . I was sexually abused by my mum . . . I was a baby in nappies . . . I remember it, when m'mum was changing me, she put her fingers into my 'gina . . . and it hurt . . . I cried and she didn't stop, . . . she put more fingers in . . . I used to get beaten up . . . really beaten . . . put in boxes with insects . . . I was terrified of insects and they'd crawl all over me . . . I hated spiders most . . . my mum shut my finger in the back door . . . deliberately and it was hanging off . . . they had to sew it back on, I was three and I had to go to the hospital alone . . . We used to have sex-parties . . . in the front room, we'd dress up but . . . the witchcraft proper began when I were 13 . . . my mother took us to a big house . . . my mother made me take some things [drugs] . . . I gave it to my children . . . it was like there was a veil there in front of me and I was a bit sleepy but I was awake as well, it was all sex and sacrifices . . . mostly babies and animals . . . and children would get sexually abused . . . I had a couple [pregnancies] when I was 14 and 15 but I don't know if they were miscarriages or abortions because my mum made me have them . . . they made me eat some of the flesh and others did too.' (Extracts from an interview with one of the four women perpetrators.)

Three women described having to prepare and control the children for sexual exploitation by the men. One woman described holding the children while they were sexually assaulted. Two of the women discussed their main duties as being to torture and inflict pain on the victims. One of these women described her role as the main person who would carry out the ritual cutting of victims.

CASE EXAMPLE 9.2

'S . . . wasn't a big woman but she had a strong standing within the group . . . the things that she used to do . . . well you wouldn't think that women would do that . . . she could be so vicious, really really vicious. That's why I have a difficult time with women . . . I was afraid of her and really, really angry. You see men . . . I know what your reaction will be . . . you see men . . . I think it's alright for a man to do that; it's normal for a man, I can cope . . . but for a woman, I just find it totally . . . women should be there to protect and that just didn't happen. It's worst . . . the betrayal is much worst. S . . . had become like a mother to me and for her to be doing that . . . She was leading me and cuddling me and all that, as she was taking me up to where I was going to have to cut someone . . . she did a good job on me . . . S . . . she told me the girl I was going to cut had told lies about me and that several of the really bad punishments that I had had was because of that . . . and S . . . also said that the girl had tried to turn them against me and take my place in their lives . . . that made me really angry . . . and I did what they said and I cut her . . . I would have done anything to please them. I was then being picked out more and more to do the punishments and I did enjoy it, partly I suppose because I was pleasing them . . . partly because it wasn't me who was getting punished . . . and also partly because I was really getting really good at it, I got a real buzz out of it. When I look back at it now I think "sick bitch", I really do . . . but then I felt that it was their destiny and that I had to do whatever I did . . . the hate was there already and it was a great way to use that hate.'

(Female perpetrator who had become involved in a ritual abuse group when she was 14. She had been enticed into the group by S and her husband C.)

REFLECTION AND COMMENT

These descriptions by the women perpetrators begin to help us understand why it is so difficult to leave such groups. As a consequence of such gross and multiple abuses and torturous acts on and by the children, at home as well as in ritual abuse group meetings, alongside the various techniques that are designed to confuse and disorientate, the children lose the ability to develop a sense of their own identity. Instead they develop a sense of belonging only to the group, a group identity, as it is only when participating in group activities that they have any sense of being valued and respected. Consequently children develop a strong loyalty to the group, and become bound to the group as they believe they cannot exist separately from it. Some children thus gain a sense of competence, enjoyment, personal empowerment and power over others, including adults, unlike anything that they experience in other aspects of their lives.

THE LIVES OF THE WOMEN

I must have had some good times in my life ... apart from being in the group ... I mean all people do, don't they? I just can't remember any.
(Woman enticed into a ritual abuse group as a young teenager)

1. How the Women Became Involved with Ritual Abuse

Two of the women described growing up within the groups, and two spoke of joining groups in their adolescence. One of these latter women was befriended as a young teenager and enticed into a group by a couple who were deeply involved in ritual abuse. She stayed in the group until she was 19 when, desperate to escape it, she committed several criminal offences in order to be put into prison, a place of safety for her. The fourth woman married a man who was involved in a ritual abuse group. None were known to be currently active within the groups at the time of the interviews.

2. Childhood Experiences

DESCRIPTIONS OF THEIR EXPERIENCES OF CHILDHOOD
'my whole childhood was related to the groups, I didn't exist as a person'
'like a never ending horror film', 'I felt very alone and isolated'
'a farce, a complete farce, to the outside world we were the perfect family; in reality I lived in hell on earth'

The women who were brought up within the group experienced many of the behaviours now described as typical of ritual abuse, both while in the groups, and in their daily lives within their own families. The other two women came from ostensibly 'respectable' families but both women described very distressing treatment within these families in their childhood prior to their involvement in ritual abuse.

3. Relationships with Their Mothers and Fathers

DESCRIPTIONS OF THEIR MOTHERS—Women brought up in group families—mothers were described as evil, inhuman, selfish, cold, cruel.
Women who joined groups—mothers were described as weak, pathetic, cut-off, subservient, no mind of her own.

DESCRIPTIONS OF THEIR FATHERS—Women brought up in group families—fathers were described as evil, violent, cruel—not as cruel as mother.
Women who joined groups—fathers were described as brutal, a fraud, a vicious calculating abuser.

The two women who were brought up within the groups described how as children they had ambivalent feelings for their mothers. Each portrayed herself as being terrified of her mother. This terror sometimes led to feelings of total physical and mental paralysis. They talked of feeling a great need to please their mothers, and wanting to be loved in return. At other times, they each saw their mother being kind and almost affectionate, but it always seemed to be towards other people. Both women recalled the intense relief and pleasure that they felt when their mothers praised them for their actions within the group. They also remembered the dread that they felt when she did not. As children, both of these women believed that their fathers were kinder, less cruel and could be more caring than their mothers. In retrospect, they felt that this had been a misconception.

The woman who married a man involved in ritual abuse, described her mother as weak. She saw this weakness mainly manifested in her mother's subservience to her father and her total inability to have an opinion or thought contrary to his. She felt that her mother was 'cut-off' from her emotionally, and this facilitated her father's behaviour. Her father was visibly a very upright and Christian man. He held a prominent position in a large company and was involved in the local Conservative Club. In the invisible world of his family, he sadistically sexually abused his daughter, from the time of her being a small child, invoking the name of Jesus Christ, and attributing all responsibility for these attacks, to 'the devil within her'. He justified his behaviour by telling her that it had to be done to drive the devil out of her. In her teens, her intense anger and hatred of her father led her to rebel totally against his stated creed, and to seek to reverse all the values he purportedly held. She sought out and became intimately associated with devil worship.

The woman who became involved in a ritual abuse group in her teens, also described her mother as weak and pathetic. As a child she felt that she needed to protect her mother against her brutal father, and had no conception of the idea that her mother could, or should, protect her. Her father would severely assault either or both her mother and herself at his whim. He would also explicitly or implicitly make her feel that this was what she wanted, or deserved to have happen. One of her clearest memories as a young child was her father raping her mother. She recalls perceiving her mother as powerless and she chose to reject any association with her mother and consciously allied herself with her father. Thus she grew to despise and loathe her mother and, despite his sadistic treatment, to idolise and idealise her father. Her father had always wanted a son, so she took the place of a son. She dressed in stereotypical boy's clothes and did everything that she thought her father would want of a son. As an adolescent, as soon as he noticed that she had started to develop breasts, he totally rejected her. Soon after this rejection, she was recruited into the ritual abuse group. Interestingly, as revealed in the Repertory Grid, the couple who befriended this woman and enticed her into the group were perceived, when not involved in the ritual abuse, as being almost identical to her ideal parents. When they were involved in the ritual abuse, she construed them as similar to her actual parents.

4. Relationships with Peers

None of these four women described having a person whom they could say was their friend, either when they were children or as adults. As young children, if they played, it was alongside rather than with other children. They never felt truly involved or connected with anyone. The abusive dynamics within each of these families set up profound competition between the women and their siblings. Each of these four women was led to believe that she had been particularly chosen and badly abused within the family while other siblings, even if also abused, actually had a much easier time. The sibling rivalries for these women, at times, bordered on flagrant hatred. Up until they left the groups, none of the women ever shared their intimate thoughts and feelings with another person.

5. Relationships with Adult Partners

DESCRIPTIONS OF THEIR ADULT PARTNERS
Vicious, perverted, violent, sadistic, insatiable

Interestingly, all the women identified their sexuality as heterosexual, regardless of their activities within the groups. The two women who grew up within the groups had each subsequently married a man who was also involved. One initially liked the man that she was to marry. However, after the marriage, he became increasingly violent towards her, at times demanding sex several times a day. If she ever refused him, he would rape her and then he would cut her in some way. The second woman felt her marriage was inevitable and said she had 'no feelings about it'. She described her husband as no better or worse than any other man, then described his violence and sexual sadism towards her.

The woman who became involved in ritual abuse when she married a man involved in Satanism, said she was drawn to him because at least he was 'honest about who he was'. She said that she chose him because he was so opposite to her Christian father. Interestingly, on the Repertory Grid she construed this man as almost identical to the father who had badly abused her and whom she hated. Unless she fulfilled all his slightest whims, her husband was as violent towards her as her father had been.

None of the three married women said that she felt emotionally close to her partner and each experienced feeling emotionally abused, humiliated, terrorised and rejected by him. All three women suffered what they felt was extreme betrayal by these men. The fourth woman (involved as an adolescent) described being engulfed by feelings of betrayal during her first experience of sexual intercourse. This young woman had not had a sexual partner before being involved in the groups.

'I was a virgin until I was 15. The group could do whatever else they liked to me sexually but not that, that was saved for someone special, the head man. The thing was, he seemed so bloody nice, he had lovely eyes, they all seemed to have such nice, kind, loving eyes, you know. He was really nice and gentle when I met him and he chose me. I was told that I was really lucky and that it was my destiny. He was the main person, the big man, that's who I lost my virginity to, over and over again it seemed, over three days that happened.'

6. Difficulties in Adult Life and Social Supports

The three married women involved in ritual abuse had equally high scores with regard to difficulties experienced in adult life, when compared to other women perpetrators of child sexual abuse. However, the women involved in ritual abuse appeared to have more social supports to help them deal with these difficulties. But further analysis indicated that all the support came from members of the group. The woman who became involved in the group during her adolescence summed up the experience of many people involved in these groups in saying 'I didn't have to worry or care for myself, they cared for me'. Cultivating this form of dependency is presumably one way in which some people are kept reliant on the group. Additionally this support prevents too much contact with outside agencies, and thus protects secrecy. One of these women and her family did rely on social services when their own resources failed and it was this that eventually led to the disclosures of the extensive abuse that was being perpetrated.

7. Perceptions of Children

As with many other women involved in the sexual abuse of children, these women perceived the children whom they sexually abused in a negative way. Unlike the other women, however, they found it very hard to know what it was about the children that they found difficult or disliked. None of the women in this group could provide individual characteristics of these children. On the Repertory Grid each woman construed the sexually abused children identically, as almost the antithesis of her ideal child. One woman said of her children 'they were ornaments, objects to be used, not children to be loved'.

One woman had had several children, the first three of whom she alleged she had tried to protect. She resisted, although not always successfully, the use of these children by the family in 'parties' or their being taken to ritual 'ceremonies'. She says that she knows that they were sexually abused by her parents and by her husband but that she, personally, did not sexually abuse them. The children were taken into care on the grounds of neglect. This woman could, however, differentiate between each of these children. She had little difficulty in describing them and gave idiosyncratic details relating to each of them. She was totally unable to do this for her other three children, with whom she had more recent contact but whom she admits to sexually abusing and involving in ritual abuse.

8. The Women's Perceptions of Their Abusers

Analogously to the inability of the women to differentiate between their victims, the women brought up within the groups found it difficult to differentiate between their abusers. They construed all their abusers virtually identically, using the most extreme and the most negative rating possible on each dimension. The women who joined the groups in their adolescence, were able to attribute differential characteristics to male abusers and to female abusers, but they were unable to discriminate characteristics of various abusers within each gender group. Interestingly, they rated the male abusers as almost identical to their fathers. They judged women to have less control than men and as being less trustworthy.

All four of these women perceived the people who had sexually abused them as being more sexual and aggressive than they perceived themselves to be as perpetrators.

9. The Women's Experience of Sex

The primary feelings for most women in the comparison group in their sexual relationships, were emotional warmth and bonding. These components were completely absent for the women who were involved as perpetrators of ritual abuse, regardless of whether that experience was with adults or children.

(a) With adults

Overall the women's perception of their sexual contacts with adult male partners was of a negative experience. All four women chose the statements 'It makes me feel invaded, at risk' and 'It makes me feel humiliated; it is a way some men/women use to humiliate another person'. The only other category that three of the women recognised as being part of their experience of sex with men, is that it gave them positive physical feelings. Three of the women talked about how *sometimes* sex with men could fulfil a physical need and reduce tension. Neither of the two women who grew up in the groups felt she could have sex with male partners, without having sexual fantasies concerning children.

> This woman had been on 'home leave' just prior to her being released from prison. She was discussing the great disgust she felt, and difficulty she had in having sex with her fiancé. When questioned about this she said 'I have thoughts of the children, the children are just standing there and I feel like I'm hurting them, and then I get aroused'.

(b) With children

All four of the women indicated that the emotions most associated with sexual acts with children were feelings of power and control. The three women who felt positive physical feelings as a result of sex with adult males, also experienced this with children. While the woman who was enticed into the groups during her teenage years described similar levels of feelings of power and control, she described no positive physical feelings. She was also the only perpetrator to say that she felt anything negative while sexually abusing children, and also that she continued to do so to give pleasure to the other perpetrators. When the women described sexually abusing children when *not* engaged in the group activities, they described anger, physical tension and a desire to hurt, as being the major feelings that prompted them to act.

(c) *Sexual fantasy*

It is of note that all four women described sexual fantasy that involved inflicting pain. Three of these women described children as the focus of their sexual fantasies, and the fourth described adults, mainly women. The major theme of these fantasies was that the women were in control of inflicting this pain.

> Q. 'What do you think of that makes you feel sexually aroused?'
> A. 'The pain and the hurting and the sexual things as well but mostly the children's pain.' (This woman then proceeded to describe fantasies of her inflicting pain on children in various ways. The interviewer stopped the discussion on this topic and changed the subject, as the perpetrator was clearly becoming highly physiologically aroused.)

> 'It's the cutting...I get turned on just thinking about scratching a person's skin with the knife, and thinking of the blood smeared on them ...'

10. Responsibility Taken for Actions

Throughout their childhood all four of these women were told by their abusers, both within and outside ritual abuse groups, that they deserved the abuses that they endured, and also that they wanted and enjoyed and had even chosen the agonies they suffered. They were told that they had control over whether or not they were physically abused and punished, or had sexual acts perpetrated against them. As adults all four women described their own victimisation and the victimisation they perpetrated against others as 'destiny'.

> 'It was my right to be there. It was my destiny. I was special. I wanted everything to happen to me ... That's why I was there ... it was my destiny.'

In the Repertory Grids all four of the women attributed to their victims more control over their lives than the women perceived they themselves had over their own lives. This indicates that the women believed the children did have self-determined control which subsequently lessened any feelings of guilt that these women felt with regard to their behaviour. The three women who been severely sexually abused themselves as children, rated the children whom they sexually abused as being 'more sexual' at the time of the abuse than they rated themselves as being while sexually abusing them. The fourth woman, who was not severely *sexually* abused by a parental figure as a child, rated the children whom she was sexually abusing at the lowest level. Interestingly, she recognised that the children did not always want, or enjoy, the sexual assaults, whereas she believed that the children did have a contributory role to play in the physical assaults that were perpetrated against them.

11. The Women's Perceptions of Themselves in Relation to Others

In the Repertory Grids, these women seemed to polarise their entire world into victims or perpetrators, which is a reflection of the actuality of their experience. These women, unlike any of the other women who sexually abused children or any women in the control groups, rarely used any ratings other than the most extreme ends of the scales. The exception to this was when they rated themselves. At times, they construed themselves as very similar to victims, and at other times, very similar to perpetrators. Again, this replicates the actuality of their experience, being both tortured victims as well as torturous perpetrators.

REFLECTION AND COMMENT

The following reflection and comment is based on my research findings from these four women. In addition, I have drawn on my clinical experience in working with other survivors of ritual abuse, and detailed discussions and sharing of clinical information with other therapists and counsellors in the UK. Thus the opinions presented are my own but are derived from a body of professional knowledge and psychological thought and evaluation.

1. The Victim/Victimiser Issue

The issue of victim/victimiser is particularly complex when a person has been born and brought up in this environment. From birth, individuals have had every aspect of their cognitions, emotions and physiology formed and distorted within an alternative framework and in some well-defined ideology. Their whole existence has been defined by being abused or abusing. They have had few or no social networks other than those involved in this behaviour. They have experienced an inordinately enhanced sense of status and power as a consequence of being involved in the groups, which was unavailable to them in any other aspects of their lives. Their attachments, however perverted, have been made to those who have abused them and to those whom they abuse. For most of them, this has been the only model of attachment they have had and thus will be the only one they are likely to reproduce. Their whole construction of the world, their models of themselves and of others, and their sense of competence, are based on these experiences. Can we then legitimately talk of choice, responsibility, and self-determination in this situation where there is no other frame of reference on which to draw? The testimony to human courage and endurance is that some people do escape and do not become or remain perpetrators. Others develop separate aspects of self to 'cope' with this psychic dilemma.

MULTIPLE PERSONALITY DISORDER AND RITUAL ABUSE

Tortured victim and torturous abuser: one woman's coping mechanism
All people present different aspects of themselves depending on the situations in which they find themselves. For example, the persona that a person presents at work is very different from that s/he presents to her/his partner, which in turn is different from the persona that is shown to one's child. Miller Mair (1977) has called this 'the community of selves'.

One of the women interviewed, who had grown up in a family involved within the groups, presents herself in very different ways, at different times. Each of these aspects of herself has very distinct levels of functioning. The differentiation between the selves is so strong as to constitute almost completely separate personalities that may have little or no knowledge of the activities of the other aspects of the self. The term most commonly used for this disorder is multiple personality and is defined in the Diagnosis and Statistical Manual of Mental Disorders III (1980, p.257) and the International Classification of Diseases. Rather than its being 'a disorder', psychologists and psychotherapists are recognising that this is an effective adaptive (at the time) mechanism; a complex form of dissociation which occurs when a young child is faced with overwhelming trauma (Spiegel, 1988). Dissociation acts as a defence to protect the individual from overwhelming pain and fear. Most young children dissociate during the severe violations that they experience during ritual abuse. For some, the dissociation results in the formation of quite distinct personalities. These distinct personalities emerge in order to deal with emotions and experiences that are intolerable and inconsistent. It appears that constitutional factors and the early mother–child relationship predispose an individual to differing degrees of vulnerability to dissociation. Multiple personality is most likely to occur in an individual whose sense of self is precariously vulnerable, and who experiences intense and acute stress. The poorer or more distorted the mother–child relationship, the weaker the child's sense of self. The experiences endured by children of families involved in ritual abuse are consistent with these factors that predispose the development of this condition.

One woman was seen presenting in at least five distinctive personalities. The personality that she exhibited most frequently, especially in the presence of people with whom she was unfamiliar, was 'the reporter'. This was the personality that knew all about the woman's life. She could recount with great detail for times, dates and situations, the most horrific and disturbing experiences, interspersed with the banalities of everyday living, and treat them as equivalent events. This personality had little or no emotion and was keen to engage in conversation. Her vocabulary was good, at times sophisticated. This reporter personality could be entertaining, socially skilled in a pseudo-refined manner, and concerned about her appearance.

In contrast, but also a relatively common presentation, was the personality of the victim, the persona who experienced at least some of the abuses. In this mode, she was very emotional and could only talk about the same experiences 'the reporter' recounted with great fear and distress. She shook and showed visible physical responses consistent with the event she was trying to describe. She became incapacitated by distress and often could not even begin to formulate words.

At other times, she presented in a very child-like way. She adopted the vocabulary, mannerisms, posture and demeanour of a child. She was noted to dress as a child at these times, and when in this mode she wore ankle socks and sucked her thumb.

On two occasions during the interviews, which were spread over approximately 15 months, this woman seemed to become almost totally 'masculine'. Her voice deepened considerably and her eyes appeared to darken and be more directly fixed. She became abrupt and aggressive. Her vocabulary was less extensive and she talked in imperatives, almost commands. She became very frightening. She talked clearly about her perpetrating behaviour, with no regret or remorse. In support of the idea that this self was 'masculine', was the statement she made when describing how she felt when she saw children in pain: 'It makes me feel ... it makes me have an erection ... you know I get randy sort of thing ... I get pleasure out of it and I just want to carry on doing it.'

At other times, she was a teenager to whom none of this had happened and who would marry her fiancé, at a big family wedding and live happily ever after. She planned her dress, the cake, the catering and even the guest list. In this mode she was coy, almost shy. She had no memory of any of the abuses she had experienced or had perpetrated. She was giggly and talked of smoking while her Mum couldn't see her. She said her Mum wouldn't let her smoke because she was too young and it was bad for her!

Over the 15 months, I became acquainted with each of these five personalities. In addition, on one occasion, I observed what appeared to be 'an idealistic and caring mother' who was extremely, and apparently genuinely, concerned for the good of all children, especially her own.

2. The Ordinariness of the Extraordinary

At times it can appear that the disclosures both from perpetrators and from victims lack the detail and specificity that one would expect from someone recounting such distinctive events. When people are involved in what, to us, seem the most extraordinary happenings, we find it surprising when they cannot be more precise about exact happenings, on certain days, in definite places. It should be remembered, however, that experiences that are extraordinary to us, for the participants have been frequent and regular occurrences, often over many years. As with *any* event that takes place repeatedly, human beings have a cognitive tendency to merge them, and to produce a generalised schema, rather than to remember particular aspects of each event. This is a functional heuristic that is used to reduce cognitive strain. It is therefore likely that there is great difficulty in separating out details of actual incidents unless they were of particular significance for that individual person. In general, testimonies are most likely to be generalised, and as such difficult to verify. It should also be remembered that the use of drugs and hypnosis, and the high state of physiological arousal during these events, will mean that some memories may be state-dependent. These factors, in conjunction with the fact that the women tell us that children are often deliberately given misinformation by the perpetrators, mean that many of the disclosures that are made are often inaccurate in part and thus 'the witness' will be perceived as unreliable. This 'lack of reliability' and of 'content validity' gives support to those who wish to maintain a position of denial, about the detail, occurrence, or even the existence of ritual abuse.

3. The Need for Denial

Ever since these cases [of alleged ritual child abuse] exploded into awareness in 1984, there's been great effort to understand how they didn't happen and why it

couldn't be true. And the best answer people seemed to come up with is the notion that therapists or police investigators are brainwashing the children into telling crazy stories. Why these people would want children to tell unbelievable stories that make them look stupid and make the investigators look stupid, has never been explained.
(Summit, 1989)

To protect ourselves from affect, we must at times avoid knowledge.
(Laub and Auerhahn, 1993)

There is still much debate, even among professionals, as to whether this type of abuse 'exists' in the form in which these women and our clients tell us it does (Putnam,1991). Opinion in the UK in the early 1990s has become significantly polarised. As with all forms of abuse, we as a society prefer to engage in a concerted denial of the very existence of ritual abuse, despite the evidence to the contrary that is readily available. Victims of all ages have disclosed, in clinically appropriate and verifiable ways, events and experiences which have a consistency across time, groups, settings, and even countries. In some cases, reports from perpetrators and victims within the same group, who have been separated from the time of disclosure, have a strong concordance. Importantly, these detailed reports are consistent with descriptions of rituals compiled from a survey of Pre-Inquisition historical documents by Hill and Goodwin (1989).

The denial is extensive. People find it very hard to accept that these acts, that can be construed as horrific, barbaric and evil, occur in our modern and sophisticated society. The atrocity, inhumanity and hideousness of what is described are too much to embrace. If we did so we would also have to embrace a part of human nature that completely opposes the basic assumptions that we need to hold if we are to feel psychologically secure in the world. It is more likely that we can believe accounts of ritual abuse if such involves one person, or even a single family, acting in isolation. These abusive behaviours can then be considered to derive from the perversity of an individual who can be construed as 'a freak', 'mad' or just 'bad', and separated as such, from our personal experience. It is far more difficult to accept that many ostensibly normal human beings, *from all strata of society*, can band together, in order to gain perverted feelings of power and pleasure, as well as at times financial gain, from committing horrific acts of torture on children, other adults and animals. To do so would be too traumatic for an individual's fundamental construction of self and personal world and thus psychologically all too threatening.

Janoff-Bulman (1992) who has carried out considerable research into trauma and victimisation, has written clearly of the psychological disequilibrium that ensues from any threat to an individual's fundamental assumptions of the world. These fundamental assumptions are part of a personal theory of reality, outside conscious awareness, constructed by assimilation of life experiences (Bowlby, 1969; Epstein, 1980; Kelly, 1955). For a sense of personal safety and psychological security, it is vital that the assumptions held are basically that: (1) the world is benevolent and people are generally good, kind, helpful and caring; (2) the world is meaningful, that events and experiences 'make sense'; and (3) the self is worthy, good, capable and moral (Janoff-Bullman, 1992). If these assumptions are not held then an individual can become perpetually anxious, or readily angry and defensive; in both cases being hyper-vigilant of potentially threatening situations. Constant confirmation of the negative aspects of humanity, the self or the meaningfulness of life can result in chronic depression and withdrawal from association with the world. If positive and affirming beliefs are those generally held, experiences that profoundly conflict with these fundamental assumptions put an individual into a state of trauma, unless they can be effectively processed. Belief that human beings, who appear similar to ourselves, can engage in activities consistent with ritual abuse, would contradict all these assumptions. The world would no longer feel benevolent as one could never tell who was or was not involved in such abuse. The behaviours alleged to occur contravene what we know to be positively and reassuringly meaningful. Also, if ritual abuse does occur, other than in individual isolated situations totally removed from 'normal life', it would threaten an individual's belief in his/her knowledge and understanding of the world and threaten a personal sense of competence. Evidence that this process does occur when people begin to recognise the existence of ritual abuse, is presented in an article by Youngson (1994). She explicitly describes the trauma experienced by professionals when they begin to work with survivors of ritual abuse.

> Commonly expressed difficulties were: disturbed sleep and nightmares; loss of appetite and resulting weight loss; psychosomatic symptoms such as headaches, indigestion and nausea, leading to an increased sickness record; and changes in affect such as increased anxiety, fear, distrust of others, anger and hostility, depression and sadness. (Youngson, 1994, pp.294–295)

This anguish has a complex aetiology: partly it is due to powerful therapeutic transference of the patient's emotional turmoil to the therapist; partly due to the sheer horror of the acts that are being recounted; and partly the need of the therapist to reassess the potential of humanity to perpetrate such horrific and torturous acts; and the realisation of the extent of the organisational networks that must exist to support the perpetuation of this behaviour. It is therefore not surprising that denial is so prevalent.

CASE EXAMPLE 9.3

I was born into a cult family. When I escaped home, at 15, the terror was indescribable. I felt that I couldn't exist because of the fear; the fear of everything, animate or inanimate. I was put into a hospital for people who were mentally ill; ironically, I began to feel safer. When I told them the fragments of memory that I had held onto, crazily, I expected them to understand that I had spent my childhood as a prisoner in hell. They listened to me with their medical ears and gave me a diagnosis, declaring I was psychotic. They traced my family to tell them of my illness. The kindly doctors were sure that they would be concerned that such a young woman was so 'ill'. The family, in their 'everyday disguises', visited the ward. The doctors attributed my terror of the family to paranoia, born out of my psychosis. They were, however, welcomed by the doctors, who sympathised with them over the fickleness of mental illness. They were told, 'It happens in the nicest and best of families'. The doctors filled me with drugs to calm my psychosis, so that they did not have to recognise theirs, and when I refused their drugs, they saw it as a confirmation of my 'lack of insight' and thus further as evidence of my 'insanity'. Consequently, they increased the recommended dose. The drugs 'succeeded', I became almost catatonic, often unable to feel or move let alone express my thoughts. I thus no longer spoke of my experiences and the doctors were pleased at my progress. They were so pleased they discharged me back to 'the care of my family'.

(Adult Survivor of Ritual Abuse)

4. The Struggle for Meaning

Human beings look at the world through transparent patterns or templates which they create and then attempt to fit over the realities of which the world is composed. The fit is not always very good [but] even a poor fit is more helpful than nothing at all. (Kelly, 1963)

When there is acceptance that ritual abuse is carried out, there then follows a struggle for meaning that would make some form of sense of these perverted, and seemingly bizarre, acts and the people who perpetrate them. The need to find a meaning by which these atrocities can be understood, appears to be more imperative for those *not* involved, than for those who are. Disclosures made by both adult and child survivors of ritual abuse, when linked with the work of Hill and Goodwin (1989) would lead to the conclusion that often (although not always) what is being described is modern-day Satanism: the worship of Satan by engaging in ceremonies during which there is a complete reversal of every tenet held in Christianity. Some writers, such as Jean Goodwin (1993, 1994), prefer to use the term 'sadistic abuse'. She argues that the behaviour can then be seen 'as part of a spectrum of child abuse accounts'. This term thus avoids attributing the behaviours to a motivational system other than sadism, and allows concentration on 'the extreme violence and destructiveness of the sadistic behaviour' (1994, p. 43). While not denying that the primary motivation of the vast majority of perpetrators involved is sadistic, or denying the extreme tortures endured by the victims, to disregard the 'supernatural element' (where it is present) is to deny a vital part of the reality of the experience for both the victims and the perpetrators. It is the 'supernatural' context within which this abuse is enacted, that confers a form of legitimacy and additional power onto the perpetrators of such intolerable tortures. It is also the 'supernatural' aspects that make the experience of those involved qualitatively different, and measurably more traumatic (Briere, 1988; Kelley, 1989) than the experience of victims of similar abuse perpetrated without the involvement of Satanic rituals. As Valerie Sinason (1994) states, the religious aspect 'creates some form of power that ensnares the victim' and as such needs recognition. Rather than acknowledge Satan as an objective reality, she uses the term 'satanist abuse'; thus recognising both 'religious' and 'human' aspects.

Finkelhor (1988), studying ritual abuse in day care, attempted to produce typologies to clarify this complexity: True Cult-Based Ritualistic Abuse (within a real belief system); Pseudo-Ritualistic Abuse (the beliefs used to frighten, confuse and titillate); and Psychopathological Ritualism (often an individual using these behaviours who has a delusional belief system). The understanding gained from the four perpetrators described in this chapter indicates these situations may frequently be linked, often within the same person as described within this case study.

CASE EXAMPLE 9.4

One woman of the women perpetrators interviewed for this research was born into a family who appeared to have had involvement in ritualistic abuse for generations. This was an ostensibly close-knit respectable family who attended the local church and specifically sent their children to Church Schools and Sunday Schools. However, from infancy she was groomed by the family to be part of the groups. Sometimes, they would have 'parties' which included extended family members. The room was decorated with Satanic signs and symbols and a table was covered with a special cloth on which were significant symbols. The floor was also covered with a cloth, on which there was a pentagram. They dressed in robes under which they were naked, and they wore masks. One outfit represented 'the devil', one 'the evil'. A fire would be lit in the grate, there would be chanting, spells, the ingestion of urine and faeces. A particular pattern of sexual acts took place in which the children had to engage in oral and anal sex, with adults, and with each other. Objects were also used to penetrate the children sexually. Photographs and videos were taken of these events. At other times, the family went to large houses, woods and barns and churches. Here similar activities took place but with many other people. These events tended to happen on particular dates consistent with the Satanic calendar. The meetings were much more 'religious', involving far more complex symbolism, chants, spells and ceremony. Apparent murders of animals, foetuses, babies and children occurred. In these circumstances they were called sacrifices and the bodily parts were ingested. At these 'ceremonies', stylised 'marriages', 'deaths' and 'rebirths' occurred. Children were caged, hung, chained, whipped, burnt, tortured, drowned, buried alive, and strapped to inverted crosses and assaulted. There was ritual cutting and the use of blood. At times 'demons' were 'conjured up' and appeared to have sexual intercourse with people who were present. The children were terrified by the use of torture and feared the devil who they believed could see their every move. From being a child victim she was trained to be a vicious and highly sadistic perpetrator, both within the family and the larger groups. When she was eventually allowed to carry her foetuses to full term and have children, they were involved, she abused them from birth, and involved them in the 'family parties' and in 'ceremonies'. She and the other members of her family were paid money for the part they played within the activities in the 'big houses' and for taking the children to be used and abused.

The woman took part in behaviours that could be classed as True Cult-Based Ritualistic Abuse. She had a true belief in the devil and evil spirits. She firmly maintained she gained great power from the ceremonies in which she was involved. Because she believed evil spirits were everywhere, she was initially certain that if she told anything about the groups she would be cursed. She was as terrified as some of the children of the spells and curses that she felt would come on her. There were many times, after she had told of these activities, that she believed that she saw images of her father, mother and other important members of the group in her room, admonishing her for having spoken and issuing all kinds of horrific threats to her. Her anxiety was expressly related to the 'higher Satanic power': 'supernatural' aspects that she felt stemmed from these meetings. Interestingly, she found it much easier to talk of the 'parties within her own home' which as an adult she knew were 'just for fun'. As a child, however, she had been almost equally terrified by these parties which could be defined as Pseudo-Ritualistic abuse.

In addition, just as her mother had done to her when she was a child, this woman would engage in the 'ritual abuse' of her own children: physically, sexually, emotionally and psychologically, when she was alone. She says that she did so 'as if she was driven'. If this activity had been 'discovered'

Table 9.2: Categories of participants involved in ritual abuse

GROUP LEADERS 'CONTROLLERS'
These people are the major money makers and gainers. They are the holders of 'knowledge', 'spells', 'tricks', therefore power

'SATANISTS' OR HOLDERS OF AN ALTERNATIVE OPPOSITIONAL BELIEF SYSTEM	'EXPLOITERS'
Have full belief in the alternative ideology and attend to these creeds. Believe that they gain power and spiritual reward as well as gain sexual and sadistic pleasure	Do not hold any alternative deology but use ritualistic practices for personal gain: power, and sexual and sadistic gratification. (May pretend 'Satanistic' beliefs in order to achieve ultimate control)

PARTICIPANTS AND/OR OBSERVERS
May pay money or do specific 'favours' to be there. May also be blackmailed due to their involvement

'BELIEVERS'   'KICK-SEEKERS'/'DABBLERS'

SPECIFIC PERFORMERS/SUPPLIERS (adult) 'ROLE PLAYERS'
May or may not be believers. Take on specific roles or duties, e.g. control the children, bring children or other victims, make videos, etc. May be paid for these duties or receive other rewards. Can be as terrorised as the child victims by the 'religious' rituals

VICTIMS (children, babies, adolescents, adults)
Used and abused in every way, silenced by terrors that they see. Are made to perpetrate abuses to bind them to the group

---

without knowledge of her other involvements, it would have been very likely that it would have been defined as 'Psychopathological Ritualism'.

WORKING TOWARDS A DESCRIPTIVE MODEL OF RITUAL ABUSE

From the available evidence from perpetrators, survivors, and the litera-ture to date, it seems that *within the same group meeting* there will be people from each of these categories involved. Various groups contain differing proportions of each category of participants and hence the degree of 'spirituality' or 'orthodox satanism' that is practised will vary. This is illustrated in Table 9.2.

Thus in Case Example 9.4 the adults in the family were 'specific per-formers' and 'suppliers' to the larger group. In their 'parties' at home, some members would have been the 'controllers'. There is clearly move-ment between the categories both within and across groups. 'Victims', 'kick-seekers' and 'dabblers' often become 'role players', 'controllers' and/or 'believers'. Women are involved in every category, including 'controllers'. Interestingly, no one has talked of sole women attending the groups as 'kick-seekers' or 'observers'. It seems that these women are always brought by men.

Thus this model is an attempt to make some sense of what seems a senseless, complex macrocosm, obscured and concealed by multifarious interconnected motivations and ideologies. Perhaps we are saying if we could just understand, make sense of ritual abuse and its perpetrators, we would be better able to cope with the actuality and the consequences both personally and professionally. Whatever sense we eventually can make of ritual abuse, we should not lose sight of the long-term and far-reaching consequences for those whose lives have been grossly damaged through their involvement, and whose psychological, emotional, and sexual functioning have been severely disrupted and impaired as a result. Hearing about ritual abuse and coming to terms with its existence is truly a world apart from living and experiencing ritual abuse on a daily basis.

PERSONAL COMMENT

The first time I interviewed a woman who described the behaviours within the ritual abuse groups in which she had been an active perpetrator, I found what she was telling me inconceivable. We were two women of similar age, who had each had a child in the same year. The house and area in which she had lived were not dissimilar to where I grew up. It was as if, for almost 40 years, we had lived in parallel worlds: worlds always touching but never mutually perceptible. We were each oblivious to the other's experience of reality, or any alternative way in which the world could be constructed other than our own. When speaking to her, and to each of the other three women who were involved in ritual abuse, I was struck by their ordinariness. They lacked any distinguishing features that would let me know that I was in the presence of women who, in some aspects of their selves, were entirely other. In fact they were persecuting and torturous abusers, gaining pleasure and excitement from the terror, humiliation and distress they inflicted on their dependent victims. Sitting in those rooms with those ordinary women, talking of experiences of womanhood common to us all, I could easily forget they were also intrinsically involved in this alternative aspect of humanity, that is the antithesis of all that we consider to be humane. I began to appreciate the banality of this evil. It is that very banality that disguises it from us, and prevents us from accepting its existence, not least because, in so many ways, those involved are so similar to ourselves.

10

SPECULATIVE
THEORETICAL MODELS

- AN INTEGRATED THEORETICAL FRAMEWORK
- THE MODEL APPLIED TO WOMEN WHO SEXUALLY ABUSE CHILDREN
- RE-ENACTMENT—A SIMILAR PROCESS TO PLAY
- POSSIBLE PHYSIOLOGICAL CORRELATES THAT MEDIATE AND MAINTAIN CHILD SEXUAL ABUSE
- SUMMARY

The frequency of physical, emotional, and sexual abuse in contemporary society suggests that such abuse is rooted in patterns of behaviour that, when expressed in benign forms are considered normal and developmentally appropriate aspects of psychological growth. (Kaplan, 1990, p.127)

The sexual abuse of a child, no matter how 'lovingly' it is portrayed by the abuser, is an act of violation and aggression. Frances de Zulueta (1993) presents a strong argument against the idea of innate aggression, and proposes that there are strong links between childhood experiences of pain, trauma and distorted and disturbed attachments and the expression of violence. Thus it can be argued that women who sexually abuse children do not do so because they are born innately 'bad' or 'mad'. They sexually abuse children because, consciously or unconsciously, they have learnt through experience that this behaviour can meet what they perceive to be their needs. This research has indicated factors that appear to be of importance in the aetiology of such behaviour. These will be described within an integrated theoretical framework based on the work of Paul Gilbert (1989) (see Figure 10.1). This is a very tentative and personal approach to the clinical observations which will of course require much further research to substantiate.

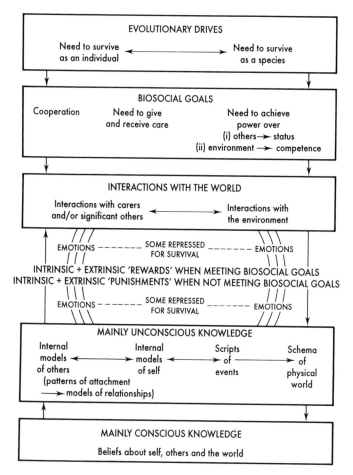

Figure 10.1: An integrated model of human functioning (from Saradjian, 1992, based on Gilbert, 1989)

AN INTEGRATED THEORETICAL FRAMEWORK

This is an holistic approach which stresses the importance of connecting a person's behaviour (cognitions and actions), environment (physical and social) and emotional and biological state (physiological correlates). At the root of this analysis is an ethological approach to human motivation which states that human beings, in common with all other living things have two ultimate goals: to survive as an individual, and to survive as a species through reproduction (Gilbert, 1989). As human beings are physically relatively vulnerable creatures, over time complex social systems have developed to facilitate this survival. Gilbert (1989) describes clinical and research evidence to support his notion that four biosocial goals have evolved which advance these ultimate goals: care-giving and care-receiving, power/control and cooperation. All behaviour when thoroughly analysed can be traced back to fulfilling one of the biosocial, and/or primary goals. Emotions act to direct and sustain behaviour (Rubin & McNeil, 1983) and thus mediate the seeking and achievement of these goals. Those behaviours or experiences that aid the achievement of biosocial goals are reinforced by physiological changes within the person that bring around a feeling of well-being (reward). People thus gravitate towards such behaviours and experiences. Conversely, those behaviours and experiences that oppose fulfilment of these goals are accompanied by physiological changes that are experienced as negative (aversive) and thus tend to be avoided or resisted. For example, the aversive emotion of jealousy acts to alert to potential loss of a source of care-giving and -receiving.

There can at times be conflict in the achievement of different biosocial goals. In these situations cognition (conscious and/or unconscious) and emotion will mediate the choice of behaviour that occurs. For example, in some instances a loss of power will be endured with the accompanying negative emotion in order that the fulfilment of affiliation and cooperative goals are met. Thus a child may endure being victimised in order not to lose a major source by which her affiliation needs can be met.

Through a person's interactions with other people and with their environment, a memory system of complex units is built up consisting of behaviours, images, tastes, smells, attitudes, etc., that are associated with particular emotion/s, 'unconscious sets' (Matte Blanco, 1975). In this way conscious and unconscious knowledge of how the biosocial goals can and cannot be achieved is developed. These complex units form a person's models of the world: their beliefs, knowledge, attitudes, etc. These models develop and change over time as new experiences are assimilated (Neisser, 1976). In differing environments, different aspects of the person's behaviour can be reinforced. Thus different selves, or aspects of self, will be predominant in different environments ('a community of selves', Mair, 1977).

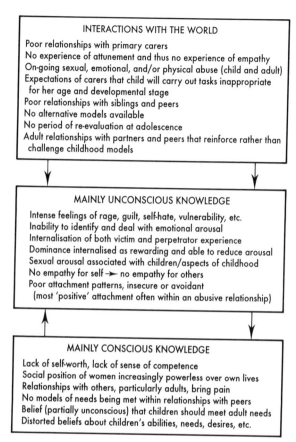

Figure 10.2: Factors involved when women sexually abuse children, placed within the integrated framework

THE MODEL APPLIED TO WOMEN WHO SEXUALLY ABUSE CHILDREN

The following analysis embeds the findings from the research within this theoretical framework in order to derive one possible formulation as to why these women may have learnt to meet at least some of their needs through the sexual abuse of children (see Figure 10.2).

A person's interactions with others and with the environment leads to the formation of 'internal models' of the world which guide behaviour. These internal models are akin to templates which lead to expectations of how the self and others will behave (Bowlby, 1980; Kelly, 1955). All the models that are formed are dynamic and can change via alternative experiences throughout the life span. These models act as a filter through which all experiences are subsequently and additionally interpreted. Experiences that are congruous with internalised models, in particular models of the self, are most likely to be accepted as valid. Experiences that are incongruous are likely to be judged as spurious and thus rejected, denied or else reframed in such a way as to maintain congruity. Hence the models of self, roles and relationships that have been developed through early experience are of vital importance. If there are no powerful mediating factors which stimulate direct challenge, the early models are resistant to change. These models influence everything that a person believes, and consequently will influence the behaviours through which the biosocial goals are met.

Initially the infant is completely dependent for developing her models of the world on her experience with her carers. Of particular importance is the responsiveness of the carers to the needs of the child (Bowlby, 1969; Bretherton, 1985; Stern, 1985). It has been proposed that congruent emotional responsiveness towards a child is necessary if that child is to learn to recognise and to modulate emotional arousal. Stern (1985) discusses the importance of 'attunement at the level of affect', that is, the carer responding to the child's feeling by accurately reflecting, mirroring and verbally interpreting that emotion as if for a brief period of time the emotion is jointly held. As the carer modulates the emotional state, the child follows, mirroring the carer. Consequently over time the child learns to identify her emotions and modulate and regulate her emotional arousal.

The women abusers who were the subject of this research generally describe having primary carers who were emotionally inaccessible and unresponsive. It is highly unlikely that any of the women offenders had any consistent experience of such attunement. This is evidenced by the fact that so many of these women offenders found it difficult to accurately identify their own emotions or to modulate them appropriately.

The women's descriptions of their victims indicate that they had little or no empathy for them. This may also have had its roots in failure of attunement. Block and Block (1980) propose that the experiencing of attunement of affect is essential for the development of empathy. Victimisers have been found to have a lack of empathy for the suffering of their victims (Staub, 1984, Beckett, Beech, Fisher & Fordham, 1994). Sadistic offenders appear to have a cognitive awareness of the pain that their victims experience but do not experience those feelings in resonance with them, hence do not have emotional empathy.

Additionally such neglect and/or denial of their needs by their primary carers that the women offenders describe is thought to lead to the development of 'narcissistic rage' (Kohut, 1985). This 'rage' may be repressed but can lead to an intensely held need for reprisal, to redress the injury (Miller, 1990). Any experience that leads to a feeling of extreme helplessness can trigger that 'rage'. This rage can be directed towards the self or to 'victimise a substitute self-object' (Wolf, 1988, p.80). Many women offenders perceive the children they target as being in some way reflections of themselves: 'substitute self-objects' which they then 'attack' (Welldon, 1988). Thus this lack of ability to identify and deal with their own emotional arousal, in conjunction with a lack of empathy and a repressed rage, may make a person vulnerable to dealing with such arousal by victimising others.

Infants that have such unresponsive and/or inappropriately responsive carers as these women describe, who may have also been physically and/or sexually abusive to them, are likely to form avoidant attachments (Egeland & Sroufe, 1981). Many aspects of the women's lives are consistent with this inference. Sroufe (1989) describes children who have histories of avoidant attachments as developing 'a model of the self as isolated, unable to achieve emotional closeness, uncared about and unworthy' (p.93). Such children are also found to have great difficulty in managing impulses, feelings and desires (Sroufe, 1983). This is the model of self in childhood held by almost all of the women abusers which they then carried into adulthood.

Main and George (1985) report that children with a history of avoidant attachment display 'negative empathy'. Negative empathy is when a child recognises another in pain and appears to gain pleasure from it and may even do something to increase the pain. Troy and Sroufe (1987) in their research on victimiser/victim dyads of children found that the victimiser was most likely to have an avoidant attachment with the primary care-taker. The victim was most likely to have had a history of ambivalent attachment but may have had a history of avoidant attachment. Sroufe proposes that either and/or both the role of victim and victimiser are open to those with a history of avoidant attachment because of 'the confluence of hostility and low self-esteem' (Sroufe, 1989, p.90).

The relationships that the women who were initially coerced by men to sexually abuse children describe with their carers, would lead to the deduction that they were most likely to have had avoidant attachments to their mothers but ambivalent attachments to their fathers. This would tend to result in these women having a great need to please men in order to maintain some form of attachment to them. This model of insecure attachment with at least one primary carer (however ultimately malevo- lent) possibly gave these women a basis to have at least some more positive, if not fulfilling, social interactions. However, as was found with this group of women, in most cases these social contacts were likely to be with men.

All of the women offenders described having experienced as a child severe rejection by primary carers. Rejection is of great psychic danger because of the child's total dependence on carers for survival. Such rejection leads to fear of annihilation (Hopper, 1991). Kohut (1985) argues that this state is so unbearable that it must be changed. Therefore in order to survive, the negative aspects of the interactions are minimised, distorted or even denied or repressed. In these circumstances the conscious beliefs about the carer can become idealised as the actuality of the experience is increasingly distorted.

Thus inconsistent models of the carers are formed (Bowlby, 1980) such as those many of the women offenders describe. To keep her 'carers' in a positive light the child will split off the 'bad' and internalise it, owning it as part of herself. Fairburn (1952, quoted in de Zulueta, 1993) describes a child's need to do this, saying 'it is better to be a sinner in a world ruled by God than to live in a world ruled by the Devil' (p.108). This defence is in keeping with the biosocial need to retain power and control. It is preferable to perceive the self as bad and hence retain an illusion of control, than to see the other as bad in which case the self would be powerless and ultimately destructible (Herman, 1990).

In addition, each of the women described when as a child feeling most cared for when she was meeting the needs of her carers: whether physical, emotional, practical or sexual. Because of the inappropriate demands made on her, she might develop distorted beliefs about what can be expected of children at various ages and stages of development. Thus she will internalise a model of children being a source of meeting adult needs. In addition, because of her own experience of abuse, she may also internalise the beliefs that 'bad' children deserve to be abused and/or rejected. In fulfilling the needs of her carers, she would have had to carry out tasks which would require abilities far in excess of her cognitive and emotional developmental stage. Consequently, as she is forming internal representations of the environment in which she lives (schema—Rumelhart & Norman, 1985) and her competence within it, she may develop a model of self as having little mastery and control over this environment.

Although these early relationships are frequently duplicated, at adolescence there is the possibility of reflecting on and challenging the models that direct those relationships (Main & Goldwyn, 1984). Within the contexts of other significant relationships, the primary relationships can be reconsidered, and models formed within relationships with early carers may be challenged. The women offenders generally describe themselves as children having poor relationships with peers and/or siblings. Consequently, these relationships could not ameliorate the effects of the adult–child relationships they experienced (Freud & Dann, 1951). For the women who sexually abused children there were no other alternative relationships, therefore there was little change in the internal models of self, others and the world.

As the women had no real alternative models, they were drawn into adult relationships which were consistent with those models of self and others developed throughout childhood. This is reflected in the finding that the women frequently used similar descriptions of their male adult partners to those they gave of their fathers and father figures. Women who initially sexually abused children in conjunction with men in almost every case minimised any negative experience with their fathers and/or idealised the relationship. These women used the same defence in their relationships with male partners so as to hold onto the belief in a 'good partner'. This was necessary as they held onto the belief that they could not survive without a male partner. Most likely as a result of modelling (Bandura, 1977) the beliefs and behaviours of their mothers, the women who sexually abused adolescents also held onto the belief that they 'needed' a partner. However, their experiences of adult partners resulted in the belief that they were 'rejecting', 'abusive' and/or controlling. As the women who sexually abused adolescents were in their own adolescence treated as adults, they perceived the children they abused to take on adult roles and fulfil their needs. An adolescent substitutes as a 'partner', thus meeting the woman's need for care-giving, care-receiving, while the woman retains a greater power and control over the relationship.

Not only were the women's relationships with their partners unrewarding, they also had very limited social networks. Positive social interactions provide care and cooperative support (i.e. biosocial goals) when faced with situations that may be stressful. This increases the chance of survival and therefore affects the reward system, bringing a feeling of well-being. In this way social interactions perform an essential part in modulating the arousal that is caused by stressful situations. Almost all the women who sexually abused children were frequently in a high level of stress. Not only because of stressful events in their adult lives, but also as a consequence of the frequent triggers to the previous trauma that will lead to emotional memories. Gorst-Unsworth (1992) proposes that even people in extreme torment obtain some degree of psychological well-being as a result of social interactions. However, these women were so emotionally isolated in childhood that they had no experience or model of meeting needs through supportive relationships with others; no model of alleviation of stress via assuagement with other people. One of the primary models that they do have of modulation of emotional arousal that they would have internalised as a result of their own victimisation, is that of the perpetration of sexually abusive acts. In high states of stress therefore they may choose to sexually abuse a child.

All the women who sexually abused children, had themselves experienced the trauma of being sexually abused as a child and/or within their adult relationships. Trauma is associated with the experience of negative emotions. A person who has experienced trauma, whether as an adult or as a child, may have repressed these negative emotions from conscious awareness or minimised them in order to cope with the immediate situation. This may be because of their dependence on their abusers and/or that some of their biosocial needs were being met within this 'relationship': needs such as care-giving and -receiving and feelings of status and competence. For many of the women abusers, this was accentuated as, at the time, their abusers were their primary attachment figures and the only resource for these needs to be met. This would tend to similar relationships being sexualised by them. Importantly, as the abusers were often the sole attachment figures, the women will assimilate, with little or no questioning, the identity projected onto them by the abusers (Salter, 1995). Subsequently they will project similar thinking errors onto their victims, as is evidenced from how the women offenders construed their target children.

Even though many aspects of the trauma are repressed from consciousness, a 'memory' will be held which involves all the aspects of that event including the associated emotions: an unconscious set (Matte Blanco, 1975). Within the unconscious set of the abuse the women abusers will have internalised both the victim and victimiser experiences (Sroufe & Fleeson, 1986). The sexual abuse of a child meets some need/s of the victimiser: affiliation needs, needs of power and control, and/or sexual needs. This will bring around a feeling of well-being within the victimiser which will be perceived by the victims. Thus the victims will internalise a model of reduction of emotional arousal, via dominance and hence victimisation of another.

The 'unconscious set' of a trauma that has been experienced can be triggered by any aspect associated with the original trauma (Perry, 1991). Internal triggers, such as feelings or body states, or external triggers, such as any environmental cue associated with the original trauma, can lead to the woman experiencing feelings similar to those felt or repressed during the original trauma (an 'emotional flashback'). Sometimes triggers can also lead to actual physical sensations that were associated with the trauma:

pain in the vagina and anus, nausea, feelings of choking and gagging, etc. These are known as somatosensory memories: 'body memories'. If the woman has completely repressed conscious memory of the trauma, triggers may still lead to 'emotional flashbacks' and 'body memories' with the accompanying physiological arousal, but without conscious awareness as to the source of distress or the triggers.

Some triggers may also lead to reliving of traumatic events through intrusive thoughts or cognitive (and even visual) 'flashbacks' and night-mares accompanied by the associated emotions. During these 'flashbacks' some women reverse the images, consciously or unconsciously, putting themselves in the role of abuser. Having such images does not necessarily mean that a person will become a perpetrator. Survivors who would never sexually abuse a child are sometimes plagued by such images. These images can be seen as coping strategies employed as an attempt to resolve the trauma. The manipulation of the 'flashbacks' may bring the women some sense of the control that is lacking as a result of their victimisation. To perceive the self as more powerful, even in fantasy, can lead to a feeling of well-being and reduction of arousal.

All the women who initiated sexual abuse were themselves victims of sexually abusive experiences. Hence, it is highly likely that through conditioning and/or modelling, some of the 'emotional', 'body' and/or 'cognitive' memories of the women's own traumas are accompanied by sexual arousal. When these 'memories' are triggered, it is as if there is a need to gain some form of 'revenge' for the abuse experienced. When that revenge is accessed via sexual acts towards a child, it can be understood as an erotic form of hatred (Stoller, 1975).

Aspects of a situation with a child or an adolescent can unconsciously trigger the repressed 'memories' of the woman's own traumas. This may lead to feelings of helplessness, victimisation and a consequent feeling of innate 'badness' that cannot be tolerated. These aspects of the self are thus 'cut off' and are projected onto the other (a child). Any aspect of the child's behaviour is interpreted by the women to fit in with those projected perceptions. The women subsequently use these same perceptions to justify the abuse that they perpetrate against the child. This is also 'justified' by the models that the women hold from their own childhood: that children should fulfil the needs of their parents/carers.

Women who have been abused in childhood but who have some other good relationships do not tend to re-enact the abuse (Ricks, 1985). However, none of the women in this study who sexually abused children had good alternative relationships. Consequently when these women were in a parental role with a child their ability to parent would have been similar to that of their parental figures. The models that the women would have developed of children's relationships to adults, would be of children being the ones meeting adult needs and not the reverse. As they themselves were not protected they do not have a model for protecting children (see de Zulueta, 1993).

For a woman to protect and care effectively for a child, she needs to have a good-enough self-concept. All of the women who sexually abused children had very poor self-concepts. Staub suggests that 'a poor self-concept makes it more difficult to extend the boundaries of the self in benevolent ways' (quoted by de Zulueta, 1993, p.129). When a woman believes herself to be inadequate and weak, she cannot obtain her biosocial goals effectively. Socialisation of women within our culture is such that these beliefs are reinforced. Other people, rather than acting as supports, pose a threat. There is a need to control others by means of aggressive and explosive outbursts and/or seductive sexual behaviour directed towards those who are culturally in a weaker position. For women in today's society, one of the few groups whom she is 'permitted' to have power over and to control is children. The findings show that the women perceive the children whom they sexually abuse to be in some way a threat, and they seek to control them by aggressive and/or seductive acts. Thus children become the commodity through which they can meet biosocial needs and modulate physiological arousal.

The women who sexually abuse children frequently experience uncontrollable stress, in addition to numerous triggers to distressing memories. They experience feelings of helplessness, vulnerability and isolation and a need to regain a sense of power and control over their lives in order to meet their affiliation needs. Being unaware of the source of their feelings, and because of the lack of empathy and emotional intimacy that they have experienced in life, the women undergo an increase in physiological arousal with no ability to recognise, interpret or modulate that arousal. The women learn to reduce arousal by a variety of behaviours. These behaviours will include re-exposure to situations similar to the original trauma (van der Kolk, 1989). Identifying with the aggressor, the woman has an internal unconscious model of reduction of arousal by perpetrating sexually abusive acts. She also has internalised a model of sexual arousal to children. Thus the woman re-enacts the abuse but in the role of the victimiser. By sexually abusing the victim, the woman regains a sense of power and control and in many cases also fulfils affiliation needs. Her sexual tension is reduced and by fulfilling her basic biosocial needs she becomes calmer. Thus the behaviour is rewarding and as such can become addictive and compulsive. The woman can become aware of the compulsion but not of the underlying rage and hatred (Welldon, 1988). Hence, the sexual act becomes associated with reduction of general physiological arousal and sexual behaviour can become the response to all forms of stress and distress. Therefore for many women the sexual abuse of a child becomes the means by which most of their biosocial needs are met.

RE-ENACTMENT—A SIMILAR PROCESS TO PLAY

Children use play in order to make sense of and integrate episodes in their lives. Children will frequently re-enact what they have experienced and learnt via play. Through play they can practise roles and act out relationships, often from all sides. Empathic intimacy can also be rehearsed and experienced. Play is used by children to help resolve any current psychological or psychosocial confusions or crises. When children play they re-enact experiences and gain control over situations, thus attempting to align their inner and outer worlds (Erikson, 1950). Often in play a child can experience, via the behaviours of other children, alternatives to the social roles he or she has experienced. Erikson (1977) also recognised that play is not confined to childhood but pursued throughout life albeit in different forms to those favoured in childhood.

It is proposed that at times adults also need to re-enact experiences in order to gain control over situations, especially when they are in a state of psychological tension or stress. They 'play' but not with toys or in games. Adults 'play' by re-enacting experiences using 'human beings' rather than toys and 'real relationships' and life situations rather than games. In the same way children create fantasies and 'play' to resolve other traumas. The women abusers created fantasies and re-enacted their traumas both as victim and as victimiser. When doing so, it is suggested that they were in a similar emotional state and stage of development to that they experienced within the original trauma. Hence at the time of the abuse they perpetrate, they feel emotionally congruent with the victims they choose to target to become involved in 'the game'. The re-enactment, however, is in itself 'rewarding' but can simultaneously be another source of trauma. Thus the behaviour becomes repeated.

POSSIBLE PHYSIOLOGICAL CORRELATES THAT MEDIATE AND MAINTAIN CHILD SEXUAL ABUSE

the physiological relations pertaining within the brain at any point in time profoundly affect our personal and social logic. (Gilbert, 1989, p.3)

All behaviour brings about physiological changes within the central nervous system. Consistent with an integrated model, an hypothesis is suggested as to some of the possible physiological correlates involved when women engage in sexual interaction with children. An argument will be made for the involvement of a key role for the endogenous opioids and the neurotransmitter, serotonin, in the inception of sexual offending behaviour. Any aspect of behaviour is modulated by *a range* of neuro-chemicals (Benton & Brain, 1988). There is evidence that these neuro-chemicals have a role to play (Saradjian, 1992) *but it is recognised that this is a simplistic and speculative model which will lead to many further questions.* In addition, it must be stressed, however, it is in no way intended that genetic biological disturbances are believed to be primarily aetiological or that pharmacological intervention is indicated.

Endogenous opioids are naturally occurring neurochemicals predomi-nately found in the emotional and motivational centre of the brain. The behaviours that have been associated with release of endogenous opioids are those essential to survival: regulation of food intake and water balance, social interaction, sexual behaviour (e.g. vaginal stimulation, see Komisaruk & Whipple, 1986), exploration and activity, and learning and memory. In these situations the endogenous opioids bring round a feeling of calm and well-being. Thus behaviours essential to survival are 'emo-tionally rewarding'. In addition endogenous opioids are also released in situations in which analgesia may be required: extreme anxiety, physical damage, the presence of a predator, anticipatory fear, novel situations, enforced immobility (Rodgers & Cooper, 1988). This brings about an insensitivity to pain which will facilitate survival when having to deal with danger. Franselow has shown that not only the actual aversive situations result in the release of endogenous opioids but also previously neutral classically conditioned cues can do so (Franselow & Bolles, 1982). These cues can be in a variety of modes: environmental cues, smells, tastes, noises, looks, physical feelings, emotions, etc., etc.

One of the common factors in the lives of all the women who sexually abuse children is experience of extensive abuse, particularly sexual abuse, as an adult, a child or both. Thus these women are likely to have been exposed to extreme anxiety, physical damage, the presence of a predator (the abuser), anticipatory fear, novel situations, periods of enforced immobility and repeatedly to be in uncontrollable situations, and suffering extensive vaginal stimulation, all of which have been shown to be associated with the release of endogenous opioids. Most victims of abuse report flashbacks of the abusive experience especially when in the presence of associated cues. These flashbacks may be accompanied by opioid-mediated, stress-induced analgesia (Van der Kolk, 1989). Fre-quency of stressful experiences and social isolation typified the lives of the female perpetrators. These experiences are also associated with the release of endogenous opioids (Guillemin, Vargo, Rossier et al., 1977). Post, Pickar, Ballenger et al. (1984) found a positive correlation between CSF β-endorphin levels (an endogenous opioid) with depression and social isolation in women. Interestingly, one often-recorded effect of extensive sexual abuse in childhood is social isolation (Tufts, 1984).

It is proposed that the lives of the women perpetrators, both as children and as adults, will most probably have led to the repeated release of endogenous opioids. Thus it is likely that the women who sexually abuse children have had such excessive exposure to their endogenous opioids that they have become 'physiologically dependent' on them (Christie & Chesher, 1982). The withdrawal phase of this form of dependency has been found to be associated with increased need for social contact and an increase in sexual behaviour and libido (Serra, Collu & Gessa, 1988). However, the women perpetrators have few social contacts available to them and no socially learned ways of gaining positive social experience with adult peers. They also have had negative adult sexual experiences. However, they do have the 'unconscious knowledge' that sexual contact will bring about a calming effect. In the women's environments there are cues that were present during their own experience of sexual abuse. These cues may, in part, account for the *initial* age-specific choice of partner for sole female perpetrators and the sexual abuse of the same child who was abused by the couple when coerced female abusers subsequently abuse alone.

Many of the women who sexually abused children described a withdrawal syndrome: a physical tension within their body that is consistent with such an experience of withdrawal. Some describe this 'tension' as a 'drive'; 'a feeling of bodily tension' or 'a sort of feeling that I know only sexual contact with a child will take away'. This may explain the finding that what so many of these women describe as a 'positive physical feeling'—particularly a sense of calm—occurs after sexual activity. The women who target adolescents tend to express similar feelings in 'romantic' rather than physical terms. These women are more likely to make statements like 'I longed for his body', 'When he wasn't there I would become agitated and distressed. I needed him to make me whole'.

Another important factor in the initiation of sexually abusive acts may be lowered levels of the neurotransmitter, serotonin. Anisman (1978), summarising the neurochemical changes associated with stress, reports that intense stress leads to depletion in levels of serotonin. Low levels of serotonin are linked with various kinds of impulsive behaviour (e.g. Linnoila et al., 1983). Collating the findings on low levels of serotonin,

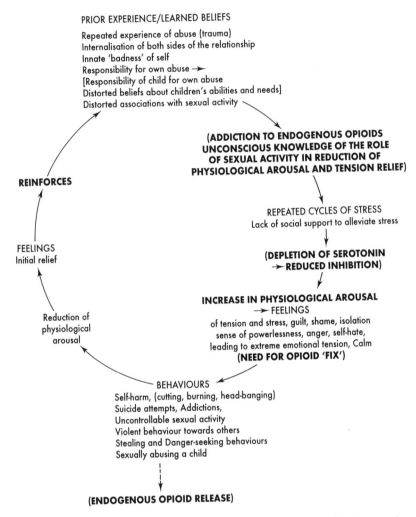

PRIOR EXPERIENCE/LEARNED BELIEFS
Repeated experience of abuse (trauma)
Internalisation of both sides of the relationship
Innate 'badness' of self
Responsibility for own abuse ➤
[Responsibility of child for own abuse
Distorted beliefs about children's abilities and needs]
Distorted associations with sexual activity

(ADDICTION TO ENDOGENOUS OPIOIDS
UNCONSCIOUS KNOWLEDGE OF THE ROLE
OF SEXUAL ACTIVITY IN REDUCTION OF
PHYSIOLOGICAL AROUSAL AND TENSION RELIEF)

REINFORCES

REPEATED CYCLES OF STRESS
Lack of social support to alleviate stress

FEELINGS
Initial relief

(DEPLETION OF SEROTONIN
➤ REDUCED INHIBITION)

INCREASE IN PHYSIOLOGICAL AROUSAL
➤ FEELINGS

Reduction of
physiological
arousal

of tension and stress, guilt, shame, isolation
sense of powerlessness, anger, self-hate,
leading to extreme emotional tension, Calm
(NEED FOR OPIOID 'FIX')

BEHAVIOURS
Self-harm, (cutting, burning, head-banging)
Suicide attempts, Addictions,
Uncontrollable sexual activity
Violent behaviour towards others
Stealing and Danger-seeking behaviours
Sexually abusing a child

(ENDOGENOUS OPIOID RELEASE)

Figure 10.3: Physiological correlates associated with the behaviour cycle

Depue and Spoont (1986) suggest that it leads to a lack of constraint. These women perpetrators were recurrently exposed to unameliorated stress. As a result they will be likely to have low levels of serotonin, leading to impulsivity/lack of constraint which can override the inhibition to sexually abuse a child.

It is proposed that these factors working together may contribute to the initiation of the sexual abuse. Once initiated, the behaviour would be reinforcing as sexual acts lead to the release of endogenous opioids. When sexually abusing a child, the female perpetrator would be in control whereas as in the past she would have been the victim. Being in control would also be associated with increase in power which, being associated with survival, triggers the reward system, releasing endogenous opioids. This is consistent with the feeling of calm they describe after they have sexually abused a child. Thus an addictive cycle is set up (see Figure 10.3).

It is further proposed that the women in this study, who would have been expected to have expressed specific symptoms as a result of their life experiences, do not do so because they are sexually abusing children. Many of the symptoms that are commonly seen as sequelae to childhood sexual abuse are also associated with an elevation of endogenous opioids: self-mutilation, suicide attempts (also associated with depletion of serotonin) especially those people who become addicted to near death experiences, eating disorders, promiscuity and drug addiction. It is of interest that, consistent with this analysis, several subjects talk about these behaviours occurring after the sexual abuse of the child/ren is no longer taking place.

SUMMARY

- Behaviour, thoughts and biological responses are inextricably linked.
- People are motivated for personal survival and the survival of the species to meet their biosocial goals: care-giving and care-receiving, cooperation and power.
- Emotions are the indicators that a human being is or is not meeting the biosocial goals.
- When the biosocial needs are met there is a feeling of well-being. When the biosocial goals are not being met there is a need which results in an increase in physiological arousal, psychological discomfort and a compulsion to reduce this arousal.
- Behaviour is a result of experiences through which a person learns how these fundamental needs can be met.
- Through their experiences women have developed the distorted cognitions and beliefs that facilitate them to sexually abuse children.
- Also, via modelling or direct experience, aspects of the woman's sexual arousal have become conditioned to triggers associated with children/adolescents.
- These women have also learnt via modelling or direct experience to meet at least some of their biosocial goals and thus to reduce arousal by their sexual behaviour with children.

- Therefore when they experience emotional arousal which they cannot modulate these women sexually abuse children which (however briefly) modulates that arousal.
- This is 'rewarding' and consequently when in similar circumstances the woman may repeat this behaviour.
- It is proposed that the neurotransmitter serotonin and the endogenous opioids have key roles in the physiological correlates of this behaviour

11

ASSESSMENT FOR RISK AND ESTABLISHING A THERAPEUTIC RELATIONSHIP

- ASSESSMENT
- ESTABLISHING AN EFFECTIVE THERAPEUTIC RELATIONSHIP
- MAINTAINING AN EFFECTIVE THERAPEUTIC RELATIONSHIP
- WORKING THE TIGHT-ROPE OF THE VICTIM/PERPETRATOR DIVIDE
- GROUP VS INDIVIDUAL THERAPY
- SUMMARY

ASSESSMENT

1. Reasons for Assessment

The process of assessment in the field of female sexual offenders involves the gathering of information in order to answer specific clinical questions. The questions most commonly posed require assessment of the woman in order:

1. To give an opinion on whether a woman is likely to have sexually abused a child or children.
2. To consider the risk a woman who is known to have sexually abused a child or children has of reoffending.
3. To consider the areas that need to be worked on in therapy to reduce risk of reoffending, including most importantly the woman's motivation to change.

4. To gain information from the woman perpetrator that may inform the therapy of her victims.

These questions are obviously interlinked so a thorough assessment should provide the information required. Also, regardless of how client-centred the therapist is, in all work with sexual offenders child protection must also be a consideration. Hence on-going risk assessment should also be a part of the therapeutic process. Therefore assessment of a woman who sexually abuses children involves collecting sufficient information in order to develop a formulation as to how the woman being assessed came to sexually offend against children. In this way those areas in which therapeutic intervention needs to be directed for change to occur can be established. In addition, assessment should be made of any of the woman's behaviours and attitudes which are likely to result in significant harm for that child. Significant harm was defined by Bentovim (1991) as abuses 'which interact with the child's on-going development and interrupt, alter, impair physical and psychological development'. The assessment should also consider and indicate specific factors for each individual perpetrator that will increase or decrease the risk. Assessment can occur at any point of knowledge of a perpetrator: from when an offence is just suspected, through to the 'end' of therapy with the perpetrator.

2. Research—the Basis of Good Assessment

Assessment is beset with hazards which attack the accuracy of the evaluation; the most important of these being the limited knowledge base in relation to the aetiology of sexual offending in general, and in particular, of sexual offending by women. The more knowledge collected as to the factors that combine and result in a person sexually abusing a child, the more accurate the theoretical model will be. The more accurate the theoretical model, the more accurate the assessment will be.

The data collected from this research on women who sexually abuse children are consistent with, *although not identical to*, the findings in relation to some male sexual offenders (e.g. Beckett et al., 1994). This therefore offers support for the model presented, until further information can be collected on women abusers which will validate or challenge this model.

3. Difficulties When Undertaking Assessment

Assessing women who sexually abuse children is endemic with similar difficulties to the assessment of male sexual offenders (e.g. Beckett, 1994);

in particular the denial, distortion and poor cooperation of the perpetrators. Additionally there are no appropriate assessment tools developed and/or normalised in relation to women offenders, and there is much research showing the dangers of applying models and tools devised for men to women (e.g. Gilligan, 1982; Belenky, Clinchy, Goldberger & Tarule, 1986). Consequently for women abusers there is an even greater dependence on self-report with all its intrinsic difficulties of reliability. There is also very little research information available on the outcome of therapy with such women, consequently the conclusions reached, as to both risk and prognosis, need to be even more tentative than those in relation to male sexual offenders.

4. Techniques for Initial Assessment

1. Unfortunately assessment is an art not a science, and a great deal of importance lies with the interviewing skills and clinical experience of the assessor. However, these can only be developed with practice, therefore *with good consultation*, professionals with appropriate training within the field of child sexual abuse can attempt such an assessment.
2. When the assessor is so reliant on the self-report of the offender it is important to elicit as much cooperation as possible without developing a collusive relationship.
3. Any woman being assessed for being a perpetrator of child sexual abuse is in personal crisis. Most women describe feelings of intense 'shame' and stigmatisation (Matthews, 1993). Shame is a very important component in inhibiting women's disclosures. Explicitly communicating to the woman the model that *all behaviour is 'explainable', if not excusable*, when viewed within the context of a person's life helps to overcome some of the 'shame'. It has also been found helpful to state that part of the task, for both the woman and the assessor, is to make sense of what has occurred.
4. It has been found that cooperation can also be facilitated by:
   (a) using language consistent with the level of understanding of the woman being assessed;
   (b) explaining the purpose of the assessment and what it entails;
   (c) acknowledging the difficulties of having to disclose to a stranger the most intimate details of one's life;
   (d) stressing the advantages to the woman of full disclosure which will help in understanding how the situation arose and in making effective recommendations for therapeutic interventions, and/or will inform the help given to the victims;

(e) remembering that an assessment carried out well can actually be therapeutic for the woman as it is often the first time she has told anyone her story and therefore encouraging her to see it as a start to sorting out difficult aspects of her life;

(f) being honest with the woman; telling her the information you have already and adding that, if it is at all possible within your remit, you will discuss your findings with her.

5. One technique that has been found to be helpful in lessening a woman's denials caused by her feelings of 'shame' is for the assessor to disclose the knowledge he or she has of women sexual offenders. For example, rather than asking 'Do you have sexual fantasies?', say 'Some women describe having thoughts about children that make them feel aroused in some way, would you say this was something you experience?' 'What sort of feelings do you have when you have these thoughts?' Many of these women, because of their emotional deprivation, genuinely cannot identify their own emotions but may be able to describe the physical sensations they experience. They say things such as 'I feel tight inside', 'my heart races', 'I can't get my breath', 'I get so restless', etc.

6. Like anyone disclosing personally difficult material, the woman is likely to tell 'the tip of the iceberg' and then extend her disclosures depending on the reaction of the listener. It is therefore important that the assessor does not appear shocked, disgusted, angry, etc., etc.

7. If possible try to collect one piece of information in a number of ways so that the internal reliability of the woman's report can be considered. For example, ask the woman to describe her mother, ask about her relationship with her mother both as a child and as an adult, ask about sources of affection, care and support as a child and use a Repertory Grid, a Dependency Grid and Garbarino's emotional abuse scale (Garbarino, 1986). Thus the woman's experience of her relationship with her own mother can be accessed in various ways and internal consistency of the woman's responses can be considered.

8. If there is inconsistency *it does not always mean the woman is deliberately lying*. It may be that the woman has idealised and denied her experiences so much to herself that she is actually describing what she believes to be the truth.

9. Audiotaping the interview can be very helpful so that the exact phrasing the woman uses can be recorded easily. This can be essential in certain aspects of the evaluation such as when assessing who or what the woman truly holds responsible for specific actions. On one level the woman may articulate that she holds herself responsible for the sexual acts, yet make attributions such as 'He came into my bed when he wanted closeness and aroused me'. Notes alone can miss

some of the more subtle attributions and can also be subject to reinterpretation.

5. The Information Collected in Assessment

It is suggested that when making an assessment of a potential woman offender a specific interview should be constructed for that woman. A suggestion for the areas to be covered in this interview, based on the research findings and theoretical model presented in this book, can be found in Appendix 5. The construction of this interview can also be informed by various resources, including the children's disclosures, reports such as those from social services, police, probation, etc. During the interview, additional information can be obtained by noting the woman's emotional and behavioural responses along with any difficulties, reluctance or refusal to answer any questions.

6. Evaluating the Information Collected

In order to make an assessment, all the information obtained should be considered in relation to what is known about women who sexually abuse children and to the theoretical model (Chapter 10). However, it must be stressed that the typologies derived from this research, and that of Speltz, Matthews and Mathews (1989), can only act as heuristic frameworks to guide the work. It is reiterated, assessment is an art; unfortunately there is no unique formula. *Typologies cannot be used purely as 'checklists'.* It is inevitable there will be other women who do not fit into these patterns who also sexually abuse children, such as those discussed as 'atypical offenders' (see Chapter 8). The information gathered from these 'atypical' offenders, however, is consistent with the theoretical model presented.

7. Factors that Increase Risk of Offending

These factors listed here which *in combination* are believed to increase a woman's risk of sexual reoffending are a result of joint work with Hilary Eldridge, Clinical Director of the Faithfull Foundation. This list should be used with great caution and it must be stressed that it can *not* act as a checklist.

(a) Issues related to the woman's history

1. Chaotic family history with blurred generational boundaries.
2. Lack of appropriate or adequate parenting and/or idealising of one or both parents.
3. Pattern of being avoidant/anxious of attachment.
4. History of victimisation, particularly sexual abuse (as a child and/or adult), especially if it was not recognised as such by the woman and/or important adults in her life.
5. Emotional abuse, emotional isolation, and/or rejection.
6. Lack of empathy for herself as victim.
7. Lack of intimate peer relationships during childhood.
8. No alternative models of herself or others have been internalised.
9. Little opportunity during adolescence to reflect on and separate out from her childhood experiences.

(b) Issues related to her current life/experience of herself

1. Low self-esteem and feelings of lack of power and control in her life; or self-esteem and sense of power and control derived from external and transitory sources (e.g. a strong partner).
2. Tendency to suppress anger, aggression and other feelings, and then subsequently behave impulsively.
3. Poor adult relationships with partners who are most often abusive: physically, sexually and/or emotionally.
4. Tendency to become involved in and unable to end abusive relationships, and/or to idealise abusive partners.
5. High levels of stress with no social support(s) available.
6. Poor social networks and an inability to form close emotionally intimate, non-sexual social contacts for appropriate support.
7. Inability to recognise and respond appropriately to emotions in self and others.
8. Sexual activity playing a central role as a response to a variety of emotions and emotional arousal.
9. Negative features in relation to her experience of sexual acts with adult partner/s.
10. Lack of, or disbelief in, the possibility that any personal or peer resources are able to meet her primary needs.

(c) Issues related to her beliefs about children

1. Distorted view of children, either idealising or denigrating, usually associated with a lack of understanding of appropriate child behaviour

and abilities.
2. Belief that children should/must meet adult's needs.
3. Perception of children as peers (at least emotionally).
4. High levels of fantasy/daydreaming/thoughts about children, accompanied by arousal (may or may not perceive this as *sexual*).
5. Use of sexual acts with children to meet her primary needs.

(d) Issues related to her offending behaviour

1. Strong denial/ minimalisation/justification about her offences, or the effects on the child; lack of empathy for her victim/s.
2. Sadistic offending, where the woman has victim awareness but has no victim empathy; intentionally maltreats the child.
3. Large number of victims. Not fixated on specific victim/s.
4. Frequency and intensity of the sexually abusive activity.
5. Heavy use of disinhibitors, such as alcohol, other psychotropic substances, child pornography, etc.
6. Use of superordinate belief system (e.g. extreme Christian belief or astrology) to claim change without offence-focused therapeutic intervention.
7. No motivation to genuinely change; nothing to gain.

8. Denying and Minimalising of Offending Behaviour

When a woman is denying sexually abusing a child, all the possible hypotheses must be considered:

1. She has done so, knows she has, and is lying.
2. She has done so, but sincerely does not recognise that her behaviours towards the child constitute sexual abuse.
3. She has abused but due to dissociation genuinely does not recognise or recall that she has sexually abused the child.
4. She has not sexually abused the child.

It is important that the final possibility is always considered along with the others.

When making an assessment of risk for court, if the woman denies any offence, it is not necessarily the task of the clinician to reach a judgement as to whether such an offence has or has not occurred. The court may reach such a judgement. The task of the person carrying out the assessment is to collect appropriate evidence to describe the woman's history; the effects of that history on her thoughts, beliefs and behaviours; how those thoughts, beliefs and behaviours could potentially increase the woman's risk of significantly harming children; and, when instructed to do so, arrive at a *clinical* judgement to put before the court.

ESTABLISHING AN EFFECTIVE THERAPEUTIC RELATIONSHIP

1. The Aims of Therapy

they are human; they are not monsters; they can change; they can develop empathy for their victims; they can lead positive lives; they are salvageable and they are worth salvaging. (Jane Kinder Matthews, 1993, p.61)

Jay Haley (1990) proposes that any symptom originates as an effective *personal* 'solution' to a problem or problems. When sexual offenders engage in therapy the symptom they present is their sexually abusive behaviour. Thus the sexually abusive behaviour is a personal 'solution' to problems within the lives of the perpetrators but such a 'solution' has very detrimental effects on the victims. Therapy should be aimed at finding what problems the sexual abuse of a child solved for that particular offender and how the offender can come to different 'solutions' and/or to change her life in such a way as not to have those problems. For each sexual offender, sexual offending is a 'solution' to an individual constellation of needs: power and control needs, affiliation needs, esteem needs, social needs, physiological needs. The therapeutic task includes working with each offender to ascertain which of their specific needs are met by sexual offending and what processes, internal or external, facilitate them to believe that these needs could be met in this way. Crucially, the psychological defences used by offenders which enable them to rationalise this behaviour as being a legitimate means to meet these needs must also be addressed. These include defences such as distorted thinking, or emotional denial and blockage, which have been employed, usually throughout life, which enable the offender to overcome internal inhibitions to sexually abusing children. Also of importance is considering the role of external factors which implicitly endorse abusive behaviour generally, such as the power imbalances in our society which bestow on males power over, and 'ownership' of, females, and give adults power over, and 'ownership' of, children.

2. Engaging the Women in Therapy

Good therapy always starts where the woman is and keeps pace with her progress.
(Rawlings & Carter, 1977, p.51)

The vast quantity of research carried out over the years relating to the process of therapy has concluded that the *single most important factor* of effective therapy is the relationship developed between the therapist and the client (e.g. Lambert, 1989). Of course, that relationship is also dependent on the perceived competence of the therapist, how well he or she uses the therapeutic techniques available, the therapist's consistency, etc. (see Garfield & Bergin, 1986). Since engaging the woman within the therapeutic relationship is so important, space will be given to this process.

3. Forming a Working Alliance: the Use of Metaphor

Almost all the women sexual offenders experience themselves as powerless, no matter how powerful they may be perceived to be by others. Therapy is yet another relationship in which the woman will feel 'the other' to hold the power. Much has been written about power issues in therapy for women (e.g. Ussher, 1991). This power imbalance is further exacerbated as, unlike most people who seek therapy, sex offenders tend to have therapy 'thrust upon them'. Many, not all, initially see it as something they have to 'go through' or 'play along with' rather than being motivated to undertake a joint venture with the aim of changing behaviour. Additionally, the woman has gained her sense of power and control by sexually abusing children. Thus if the power imbalance of the therapeutic relationship is not managed, her feelings of powerlessness within it could become a source of more triggers for the woman to sexually abuse a child.

Therefore the aim is to attempt to achieve with the woman a collaborative relationship which does not exacerbate her feelings of powerlessness. To form such a relationship it is helpful if there is an *explicit* mutual understanding between the therapist and the client as to what therapy entails: the task and the role of both the therapist and client. Using metaphor can be very helpful in this. For example, therapy can be likened to a person writing her life story. She is some way through the book but has got stuck. She finds herself going over and over the same piece of plot and cannot move on. She has dropped all the pages of the previous chapters and these are scattered around, some may even be mislaid. Although she vaguely knows the plot, she is not really sure of exactly how and why she got to the place at which she is stuck. So she cannot move on and repeats that part of the plot over and over. The role of the therapist is to help her to collect all the pages, read them, trace the paths of the subplots, and put them in order. Thus together they can make sense of how she got to the place she is at and consider what options she has to move on with the rest of her story.

Such a collaborative relationship does not preclude challenge. Indeed challenging the woman's beliefs and reasoning, and thereby offering alternatives to her set patterns of attitude and beliefs, is likely to aid effective therapy.

4. Making a Contract

Therapy is not an 'easy option': it can be an extremely painful process. These women are very likely to have had a history of relationships that have seemed 'good' and became 'bad'. This can appear to be what happens in therapy if the process of therapy is not made explicit to the woman. This is especially true when (as is likely) she has herself experienced severe abuse and had to repress the painful feelings associated with that abuse. These painful feelings are then experienced via therapy. If the woman is not forewarned, she is likely to perceive this as a failure either in therapy, in the therapist, and/or in themselves and stop attending. The therapist needs to make a contract with the woman so she is fully aware of what therapy entails. Explicitly stating what is expected of the woman and what she can expect from the therapist can in itself be therapeutic for the woman. Such a contract between the woman and the therapist can help the woman to feel contained enough to work through difficult times.

Again a metaphor can be usefully employed to illustrate the therapeutic process. It is likely you have been cut severely, but have no one whom you can tell and thus you cannot obtain help for the injury. So you have to cover it up, block out the pain or take strong painkillers so that all appears to be well. On the surface the cut appears to heal but because it has not been properly looked after, it becomes infected and that infection travels around the body and causes secondary symptoms in ways that at first viewing appear to be totally unconnected to the original injury. Sometimes treatment is given to these symptoms but because the source of the problem has not been tackled, they reoccur either in the same or a different form. Therapy involves looking at the original injury, reopening it, and cleaning out the infections that have become systemic. This can be extremely painful. Good therapy then involves sewing up the original injury, but neatly so that it heals well. The scar will always be there, and from time to time it may begin to flare up. Therapy can help a woman to recognise the signs when this begins to happen, how to deal with it and how to get help quickly if this is required.

Providing a framework which promotes emotional safety can also be done by discussing the woman's assessment with her and indicating the areas which will be addressed in therapy.

5. The Areas to be Covered in Therapy

This is an outline of the areas which the research has indicated are most likely to need to be worked on in therapy. Which areas are most pertinent for a particular woman can be ascertained by an individual assessment. These areas are not a checklist that can be worked through 'in order'. Many components are dependent on each other to obtain resolution (see Chapter 12).

1. Facilitating the woman to accept she has sexually abused a child or children and to take responsibility for her behaviour.
2. Gaining an understanding of her pattern of offending, particularly:
   (a) identifying triggers that lead to her offending;
   (b) the beliefs that lead her to offending;
   (c) the way she targets and grooms children;
   (d) the part played by sexual fantasy in her offending.
3. The woman's own victim issues (i) as a child (ii) as an adult.
4. Identification and reattribution of emotional feelings.
5. The development of both intellectual and emotional empathy (not just victim awareness).
6. Relationship issues—partners, parents, peers, children (including developmentally appropriate behaviour).
7. Facility to develop emotionally intimate relationships.
8. Social skills and social network development.
9. Self-esteem issues.
10. Relapse prevention—the whole process of therapy is part of relapse prevention, this specifically applies to the conscious understanding the woman has of how to control her own behaviour.

6. Overcoming Specific Resistances to Engaging in Therapy

Women who have sexually abused children in different ways often have specific resistances to engaging in therapy. Carefully considering the order in which issues are addressed in therapy has been found to be helpful in overcoming these resistances.

(a) 'I don't need therapy because I've lost my children. There's no point any more'

For the women who sexually abuse very young children, particularly their own, the greatest resistance seems to be that they see no point in going through the therapy, as they believe it is unlikely they will ever be allowed contact with children again. These women appear very determined they will not sexually abuse children again and that therefore they will have no need of therapy. However, if the therapy begins by looking at their history of childhood, and an empathic therapeutic relationship is developed, the links between their own abuse and their perpetrating behaviour can begin to be made. This is likely to be the first time in the woman's life she will have another person's undivided attention in a genuine, non-judgemental, empathic relationship with appropriate boundaries. If such a relationship is established the woman is highly likely to continue with the therapy.

(b) 'I don't need therapy because I did nothing wrong'

The most difficult women to engage in therapy are those who target extrafamilial adolescents. They tend to maintain extreme denial that their behaviour is actually sexual abuse. This is particularly true when the women target adolescent boys. This denial is based on, and reinforced by, society's construction of male sexual aggression and female passivity and the widely held belief that young males want to be 'seduced' by older women. The denial is also strengthened by the tendency of these women to deny that their own sexual experiences during their adolescence were actually sexual abuse. However, research indicates that this group of women generally have the least entrenched pathology and, when they enter therapy, have an excellent prognosis. Direct challenge tends to result in further entrenchment of ideas, superficial compliance and/or non-attendance for therapy. One method that has proved helpful in motivating this group of women is by initially focusing on a woman's life experiences and relationships with adult partners. Through facilitating the woman to look at the power imbalance in these relationships, the societal influence in that imbalance can be explored. The woman's 'relationship/s' with the adolescent/s can be challenged.

(c) 'I don't need therapy because he made me do it'

Women who were initially coerced into sexually abusing children tend to attribute responsibility onto their male partner. They are likely to insist they have no sexual arousal to children and therefore, as they are no longer with those partners, they do not need therapy. Such a woman can often be engaged in therapy by looking at how and why she became involved with the man, and the effects on her of her life with him. This will then include the effects of the abuse they perpetrated together and hence inroads into her responsibility can be made. During this work the woman's own sexual arousal to children and any abuse she initiated can then be seen in context and hence worked through. Due to the domination these women's partners have over them, it is usefully more beneficial to the therapy if contact between them is broken before therapy begins.

MAINTAINING AN EFFECTIVE THERAPEUTIC RELATIONSHIP

1. Support for the Woman during Therapy

Women who sexually abuse children also tend to have very poor social support networks. Therapy will raise many emotional problems for these women, and they will need support to help deal with these. It would be useful if support could be put in place before therapy begins and maintained until the woman is able to form a network for herself. This would also give the woman experiences of positive gain from adult relationships.

If the woman has another child or children, it may be important that she does not have care of the child or children directly after the therapy sessions. At such times the woman is likely to project the feelings raised in the therapy onto these children until she learns to deal with them appropriately.

2. Looking at Feelings Raised within the Therapeutic Relationship

(a) Supervision, support and personal therapy

Working with women who sexually abuse children is difficult, personally as well as professionally, and it is the ethical responsibility of the therapist to ensure that he or she has the necessary resources to be effective. The importance of good honest supervision for all casework cannot be stressed enough. Supervision is related to examining the therapy and the therapeutic process between the therapist and the client. This should enable the motivation and validity of the therapist's interventions to be carefully considered. Distinct from supervision, a therapist working in this area will also need support. This relates to the personal effect the work the therapist is undertaking with his or her client has; the way that carrying out this work makes the therapist feel. If through the support sessions it becomes clear there are underlying issues for the worker that have been triggered by his or her work with this case then personal therapy should be sought (Youngson, 1994).

(b) Boundaries

Women who sexually abuse children are primarily in therapy because each of them has had a relationship with at least one child where there were no boundaries. Research indicates almost all of the women had frequently had their own personal boundaries breached; many had never had a relationship in which appropriate boundaries were maintained. These women are very likely to challenge the personal boundaries of the therapist. However, it is crucial for effective therapy that the therapist maintains the appropriate therapeutic boundaries with the client. A therapist who is self-aware, alert to, *and mindful of*, the transference and counter-transference issues is unlikely to breach therapeutic boundaries.

(c) Transference and counter-transference

Although transference and counter-transference were originally psychoanalytic terms, these phenomena occur in any therapeutic interaction; some people claim they occur in all human interactions (Jacobs, 1988). When one is working with a woman who has sexually abused a child a key feature of the work will be examining inappropriate feelings, attitudes and behaviours within her relationships, both as an adult and as a child. Whether or not transference and counter-transference are used overtly as interpretations to the client, it is fundamental that the therapist be aware of them.

It is the role of the therapist to provide an environment safe enough for the woman to re-experience the traumas in her life but different enough to prevent her from becoming retraumatised by the therapy (Casement, 1990). If the therapist is not aware of the transference and the resulting counter-transference, he or she will act/react inappropriately and have difficulty in maintaining the necessary boundaries, thus possibly re-traumatising the woman and/or precipitating the breakdown of the therapy.

(i) Defining transference and counter-transference
Casement (1990) describes how aspects of objective reality within the therapist–client relationship can unwittingly trigger emotions and expectations associated with the original trauma. These feelings, attitudes and associated behaviours which are generated are related to past relationships of *both* client and therapist which may be introjected into the therapeutic relationship.

Transference. This is the term given to the displacement of emotions, attitudes, and behaviours applicable to other people in the client's life onto the therapist. It has been described as 'a concentration of a past attitude or feeling inappropriate to the present and directed *quite specifically* towards the other person' (Sandler, Dare & Holder, 1970, p.671).

Counter-transference. This is the term used for the feelings, attitudes and behaviours generated in the therapist. These feelings may be generated in the therapist by the transference of the client and thus are important in helping the client to gain insight into her behaviour. Additionally it may be the therapist's own emotional issues which are triggered by aspects of his or her work with this particular client (Casement, 1985). These feelings can be very detrimental to effective therapy. It is the task of the therapist to separate out what is current and real to the on-going situation with the client, what is transference, and which aspects of the counter-transference are a response to the client's transference and which are due to the therapist's own issues. Good clinical supervision, support and in some cases personal therapy, are essential to help the therapist to do so.

(d) Common transference issues

There are particular transference issues that it is important to be aware of when working with women who sexually abuse children. A common transference is the eroticising of the therapeutic relationship. This can occur whether the therapist is male or female. As many of the woman's previous one-to-one relationships have become sexualised, it is likely the woman will interpret actual, ostensibly innocuous, cues from the therapist as being associated with the therapist wanting a sexual interaction with her. Consequently she may act seductively or be very resistant to attending/participating in sessions, etc. Also when the woman experiences appropriate physiological arousal in therapy consistent with the emotional response to the matters being raised in therapy, she can inappropriately interpret this as sexual desire for the therapist. One woman eventually disclosed having sex with her partner as soon as she could after therapy. She said she felt it was the only way she knew how to deal with her 'sexual feelings' for the therapist. When she began to recognise and identify the actual emotions associated with her physiological arousal, she could act appropriately on them and her 'sexual desire for the therapist' was resolved. Working through these issues helped greatly in facilitating the woman to recognise how she had previously dealt in her life with any emotional arousal, that is by engaging in sexual activity.

Other typical transferences are derived from other aspects of the woman's own victimisation. She experiences herself as powerless, and expects the therapist to punish, criticise and/or reject her. Therefore the woman may become defensive. This defensiveness could manifest itself either as passivity and compliance or as hostility and threat. Additionally, the woman has learnt to gain some power and control over her environment by meeting the needs of others. Therefore she may either overtly and/or covertly, consciously and/or unconsciously attempt to discover many circumstances about the therapist and behave in a manner consistent with meeting what she perceives to be the needs of the therapist.

A woman is also likely to develop a perpetrator transference towards the therapist. This is evidenced by the woman *appearing* to use the therapy to obtain her needs in an unhealthy way. She will use similar techniques to those she used with her victims in her relationship with the therapist. These may be very subtle and are most easily accessed by the feelings these behaviours generate in the therapist. The therapist may begin to feel used, victimised, manipulated and/or deceived by the client.

(e) Common counter-transference issues

In consultation and supervision of several cases involving women who have sexually abused children, two specific patterns of counter-transference have been observed: over-involvement leading to protective behaviour towards the woman; and anger leading to punitive behaviour towards the woman. It is suggested that both these responses are related to the therapist's schema of women which has been challenged by the woman having sexually abused a child. Anger and minimalisation are typical and predictable responses to such a challenge (see Chapter 1).

The therapist who becomes 'over-involved' identifies with the woman's victim experience and colludes in minimising and/or excusing the perpetrating behaviour. This therapist may insist he or she is the only person the woman can, or will, work with. This therapist tends to break many boundaries with the woman and the case takes up a disproportionate amount of time. He or she tends to become very protective of the woman and shields her in every way possible. The therapist can be in greater denial than the woman with whom he or she is working and is easily convinced that, once the woman 'knows' it is wrong, she will not sexually abuse again. This response is likely to be a defence to protect the worker from addressing his or her own preconceptions of the sexuality of women. The therapist can facilitate the woman's having unsupervised access to children in order to prove she is trusted and/or rehabilitate her children with minimal therapeutic or practical intervention. The therapist tends to concentrate on the victim experience rather than the perpetrating behaviour. Therapists who behave in this way can exacerbate the likelihood of women reoffending by encouraging denial, endorsing the lack of responsibility for their own actions and consequentially of power and control in their own lives. Consequently in situations of stress the woman is likely to reoffend.

Although suppressing *overt* anger, other therapists while appearing to be firm and challenging, can go to the other extreme and become punitive towards the woman offender. They can harangue the woman to disclose offences she has not committed and admit to motivations she does not have. With no valid theoretical model underlying their actions, they tend to insist that the woman should engage in extreme, and often inappropriate, disclosure to her victims and other people in her life. Without any consideration of the children's wants or needs, they forbid access to all children, even supervised access. They will not consider the possibility of working with the woman and the child/ren, and thereby if at all possible, maintaining any positive aspects of the relationship between them. This behaviour is also a defence on the part of the therapist against the schema of women. These behaviours exacerbate the risk of the women reoffending by increasing their shame, isolation and feelings of powerlessness. These therapists concentrate on the offending behaviour and minimise the work on the woman's victim experience. Rather than having a collaborate relationship in which the woman can build up a sense of power and control in her life, she reinforces her model of adults as being punishing and rejecting. This in itself can make the woman feel more emotionally congruent with children and further exacerbate perpetrating behaviour.

Similar reactions such as those described as occurring in therapists have also been observed in agencies involved with women who have sexually abused children. Some workers identify, defend and virtually collude with the woman perpetrator while others can act punitively against her. Some workers trying to act realistically towards a woman who has sexually abused a child have found themselves professionally isolated.

CASE EXAMPLE 11.1

Two social workers had great difficulty in their area office when several members of their team refused to cooperate with them in any area of work after they persisted in their stand against returning children home to a coerced female offender. The woman was holding onto the defence that she was always 'forced' into sexually abusing her young children. She denied ever sexually abusing the children alone and appeared to be a concerned caring mother. She said she now had the full support of her 'estranged' father and stepmother who would help her care for the children. The children's anger and their reluctance to return to their mother was considered to be their response to her coerced behaviour and the social workers in favour of rehabilitation wanted to work with this. The dispute among the social workers, and the children's reluctance, led to the children being assessed over a long period of time by a child psychologist. The children eventually disclosed to the psychologist that their mother instigated a great deal of the sexual abuse as a sole perpetrator. At times the abuse was sexually sadistic and she had also watched their grandfather, her father, sexually assault them on many occasions.

CASE EXAMPLE 11.2

A child, aged $2\frac{1}{2}$, had a sore vagina. Her mother took the child to the GP who referred the child for paediatric examination. There were anal and vaginal signs consistent with digital penetration. The mother was extremely distressed and appeared desperate to find out who had sexually abused her daughter. She was a single parent who had no contact with the father and apparently had no other males in her life. The professionals made the assumption that the mother was the perpetrator and the child was removed from the home. All the mother's protestations were regarded as lying. Even the child's very good relationship with her mother, and her obvious distress at being removed from her mother, were seen as part of the mother's enmeshment with the child. The social worker told all the woman's family, friends and neighbours who had small children that she was a sexual offender. The woman became a complete recluse and made a very serious suicide attempt. Fortunately the child was placed with an excellent foster mother who noted statements the child had made consistent with it being a man who had sexually abused her. Gentle questioning by the foster mother resulted in the child disclosing in a non-sequential but very clear way that the abuser was the next door neighbour. When she was in her 'safe' enclosed back garden playing, the neighbour would call her, carry her over the fence and give her sweets and the odd small toy. He would penetrate her with his fingers and masturbate her, or get her to masturbate him. Even after the foster mother reported these disclosures to social services, two of the workers involved in the case still resisted the child being returned to her mother.

WORKING THE TIGHT-ROPE OF THE VICTIM/PERPETRATOR DIVIDE

Although it must never be denied that a woman who sexually abuses children has responsibility for the abuse she has perpetrated, until her victim issues are addressed it is doubtful whether she will be able to fully gain insight into her perpetrating behaviour. If it is solely the victim issues that are addressed prior to her perpetrating behaviour, there is often the tendency to use the victimisation as an excuse rather than as 'an empathy bridge' to her victim's experience. From experience, it seems that the most effective therapy has been done by walking the tight-rope of the victim/perpetrator divide (Eldridge, 1994). The victim issues are addressed and the insight gained applied in relation to the woman's perpetrating behaviour; why she sexually abused a child, how she facilitated that abuse and the effects on her victim.

GROUP VS INDIVIDUAL THERAPY

There is currently a general acceptance that group work is a preferred and useful method of working with male sex offenders. However, the most effective sex offender programmes contain additional individual work (Beckett et al., 1994). Matthews (1993) has also found group work to be effective with women who have sexually abused children. There have been very few reported attempts in this country to run groups for female sexual offenders. In the main this is due to not enough known female sexual offenders at compatible stages of treatment being in one place at one time. One group was run with women in a prison. Six women attended for ten sessions. The outcome measures indicated therapeutic improvement for the women. However, non-group workers were struck by the negative effect group participation appeared to have outside the group. The women became isolated and alienated from the other prisoners with whom they lived since, because of their group attendance, they became known as sex offenders. The women's only allies were each other and they became unhealthily supportive and collusive. Rather than challenge each other, they frequently found excuses and explanations for each other, thus inhibiting the development of a sense of responsibility for their own behaviour. These reactions may be a consequence of the relatively short length of the group, or of the fact that the women had to live with each other as well as attend the group. However, the reason might be because the programme was based on one devised for male sex-offenders and the women responded differently because of their differential socialisation.

These are important factors to consider when thinking about devising a group programme for women who sexually abuse children along the lines of those run for men. There have been many valid arguments against applying male models to work with women (e.g. Belenky et al., 1986; Gilligan, 1982). Group work can be an excellent, and in many cases a vital, adjunct to treatment but for women who sexually abuse children it is proposed that individual work is of primary importance. Until centres where such women can undergo full integrated treatment programmes are established individual therapy will be the main intervention for women.

SUMMARY

- Assessment of a woman who sexually abuses children aims to (i) make a judgement as to a woman's risk to children; (ii) assess which areas need specific work in therapy.
- Good assessment requires a theoretical model as to the factors that combine together to precipitate and increase and decrease risk of sexually abusive behaviour.
- The aims of therapy are to:
    (a) identify what problem/s her abusive behaviour solves;
    (b) find out how she has come to that 'solution';
    (c) find alternative 'solutions' to prevent relapse.
- Most women do not initially seek therapy of their own volition, thus work needs to be done to establish an effective relationship and overcome initial resistances.
- As a result of the inappropriateness of the boundaries in the lives of women who sexually abuse children, the importance of maintaining firm professional boundaries is emphasised.
- The most likely tranferences are to erotise the relationship with the therapist, to perceive the therapist as an abuser, and/or to emotionally threaten the therapist and try and gain power and control.
- The most common counter-transferences are protectiveness, due to identification with her victim experience, or an angry/punitive transference related to her confronting the therapist's schema of women as nurturers, sexually non-aggressive etc., because of her perpetrating behaviour.
- It is suggested that the most effective therapy is carried out by addressing victim issues and relating these to perpetrator issues.
- While the usefulness of group therapy is acknowledged the necessity for individual work is emphasised. Caution is given as to the dangers of taking methods successful with men and applying these directly to women.

12

THERAPEUTIC INTERVENTION

- THE PROCESS OF THERAPY
- ACCEPTING RESPONSIBILITY FOR PERPETRATING CHILD SEXUAL ABUSE
- DEVELOPING AN UNDERSTANDING OF HER PATTERN OF OFFENDING: CYCLES
- WORKING ON THE WOMAN'S VICTIMISATION BOTH AS A CHILD AND AS AN ADULT
- IDENTIFICATION AND REATTRIBUTION OF EMOTIONAL FEELINGS
- THE DEVELOPMENT OF BOTH INTELLECTUAL AND EMOTIONAL EMPATHY
- SEXUAL ISSUES
- RELATIONSHIP ISSUES: WITH PARENTS, PARTNERS, PEERS, CHILDREN
- AIDING THE DEVELOPMENT OF EMOTIONALLY INTIMATE RELATIONSHIPS
- SOCIAL SKILLS AND SOCIAL NETWORKS
- SELF-ESTEEM ISSUES
- POWER AND CONTROL
- RELAPSE PREVENTION
- SUMMARY

The purpose of this chapter is not to provide a prescription as to 'how to' conduct therapy with a woman who has sexually abused a child. The purpose is to highlight for experienced therapists the areas that are most likely to need addressing with such a woman along with some suggestions as to how it has been found useful to do so. The specific areas chosen as a focus for therapeutic intervention are based on the theoretical model presented in this book, which in turn is based on the research findings. For each of these areas the role of therapy in bringing about change will be considered, although it must be stressed that working on any one area will clearly involve facilitating change in other areas.

THE PROCESS OF THERAPY

The process of therapy aims to integrate knowledge, understanding and emotional experience in order to effect a change in behaviour. Eldridge (1995) describes this process as word and thought change, followed by feeling and belief change, which then leads to a behaviour change. Therapy aims to facilitate a better understanding of the factors, internal and external, that determine feelings and behaviour (Woodward, 1988). Thus a woman who sexually abuses a child needs to work through: (i) which need is being met by the sexual abuse of the child, (ii) how she came to believe that that was an effective and/or acceptable behaviour; (iii) how she manipulated the situation so she could act in the way she chose; (iv) the emotional effects both for her and the child of that experience; (v) what factors precluded her needs being met in other ways (internal and external); and (vi) ways other than offending to meet these needs in the future.

ACCEPTING RESPONSIBILITY FOR PERPETRATING CHILD SEXUAL ABUSE

Until a woman can take personal responsibility for the sexual abuse she has perpetrated she is more vulnerable to relapse, as she can still attribute some portion of blame away from herself. Some women apportion at least some responsibility and/or desire to the child. Some women describe sexual acts as the only way they know to love a child, as a result of their own childhood experiences. Other women, particularly co-offenders, attribute responsibility to the other abuser/s. In addition, women may also minimise their intention to harm and/or the use of the abuse to meet their own personal needs and/or the negative effects of the abuse they have perpetrated. Both denial of responsibility and minimisation are cognitive defences employed to make it more psychologically comfortable to engage in the behaviour. These defences are entrenched and can rarely be breached solely by argument. There are different levels of accepting responsibility. A woman may verbally accept responsibility for the abuse but still hold beliefs that also attribute blame to others and minimise the effects of the abuse. Even when these beliefs change, the woman may lack emotional empathy for her victims. The level at which the woman can accept responsibility for her behaviour often changes during therapy.

DEVELOPING AN UNDERSTANDING OF HER PATTERN OF OFFENDING: CYCLES

As they have such ready access to children, it can be easier for women than it is for men to deny that they plan their offending or that there is any pattern in their behaviour. However, it is important that a woman should recognise her pattern of offending if she is to gain any control over this behaviour. Particularly:

1. Identifying triggers that lead to her offending.
2. The beliefs that lead her to offend.
3. The way she targets and grooms children.
4. The part played by fantasy in her offending.
5. Her emotional and cognitive response to her own offences.

One way in which a woman can be helped to recognise her own pattern of offending is to use the notion of cycles of behaviour. If sexual offending were not rewarding for the perpetrator, she would not do it. As it is rewarding, it can become addictive. Everyone has the potential to become addicted to rewarding behaviours that may also have detrimental effects on ourselves and/or others (e.g. drinking alcohol, smoking, eating choc-olate, gambling, shopping, etc.). Such addictive behaviours usually form part of a cycle of behaviour (Figure 12.1).

Cycles can be inhibited or continuous (Figure 12.2; Eldridge, 1995). A cycle is inhibited if the person has any compunction about the behaviour and has to justify it to him/herself. A cycle is continuous if the person has no overt internal compunctions about the behaviour, therefore does not need to engage justification. Women who sexually abuse children can have inhibited or continuous cycles. Deriving a woman's cycle of abusing behaviour is a useful starting point, once the woman has committed herself to therapy. These cycles as applied to women offenders are the work of Hilary Eldridge and are included here with her permission.

The woman's cycle of offending can be used as a framework for therapy, and as a result of that therapy, the woman's cycle can be expanded and developed over time. For example, some women recognise they have

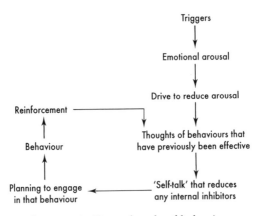

Figure 12.1: General cycle of behaviour

different cycles for different sexual behaviours. Some women realise that different triggers lead to different behaviours. Many women initially denied sexual fantasy but then after some work recognised they did think of sexual acts they had committed or wanted to commit.

CASE EXAMPLE 12.1

Sandra had a continuous cycle for sexual acts with her son such as intimate kissing, caressing, and mutual masturbation. She felt no guilt at these acts which occurred daily. However, she had an inhibited cycle in relation to sexual intercourse with him. After intercourse she would feel guilt and resolve never to do it again. Yet, particularly when Sandra felt she was at risk of 'losing him', she would convince herself that *he* wanted the additional bond and therefore would engage in intercourse with him.

CASE EXAMPLE 12.2

Doreen describes when she felt a need for intimacy she would engage in 'loving', 'gentle' sexual acts with her daughter. At other times when she was feeling hurt, or angry she would 'hurt her...sexually'. Both of these cycles were inhibited cycles.

Each aspect of the cycle can in itself be a focus of therapeutic sessions. This is especially useful for helping a woman begin to describe her triggers to offending; thus enabling the woman to begin to establish for herself the needs she met via the sexual abuse of a child. Different needs emerge over time as the woman develops greater knowledge of herself via therapy and

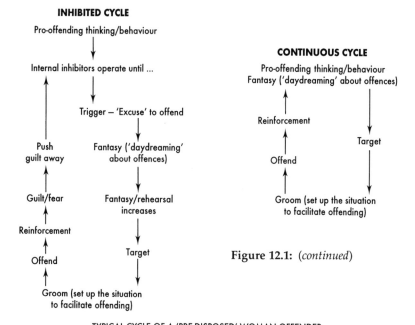

INHIBITED CYCLE

Pro-offending thinking/behaviour

Internal inhibitors operate until ...

Trigger — 'Excuse' to offend

Push guilt away

Fantasy ('daydreaming' about offences)

Guilt/fear

Fantasy/rehearsal increases

Reinforcement

Target

Offend

Groom (set up the situation to facilitate offending)

CONTINUOUS CYCLE

Pro-offending thinking/behaviour
Fantasy ('daydreaming' about offences)

Reinforcement

Target

Offend

Groom (set up the situation to facilitate offending)

Figure 12.1: (*continued*)

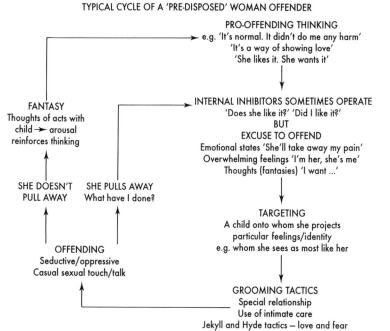

TYPICAL CYCLE OF A 'PRE-DISPOSED' WOMAN OFFENDER

PRO-OFFENDING THINKING
e.g. 'It's normal. It didn't do me any harm'
'It's a way of showing love'
'She likes it. She wants it'

FANTASY
Thoughts of acts with child → arousal reinforces thinking

INTERNAL INHIBITORS SOMETIMES OPERATE
'Does she like it?' 'Did I like it?'
BUT
EXCUSE TO OFFEND
Emotional states 'She'll take away my pain'
Overwhelming feelings 'I'm her, she's me'
Thoughts (fantasies) 'I want ...'

SHE DOESN'T PULL AWAY

SHE PULLS AWAY
What have I done?

TARGETING
A child onto whom she projects particular feelings/identity
e.g. whom she sees as most like her

OFFENDING
Seductive/oppressive
Casual sexual touch/talk

GROOMING TACTICS
Special relationship
Use of intimate care
Jekyll and Hyde tactics — love and fear

Figure 12.2: Offending cycles: typical cycles of women in each primary typology (reproduced with permission from Eldridge, 1995, p.T5) (*continues overleaf*)

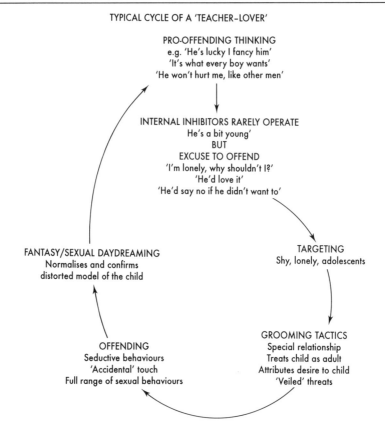

Figure 12.2 *(continued)*

other changes in her life. Once the needs are identified, other more appropriate ways in which the needs can be met can be cultivated.

An extension of the cycle work is to use the cycle to establish how the woman may have come to those beliefs or to engage in those particular patterns of behaviour. In doing so, the link between the patterns of abusing behaviour and her own experience of victimisation can begin to be developed.

WORKING ON THE WOMAN'S VICTIMISATION BOTH AS A CHILD AND AS AN ADULT

Over the past 20 years we have learnt much about the extensive and complex symptoms that human beings experience as a result of victimisa-

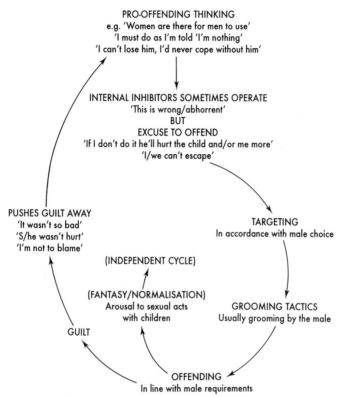

TYPICAL CYCLE OF A MALE-COERCED WOMAN OFFENDER

PRO-OFFENDING THINKING
e.g. 'Women are there for men to use'
'I must do as I'm told 'I'm nothing'
'I can't lose him, I'd never cope without him'

INTERNAL INHIBITORS SOMETIMES OPERATE
'This is wrong/abhorrent'
BUT
EXCUSE TO OFFEND
'If I don't do it he'll hurt the child and/or me more'
'I/we can't escape'

PUSHES GUILT AWAY
'It wasn't so bad'
'S/he wasn't hurt'
'I'm not to blame'

TARGETING
In accordance with male choice

(INDEPENDENT CYCLE)

(FANTASY/NORMALISATION)
Arousal to sexual acts
with children

GROOMING TACTICS
Usually grooming by the male

GUILT

OFFENDING
In line with male requirements

Figure 12.2 *(continued)*

tion (e.g. Briere & Runtz, 1993; Herman, 1992; Salter, 1995; Wyatt & Powell, 1988). The evidence for the helpfulness of abuse-focused therapy in dealing with the symptoms resulting from such victimisation is undisputed. It is very curious therefore why some people still resist working with the victimisation issues of perpetrators. Every woman who has been interviewed for this study has experienced victimisation, as a child, or as an adult, and for many throughout their lives. None of these women had received effective therapy for her own victimisation. The women's stories showed clear and often direct links between their own experience and that of their victims. It is proposed therefore that it is essential that the woman's victimisation should be worked on, if *real* change is to be established.

For each woman, her primary or most important attachment figure at the time she was being victimised was the person who abused her. Consequently, the woman is likely to have internalised the beliefs of the offender along with the associated emotional responses. Many cognitive distortions (thinking errors) she carries, she uses to justify the abuse she perpetrates. She in turn implants similar thinking errors into the minds of her victims (see Salter, 1995). She is unlikely to have had any alternative model of self, others and the world. Thus for psychological security, she will have selectively perceived aspects of any situation which reinforced this distorted view of the world and rejected any that challenged it. Direct challenge is thus likely to be unsuccessful whereas the whole of the therapeutic relationship can provide the woman with an alternative so that she can explore and challenge her own views. The woman needs to be helped to feel safe enough to tell her own history of victimisation: sexual, physical and emotional. She needs to have the space to understand how she gained the beliefs that she held and used to justify her perpetrating behaviour. She needs to make sense of her experience and the consequences of that experience for herself and her victims. It is walking this tight-rope between her experience of her victimisation and the abuse she perpetrated that has been found to be so useful.

IDENTIFICATION AND REATTRIBUTION OF EMOTIONAL FEELINGS

Survivors of abuse in childhood have great difficulty in modulating emotional arousal (van der Kolk,1988). As a result of the poor attachment patterns she had in her childhood, and the abuse she suffered as a child, each woman will have experienced difficult emotions for which she was unable to obtain appropriate care giving and thus assuagement (comfort).

> Stress → demand → caregiving → assuagement → latitude
> (Hanks & Stratton, 1988)

The children, however, must have latitude (freedom to act) so in the absence of care-giving they have to find a way of coping with such emotions. Therefore they become repressed and 'encapsulated' as 'unconscious sets' (Matte Blanco, 1975). This 'encapsulation' allows the children the latitude (freedom to act) but prevents learning about (i) relying on other people for care-giving and comfort, and (ii) appropriate modulation of emotional arousal (Figure 12.3).

Stimuli associated with the original trauma can trigger the repressed emotions (Casement, 1990); stimulus 'opens the unconscious sets'. These emotions are felt but they cannot be identified or modulated so alternative methods are resorted to (e.g. eating disorders, substance abuse, self-harm, stealing, re-exposure to trauma, etc.). Women who sexually abuse children

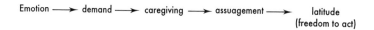

ATTACHMENT FIGURE IS RESPONSIVE/AVAILABLE

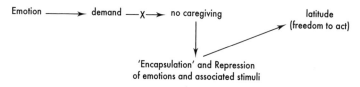

ATTACHMENT FIGURE IS UNRESPONSIVE/UNAVAILABLE

Figure 12.3

often misattribute other forms of emotional arousal to sexual and/or aggressive arousal and thus they modulate their arousal by the sexual abuse of a child.

During therapy it is hoped that the woman will experience feelings that throughout her life she has had to repress in order to survive. The therapist's role is to help her make connections between the source of the emotion and the emotion that she is feeling. It is likely however that the woman will be unable to identify and modulate these feelings. Salter (1995) describes how essential it is for the therapist to be 'affectively present'. She argues 'affective change does not occur in the absence of affect' (p.258). Throughout therapy the therapist needs to be 'affectively present' so that s/he can become aware of the emotional state of the client. At appropriate times, the therapist can explicitly reflect to the woman the emotion s/he believes she is feeling. Additionally, the woman can then be helped to identify the source of that emotion. This process is attempting to recreate for the woman the attenuation that she is likely to have missed in her early infancy (see Chapter 10). Therefore through acknowledging her emotions, helping her to identify them, and allowing her to express them within the safe environment of therapy and dissipate them, the woman can learn, over time, to modulate her own emotional state. She can also learn that sharing her emotions can become a source of appropriate comfort.

THE DEVELOPMENT OF BOTH INTELLECTUAL AND EMOTIONAL EMPATHY

The research shows that the woman who sexually abused children had no empathy for herself as a victim and hence had no empathy for her victim.

As the woman offender was psychologically blocked from recognising and modulating her own emotions, she would be equally psychologically blocked from recognising any negative emotion in others. Staub (1984) argues that empathy is an inhibitor of aggressive behaviour. This view has been endorsed by many who have worked with sexual offenders (e.g. Pithers, cited in Beckett et al., 1994). A distinction must, however, be made between intellectual empathy and emotional empathy. Intellectual empathy is being able to know and understand what a victim may feel and why. Emotional empathy is the ability to have an emotionally resonant response to the experience of another person. To develop intellectual empathy without emotional empathy might *increase* the likelihood of the sadistic offender abusing.

Emotional empathy is highly unlikely to be developed by cognitive challenge alone. When the woman is able to talk of her own victimisation and recognise the associated emotions, she will then be able to begin to recognise the emotional effects on her victims. By learning how to tolerate and modulate her own emotional distress, she is more likely to be able to tolerate and thus recognise distress in others. The level of emotional abuse that these women have experienced in their childhood means that they are very unlikely to have ever experienced emotional empathy. Therefore the therapist being emotionally present for the woman, feeling with her and reflecting back her emotional state, is likely to be essential if the woman is to learn to feel emotional empathy for her victims.

It is of interest that at this stage of therapy several women revealed more offences than they had previously disclosed. Some women also described a change in their affective reaction to 'sexual thoughts of children'. These women said that the sexual thoughts that used to be associated with arousal and excitement began to make them feel uncomfortable, distressed, and to experience great shame. Not all women experience this change, and specific work focusing on changing their patterns of sexual arousal is needed.

SEXUAL ISSUES

Many women, particularly those who have experienced sexual assault, whether as a child or as an adult, have deviant sexual thoughts that they find intrusive but which lead to sexual arousal. However, unlike the female perpetrators, very few of these women actually further develop and/or act on these thoughts. It seems important to enable the women perpetrators to talk about these thoughts without fear of censure. Thus they can be helped to learn to stop the thoughts and/or to manipulate them to become aversive rather than arousing. Sexual education has also been found to help reduce these thoughts and arousal to them (Larson & Maison, 1987).

Although these women have been involved in a great deal of sexual activity in their lives, they often have very limited knowledge about sex and sexuality. As a result of their life experience, the knowledge they do have is frequently distorted or completely inaccurate. For some women these distortions can be addressed as part of therapy but others may actually need a didactic programme of sex education. Larson and Maison (1987) have developed a sex education programme for women sex offenders in a prison setting. They suggest that the areas that need to be covered are: Childhood Sexuality; Puberty; Adolescent Sexuality; Body Image; Anatomy and Physiology of Sex; The Meaning of Sex; Masturbation; Sexually Transmitted Diseases; Male Sexuality; Homosexuality; Sexual Fantasy; Sexual Relationships; Sexual Dysfunction; Pregnancy and Childbirth; Prostitution; Rape; Sexual Variations; Sexual Abuse; Female Sexuality. Similar group learning courses are often put on by Women's Centres, Women's Groups, and Women's Therapy Centres. If such a course is not available, a professional involved with the woman, other than the primary therapist, may agree to undertake such an educative programme. This type of sexual education will raise many issues for the woman about her own past and present relationships.

RELATIONSHIP ISSUES: WITH PARENTS, PARTNERS, PEERS, CHILDREN

The woman offender will have learnt two primary patterns of interacting in relationships: as victim or as perpetrator. Consequently she is likely to have developed distorted views of relationships: particularly adult–child relationships and male–female relationships. The woman's patterns of, and beliefs about, relationships may be experienced in her relationship with the therapist (Chapter 11). She may also need to explore the similarities and differences in the relationships she has had throughout her life. For example, it may emerge that she has a specific pattern in her response to men and another in response to women (this can usually be seen in the relationships of many male-coerced offenders). It may be that she can be a moderately good-enough parent to boy children but sexually, physically and emotionally abuses girl children.

It is also highly likely that the woman will have developed inappropriate expectations about the needs and abilities of children, adolescents, and adults. These issues may partly be redressed by her working through her own victimisation. However, it may also be necessary for her to learn about developmentally appropriate interactions and behaviours through new experiences and/or reading and/or exploration.

If the woman is to remain in contact with other family members it may also be important that some joint work is carried out, preferably by another therapist or agency.

AIDING THE DEVELOPMENT OF EMOTIONALLY INTIMATE RELATIONSHIPS

None of the women who sexually abused children described experiencing emotional intimacy with anyone who did not abuse them. For these women emotional intimacy had always been associated with betrayal of trust and further exploitation. Developing an emotionally intimate but safe and clearly boundaried therapeutic relationship has been found to encourage the woman's ability to develop appropriate emotionally intimate relationships in other areas of her life and to find these rewarding and supportive rather than threatening.

SOCIAL SKILLS AND SOCIAL NETWORKS

For women who have never had the extended social networks most of us take for granted, this is one of the most difficult areas to deal with. This is particularly the case since it relies on the woman's acting alone: proactively. Often her self-esteem is too low to engage in activities that can lead to developing acquaintances and friends. For some women a first step can be to 'practise' by attending health or social service day centres or drop-in social centres. This will also give the woman some extra support during difficult times in therapy. For other women this is either not available or is not a suitable option. It may be possible there are people in the woman's life with whom she can begin to develop social contact. There may be people who previously she had kept herself away from: either physically or emotionally. Local social skills courses or assertiveness courses may also be of help in this area of work.

SELF-ESTEEM ISSUES

The very process of the therapeutic relationship in which the woman will experience a genuine, empathetic relationship and the unconditional positive regard of another human being, will undoubtedly raise her self-esteem.

One of the most persistent effects of long-term victimisation such as these women experienced is lowered self-esteem. Contributing to this lowered self-esteem are the internalised beliefs of the perpetrator and self-blame for the victimisation (Herman, 1992). Therefore making sense of a woman's life history, particularly her history of victimisation, as well as her perpetrating behaviour, can act to raise the woman' self-esteem.

Throughout therapy, facilitating the woman to find a sense of who she is *other* than a victim or a perpetrator can give her a foundation to develop other aspects of herself. In addition, improvements in the woman's social networks, activities she begins to undertake no matter how small and circumscribed at first, and being able to stop offending and thus not have to keep censurable 'secrets' will also add to an improved sense of self.

POWER AND CONTROL

Almost all the women perpetrators cited issues related to power and control as feelings related to the sexual abuse of children. Therefore it is important that the woman finds an alternative source for such feelings. Increases in self-esteem will give the woman an improved sense of control over her life. Also, stopping offending and finding other, more appropriate and ultimately more effective ways of dealing with her emotions is likely to make her feel more in control. Learning to be assertive in relationships and to solve problems effectively are also routes to improving her sense of competence and efficacy within her own environment. If she is still to have care of a child, child development and child-care work will help her to gain a better understanding and develop an appropriate level of control through good child care.

RELAPSE PREVENTION

Even after effective therapy, there will be times when a woman will find herself vulnerable to reoffending. Relapse prevention is a cognitive-behavioural intervention, *individually* formulated with each client, aimed at facilitating that client's maintaining control of the problem behaviour over time and across situations (Salter, 1988). The whole process of therapy should be part of relapse prevention, that is, learning aimed at preventing the recurrence of offending behaviour. A relapse-prevention plan requires

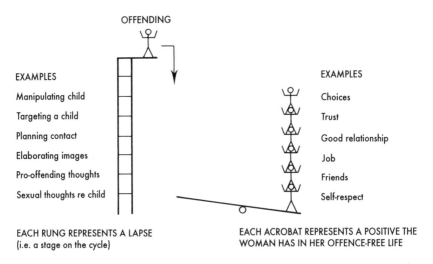

Figure 12.4: See-saw and diving board (reproduced with permission from Eldridge and Fairfield, 1993)

the woman to have specific conscious understanding of how to control her own cycle of behaviour. Eldridge (1995) describes how a personalised relapse-prevention plan is formulated with the offender so that she knows her own pattern of offending behaviour, recognises lapses when/if they occur, recognises her triggers to offending—be those feelings, thoughts, sights, smells etc.—finds alternative ways of dealing with these triggers, avoids high-risk situations, is able to recognise the difference between a lapse and a relapse, and to use effective coping mechanisms to prevent lapses leading to another offence against a child. Pithers (1990) suggests that in order to prevent offenders experiencing relapse prevention as 'an interesting intellectual exercise', it is best introduced after the woman has developed emotional empathy for her victim/s. Eldridge's relapse-prevention manual *Maintaining Change*, although written for men, can be used selectively with women offenders.

1. Lapse and Relapse

A lapse is one of the steps that lead up to offending; a relapse means committing a sexual offence against a child. The see-saw and the diving board is an analogy devised by a male perpetrator to illustrate the relapse-prevention process and the difference between lapse and relapse (Eldridge & Fairfield, 1993; Figure 12.4). The woman is first asked to describe each of the positive aspects that she would include in a life without offending. For each positive aspect an acrobat is drawn and labelled. The woman is then introduced to the idea that if she reoffends it will be like jumping off the diving board onto the other end of the see-saw; all the good aspects of her life that she has built up will be shattered. However, there is a build-up to the offence which is personal to each offender. Each step of the ladder is labelled with one aspect of that build-up (lapses). Her cycle of behaviour can be used to inform this process. It can then be seen that the woman can stop and reverse the process at any time up until the actual offence (relapse). A lapse can be reversed and not harm the positives in her life. A plan of intervention to prevent proceeding onto the next rung of the ladder can be worked out with the woman in order to prevent her committing the offence. Initially the woman writes down her plans but eventually it must become as integral a part of her life as offending once was.

SUMMARY

- The areas to be addressed in therapy are based on the assessment of the woman's individual needs.
- As the woman gains deeper understanding of the choices she made and the effects of her behaviour, the level of the acceptance of responsibility for the abuse changes.
- The woman's cycle of behaviour forms a good framework for beginning therapy. It is also vital for the development of a relapse-prevention plan.
- While not denying the importance of the woman's perpetrating behaviour, it is also important to work on her victim issues early in the course of therapy.
- Understanding her own victimisation and helping the woman to identify and express her emotions appropriately will 'free' her to be able to develop both intellectual and emotional empathy with her victim/s. Intellectual empathy is knowing the effect of the behaviour. Emotional empathy is being able to feel an emotional resonance with the victim's experience.
- An empathetic therapist can mirror the process of attenuation so that the woman learns to recognise and deal with her emotional feelings in a safer way.
- The woman may experience sexual arousal to deviant sexual thoughts and images. These thoughts can be managed by cognitive techniques of thought stopping and/or elaborating the images to include the effect on the child and the consequences for the woman should she act out the thoughts.
- The woman's beliefs, feelings and behaviour within relationships can be

explored via the therapeutic relationship and looking for patterns within specific types of relationship.

- The therapeutic relationship can help the woman experience a non-sexual, non-exploitative relationship.
- Outside agencies often need to be engaged in helping the woman develop an appropriate social network.
- The therapeutic process in itself will help improve the woman's self-esteem as well as helping her to feel more in control of her life and to develop aspects of herself that are not involved in victimisation and/or perpetration.
- Relapse prevention is an essential and integral part of therapy. It helps the woman to know her own patterns of behaviour and to develop appropriate responses to any lapses in order to prevent reoffending.

13

FINAL WORDS

Although not enough work has been carried out with women who sexually abuse children for research outcome studies of therapeutic intervention, individual case studies with good outcomes have been reported (e.g. Matthews, 1994). To end this book, three vignettes will be presented of women who have done well in therapy and for whom there is no evidence of reoffending.

CASE EXAMPLE—ANN

BACKGROUND

Ann was an only child and felt very neglected and isolated in her childhood. Her parents worked abroad and Ann was left with her maternal grandparents. When they had leave they often went on holiday and did not take Ann with them. Ann describes both her mother and grandmother as cold, rejecting and controlling women and her father as violent and selfish. Her grandfather seemed loving and caring but Ann was also frightened of doing anything to upset him. She described him as the only friend she ever had. Her grandfather sexually abused her during her childhood and even touched her sexually on her wedding day 'for old times sake'. Ann says the sexual acts with her grandfather was what made her feel loved, wanted and cared for.

Ann married when she was 16 and pregnant. On honeymoon Ann was beaten up by her husband and ended up in hospital. He left her the day their baby was born as it was a girl and he wanted a boy. When he left, Ann's grandfather would come to her home and have sex with Ann.

Ann said Mary had always been a disobedient and difficult child. Ann does not remember when she first started sexually abusing Mary, but they had always shared a bed and that it was then that she felt close to her and wanted to love her and be loved by her. The abuse was discovered when some things Mary said at school about their home life led to an investigation.

Ann was imprisoned for her sexual offences and in prison met and eventually married a Christian prison visitor. Ann described her life as 'totally changed'. She has no contact with her family of origin. She had become a Christian herself, described the man she married as totally wonderful. She had many friends within the church who knew of her offences but believed she was forgiven. The only mar to her happiness was that she had just given birth to a baby boy who had immediately been taken into care, due to her offences. She saw him for two hours daily and described him as a perfect child.

PRIOR TO STARTING THERAPY WITH ANN

An initial assessment was carried out with Ann. It was also recommended that a full risk assessment should be carried out with her new husband and of them as a couple. An independent assessment of Ann's relationship with her child was also carried out.

SOME ASPECTS OF THERAPY

Ann had excellent motivation to engage in therapy: the chance to care for her son. Even so, initially, she found it very difficult to engage in the work. She felt as if her new life was so perfect she would never sexually abuse a child again. She found it very difficult to revisit her past. The turning point in therapy came when she began to allow herself to recognise her feelings about her own abuse and then what she had done to her daughter. When she first came to therapy Ann admitted the abuse and said that she felt guilty about it. Later she was able to say that this was what she thought people wanted her to say but 'deep down' she did not feel she done any real harm to her daughter. She also confessed to thinking that people made too much fuss about sexual abuse as she did not feel bad about what had happened to her. However, while working on her own sexual abuse by her grandfather, Ann began to get terrible nightmares and daytime flashbacks, including powerful body memories of her grandfather's sexual acts with her. She described dreadful feelings of fear, disgust, and total helplessness. At this stage she wanted to give up therapy, saying it was destroying her new-found happiness. The nightmares and flashbacks proved vital in helping Ann recognise the feelings she had repressed for so long about her own abuse. Subsequently Ann was able to gain emotional empathy with her daughter's experience. The most difficult feeling Ann had to deal with was her guilt for what she had done to her daughter. Ann's distress at recognising this led to a real risk of her harming herself. She needed constant support from her husband and the friends she had made in the Church. If these people were not in her life, it is likely she may have had to have been admitted to hospital. Ann learnt to experience and recognise difficult feelings and also that her husband and friends could help her deal with them appropriately. Ann recognised that in the past virtually all her feelings were dissipated by the sexual abuse of her daughter. Ann also recognised she did not really know how to care for a child and thus acknowledged the work she needed to do to care for her son effectively.

WORK IN OTHER AREAS OF ANN'S LIFE

Unlike many situations with sexually abusing mothers there was a nonoffending parent. Ann's husband knew about Ann's offending but initially believed that now she was a Christian and married to him, she would not do it again. Work was carried out with him to educate him and to help him learn to protect the child and work with Ann to prevent her reoffending. The couple assessment led to the recognition of how childlike Ann was in her relationship with her husband. Couple work was carried out, focusing on developing a more equal relationship. The more work that was carried out with Ann in her individual therapy, the more assertive she became, which facilitated the couple work. Ann was also encouraged to develop a support network outside the Church. She went to mother and child groups where she met other young mothers and also met other women at college. Both Ann and her husband went to child-care classes and Ann also enrolled for child development courses at the local college as well as other courses such as word processing and computer skills. The contact time between Ann, her husband and the child was increased gradually until eventually they had full care of the child.

OUTCOME
The child was subject to a full care order but with residency with his parents. Ann, her husband and baby are still together and the child is now four years old and thriving. Ann has a part-time job and they have a social network both within and outside the Church community.

CASE EXAMPLE—ELLEN

INITIAL PRESENTATION
Ellen was 39 when she first came to therapy. She was reluctant to attend but it was a condition of her probation. She was referred because of her sexual 'relationships' with several teenage boys. She said she could not see any harm in what she was doing. She described the therapist, the probation officer and the courts as 'stuck-up', 'prudish' and 'jealous because she could attract young men'. For several sessions it appeared Ellen was saying what she thought people wanted to hear rather than accurately communicating her own inner thoughts and feelings.

BACKGROUND
Ellen was put into care when she was 12 as she and her two younger siblings had been abandoned by their mother when her mother's partner took a sexual interest in Ellen. Ellen had always been very independent, having been made to care for her siblings and her mother for many years. Ellen hated the restrictions of 'care' and constantly ran away. Once when on the run, she was given a lift by a middle-aged man who rented a flat for her to live in in return for sex. She describes him as 'a saviour who rescued her from care'. He 'sold her' to several of his friends but she describes it as 'paying her way'. This situation lasted for five years until she was 17 and ended when the man said his wife

had found out and threatened him. Ellen said she was devastated as she 'loved this man'. Ellen moved to London and got her own flat and a job in a hotel. She had many relationships with men all of whom ended up using and abusing her. She became pregnant in her early twenties. When her daughter reached her teenage years, it was her daughter's friends whom she engaged in sexual relationships.

SOME ASPECTS OF THERAPY
Ellen first appeared to become committed to therapy when she began to discuss how distressed and abused she felt within her relationships with male partners. She was helped to see the power imbalances in those relationships but she also held firmly onto the belief that she would not be happy unless she had a partner and was 'in love' and 'loved'. She also saw nothing at all abusive in her relationship with the middle-aged man who had had sex with her from when she was 12 until she was 17 and sold her to other men for sex. Ellen even blamed herself for the abandonment of her mother, as she had believed her mother who said Ellen had lured her partner away from her. These beliefs seemed very fixed and Ellen appeared to be repressing all her emotions in relation to these experiences. The breakthrough came when Ellen heard in discussion with another mother how that woman would have felt if it had been her own 12-year-old daughter who had been sexually approached by her partner. This woman also went on to reflect how she would feel if her daughter had been set up in a flat and sold for sex. As Ellen told of this experience, the therapist reflected back the feelings she detected from Ellen. Ellen began to cry. The next session Ellen attended therapy having written a detailed account of her sexual experiences as a teenager and the associated feelings. She had also drawn up a chart to show how her experiences were similar to those of her victims. From then the therapy was completed very quickly. Interestingly, Ellen initially dressed in clothes that would be described as 'teen-fashion'. During this period her whole manner of dress became far more age-appropriate.

OUTCOME
Ellen was a bright and efficient woman. She had previously done very well in the hotel business. She got a job as a receptionist and then was promoted to reception manageress and wants to develop her career further. She also has had two relationships with adult men. The first was with a married man but when she found out he was married, for the first time in her life, she ended a relationship. She is still happy in the relationship with her current partner.

CASE EXAMPLE—SUSAN

BACKGROUND
As a child Susan was sexually abused by her brother from when she was 11

until she was 14. She felt very rejected by her mother and had a much more positive relationship with her father. Susan was initially coerced into sexually offending by her husband Ted (see Case Example 4.13). Susan also sexually abused the children at times when Ted was not present. Like many male-coerced offenders, Susan attributed much of the responsibility for the sexual offences committed against her children to Ted but also minimised the seriousness of the effects and found excuses for his behaviour. Additionally, she also attributed some blame to the children they sexually abused. She saw them as 'very cooperative' and 'enjoying what was going on'. She seemed very angry with the children, who she perceived as coming between her and Ted, and she was able to say how jealous she was of their ability to 'get him aroused and make him happy'.

SOME ASPECTS OF THERAPY

Having made an assessment of the resistance Susan showed in her beliefs about the sexual abuse, the therapist asked her to focus on her relationship with Ted. Together they unpicked all the tactics that he had used to get her and her children into the situation in which she agreed to sexually abuse them with him. This gave her insight into just how calculating and premeditated his plans were but she still seemed unable to let go of her positive feelings for him. The therapist therefore asked Susan to think about her feelings towards men generally and the role they had played in her life. This led to Susan focusing on her relationship with her father; how important he was to her. During one such session Susan appeared to regress and described feeling that if she did not have her father's love she would face some indescribable terror. She then had the insight that this was what she had felt in her relationship with Ted; a complete terror of losing him which he fed by what he said and did to her. Susan was able to say how she feared that her daughters had a 'better' relationship with Ted than she did and that he wanted them more, and she was able to relate this to her childhood in which she believed she had a better relationship with her father than her mother had. After this session Susan seemed able to let go of the positive feelings of Ted and began to describe again the abuse they perpetrated against her daughters. This time she could do so in much more detail and was able to re-experience the feelings she had repressed, including envy, anger, and feelings of power and sexual arousal to the acts. She said that initially she felt that unless she agreed she would lose Ted and her daughters too as they would prefer to be with him. She herself made links between her feelings during these acts and her beliefs about the sexual acts with her brother. She talked about how she had told herself when she was abusing the girls how much they were enjoying it and how she had convinced herself that they had seduced Ted away from her. She also believed that the sexual acts did make them belong to each other. She described believing her brother when he said the sexual acts made them belong together. She described how as a child her body had responded to the sexual abuse by her brother, and his using this to convince her that she had seduced him, that she enjoyed and wanted the sexual acts and he was only doing it to please her. This was reinforced when her mother had walked in once on them having sex and her mother beat her and called her 'a little whore' and a 'slag' while saying nothing to her brother. During the session in which Susan 'relived' some of the abuse she experienced from her brother, she became extremely distressed, sobbing, rocking and holding her body to her. She said she felt as if she had *told herself for the first time* what she had really experienced and felt. After this Susan was able to recognise the feelings her daughters may have experienced during the abuse she perpetrated against them, both when she was coerced and as a sole perpetrator. Susan described her grief, shame and guilt as almost unbearable.

OUTCOME
Susan's daughters were in care while she was in prison. Unfortunately this was not a good experience for them and they had been in three different foster homes and two children's homes. They had both been in therapy and the therapy with their mother informed the therapy with the girls. Both girls had individually asked to see their mother. Susan initially said she felt too ashamed to face them but was persuaded by their need to do so. Individual meetings were arranged during which each girl was able to tell her mother what she felt about what had happened. Therapy continued for all three of them and the girls, who are now in their mid-teens, visit their mother frequently and stay with her some weekends. Susan lives alone for the first time ever and is building a life for herself. She is beginning to make friends and has joined an aerobics group to try and meet more people. Although she says that she would like another relationship sometime, she says she feels that will be in the distant future; she needs to know who she really is first.

APPENDICES

APPENDIX 1: THE CHILDREN THE WOMEN TARGETED

Women Who Targeted 'Prepubertal Children'

CASE	AGE OF WOMAN AT INTERVIEW	CHILDREN (OWN) AGE OF CHILD WHEN WOMAN INTERVIEWED	CHILDREN (OTHER) AGE OF CHILD WHEN WOMAN INTERVIEWED	AGE OF CHILD/REN WHEN ABUSED
1A	24	♀* ♂ 5 1	none	1–4 #
2A	25	♀* ♀* ♀ 7 5 3	none	2½–6 # 2–4#
3A	56	♀* 39	none	1½–8 #
4A	26	♂ ♀* 9 6	none	birth–4 #
5A	29	♂ ♂ ♂* 7 6 4½	none	¼ –4½ #
6A	30	♀* ♂ 11 ½	none	4 mths–5 #
7A	40	♂* ♂* 19 17	none	2–14 # 2–8 ~
8A	28	♀* ♂* ♀* ♀* ♂ 11 9 7 5 2	♀* ♂* ♂* 4 14 14 + others mainly 0–6	½–5 # 1–3 # birth–½ # birth # 3–4 # 13–14 # 14 # others #
9A	22	♂* ♀* 5 3	none	2½–4 # 2–2½ #
10A	26	♂ ♂ ♀* ♂* 10 8 6 4	none	1½–5 # 3 (once) ~
11A	22	none	♂* 6 (nephew)	5–5½ #
12A	32	♂* ♀ ♀ 16 8 8	none	3–14 #
13A	24	♀* ♀* 7 6	♀* 11 (niece)	4–5 # 3½–4 # 3 (twice) ~
14A	44	♂* ♂* ♀* 27 26 24 ♀* ♂* (d.17) 21	none	birth–6 ~ birth–5 ~ birth–12 @ birth–6 ~ birth–11 ~

KEY: *–sexually abused child; ~–woman stopped the behaviour; @–child stopped adult, ran away or told; #–found out or stopped by others

Women Who Targeted Adolescent and/or Preadolescent Children

CASE	AGE OF WOMAN AT TIME OF INTERVIEW	CHILDREN (OWN) AGE OF CHILD WHEN WOMAN INTERVIEWED	CHILDREN (OTHER) AGE OF CHILD WHEN WOMAN INTERVIEWED	AGE OF CHILD/REN WHEN ABUSED
1B	42	♂* ♀ 17 14	none	10–17 @
2B	32	♂* 17	none	10–15 #
3B	27	none	♂* ♂* 16 17 nephew	13–14 @ 12–13 #
4B	48	♀ 32	♂* 28	13–15 @
5B	37	♂* ♀ ♀ 21 17 14	none	8–17 @/#
6B	34	♀ 2½	♂* 16	14–15 @
7B	26	none	♀* ♀* ♀* 14 15 14	13 @ 14@ 13@
8B	43	none	♀* 21	13–15 #
9B	34	♂ ♀ ♀ 17 13 12	♂* 17	14–16 #
10B	44	♂* 35 (stepson)	none	13–14 @

KEY
*–sexually abused child
~–woman stopped behaviour
@–child stopped adult, ran away or told
#–found out or stopped by others

Women Initially Coerced into Sexually Abusing by Men
(Þ = women who also abused as sole perpetrators)

CASE	AGE OF WOMAN AT TIME OF INTERVIEW	CHILDREN (OWN) AGE OF CHILD WHEN WOMAN INTERVIEWED	CHILDREN (OTHER) AGE OF CHILD WHEN WOMAN INTERVIEWED	AGE OF CHILD/REN WHEN ABUSED
1C	37	♀* ♂ ♂ 17 5 4	none	13–15 ~
2C	39	♀ ♀* 13 10	none	8–10 ~
3C Þ	36	♂* ♂* ♀* ♂* 25 24 17 16 (own & stepchildren)	♀ * 24	12–16 # 11–15 # 4–8 # 3–7 # 15(once) #
4C Þ	36	♂ ♀* ♀ 16 15 13	none	birth -11 #
5C Þ	34	♂* ♂* ♀* ♀* 17 15 14 12	♂* ♂* ♀* ♀* 15 13 13 11 (nephews and nieces)	9–14 # 8–13 # 9–11 # 8–9 # 11–12 # 10 (once) # 9–10 # 8 (twice) #
6C Þ	31	♀* ♀* 13 11	none	12–13 # 10–11 #
7C Þ	26	♀* ♀* 8 7	none	4–7 # 3–6 #
8C	21	♀* 6	none	4–5 ~
9C Þ	46	♀* ♂ ♀ 26 23 20	none	1–15 @
10C	44	♂ ♀ ♀ ♀ ♂ 24 23 21 18 16	♀* 19	14–16 @
11C Þ	28	none	♀* 15	14 @
12C Þ	20	♀* 5	none	2–4 #

KEY
*–sexually abused child
~–woman stopped the behaviour
@–child stopped adult, ran away or told
#–found out or stopped by others

APPENDIX 2: THE WOMEN'S OWN EXPERIENCE OF SEXUAL ABUSE

The Women's Experience of Sexual Abuse in Their Childhood
(Women who initially target young children)

WOMAN	WHEN ABUSE BEGAN	DURATION	PERPETRATOR/S
Jenny 1A	From as young as can be remembered	On and off →12	father & male babysitter
Jean 2A	From as young as can be remembered	→ 16 then left	father
Sophia 3A	From as young as can be remembered	→ 6 when abuser died	grandfather
Doreen 4A	From as young as can be remembered	→ 19 when able to leave foster home	father → age 6 foster father 6 → 19
Connie 5A	From as young as can be remembered	→ 13 she ran away 14 →in care 15 →prostitution	father various various
Amanda 6A	From age 3 when left to live with grandparents	→ 16 left to get married	grandfather
Mavis 7A	From as young as can be remembered	→ when went into prison age 36	father brothers
Mary 8A	From age 3 when went to live with grandmother	→adulthood when her perpetrating behaviour was discovered	older brothers various men in the village & male relations
Rebecca 9A	Thinks from age 3 after mother died can't remember before	→ 17 left home when pregnant	father first child father's baby
Karen 10A	From as young as can be remembered	→ 6 mother remarried	mother
Pat 11A	From about 4/5	→ 22 when arrested	stepbrother 12 years older
Sarah 12A	From as young as can be remembered	→ 22 when grandfather died	mother →5 grandfather →22
Theresa 13A	From as young as can be remembered	→ 8 grandmother died	grandmother
Vera 14A	From as young as can be remembered	→ 20 when left home to marry	father then also brother

The Women's Experience of Sexual Abuse in Their Childhood
(Women who initially target adolescents)

WOMAN	WHEN ABUSE BEGAN	DURATION	PERPETRATOR/S
Glenda 1B	14	→ 15	47-year-old 'boyfriend'
Sandra 2B	12	→ 16	male teacher
Nancy 3B	13/14	two incidents	raped on two separate occasions by mother's lovers
Liz 4B	14	→ 16	37-year-old 'boyfriend'
Pam 5B	8	→17	stepfather
Angela 6B	11	→ 14	mother's 'live-in' lover
Alice 7B	11 13		raped by her first 'boyfriend' gang-raped on way home from school
Rosie 8B	12	→ 16	'relationship' with female teacher (age late 30s)
Melanie 9B	10 12 13	one-off →13 →14	uncle another uncle mother's lover became 'her lover' (age about 40)
Fiona 10B	7	→ 17	stepfather

The Women's Experience of Sexual Abuse in Their Childhood
(Women who were initially coerced offenders)

WOMAN	WHEN ABUSE BEGAN	DURATION	PERPETRATOR/S
Joanne 1C	7	→ 11	stepbrother
Joan 2C	Not sexually abused in childhood		
Cathy 3C	Not sexually abused in childhood		
Diane 4C	14	2 weeks	brother
Celia	7	one off	mother's lover
5C	9	one off	coach driver on school trip
	11	over 6 months	16-year-old neighbour
Susan 6C	11	→ 14	older brother
Paula 7C	8	→ 10 intermittently	brother
Penny 8C	Not sexually abused in childhood		
Carol 9C	From as young as can be remembered	→ 17	father and mother
Tina 10C	7	one off	stranger
	10	→ 14	older brother
Carrie 11C	From as young as can be remembered	→ 27 when arrested	father
Nicola 12C	10	→ 15	mother (perverse abuse see Case Example 1.3)

The Women's Experience of Sexual Abuse in Their Childhood
(The comparison group)

WOMAN	WHEN ABUSE BEGAN	DURATION	PERPETRATOR/S
Judy 2D	11	two incidents	'friend' of the family
Christine 8D	15	→ 17	grandfather
Sharon 14D	7	→ 8	uncle
Gillian 17D	6	→ 10	stepfather
Carol 23D	9	one off	stranger
Frances 30D	From as young as can be remembered	→ 14	father
Wendy 31D	12	14	brother

APPENDIX 3: THE QUESTIONNAIRES USED

(For details of the construction of these questionnaires see Saradjian, 1992)

1. 'What Sex Means' Questionnaire

TICK THE 6 STATEMENTS THAT BEST DESCRIBE WHAT BEING SEXUAL
WITH SOMEONE MEANS TO YOU—You may add your own if you prefer

——It brings me pleasure

——It is the way to really feel part of someone's life

——It is an ordeal I go through to keep my relationship

——It makes me feel warm and cared for

——It makes me feel used

——It's how you show someone you really love them

——It makes me feel very close to someone

——It's how I can completely give myself to someone I love

——It gives me a sense of being in control

——It gives me a release of tension and makes me feel calm

——It's a bonding with someone

——It makes me feel invaded, at risk

——'It's the most fun you can have without laughing'

——It gives me a feeling of power

——It makes me feel loved

——It makes me feel glowing, alive and physically good inside

——It gives me a way to hurt someone, get my own back

——It makes me feel attractive and desired

——It means absolutely nothing to me

——It is a way of giving pleasure to someone I love

——It makes me feel humiliated

——It fulfils a physical need in me

——The very thought of being sexual makes me feel nauseous

——Being sexual means forming a complete union with someone

CATEGORIES INTO WHICH THE STATEMENTS ARE CLASSIFIED
Positive Physical Feelings—to experience a positive physical feeling
Negative feelings—any negative feeling as a result of the sexual act
Bonding—to engage in a sexual relationship in order to form or maintain a specific involvement in the life of the partner
Emotional Warmth—to feel warmth, intimacy and care
Give Pleasure—to give pleasure to the partner
Own Pleasure—for one's own good feelings that are not related to other positive feelings
Power and Control—use of the sexual act to gain feelings of power and control over others

2. Repertory Grid

The Repertory Grid (Kelly, 1955) was used to explore how the women experience various aspects of their lives. The women rated on a scale of 1–7 aspects of themselves and also of other people (elements) on various characteristics (constructs). Eight constructs were provided so comparisons could be made on these constructs. Four further constructs were elicited from each woman and added to the list of constructs. The final version of the Repertory Grid used for this study had the following elements and constructs.

ELEMENTS
Self
Ideal self
Self as a child
Self as an adolescent
Self as an abuser
Mother
Father
Childhood abuser (if any and if more than one major abuser the major ones)
Partners (major ones)
Child (1)
Child (2) etc.
Other major people in the woman's life
An ideal mother
An ideal father
An ideal child
An ideal partner
CONSTRUCTS
Affectionate/loving/Non-affectionate/cold
Able to cope alone/ dependent
Can form close relationships/ Finds it difficult to form close relationships
I can trust/ I cannot trust
In control of own life/ No control over own life
Wanting sexual contact/ no desire for sexual contact
Aggressive/ Unaggressive
Cares for me/ Does not care for me
PLUS 4 ELICITED CONSTRUCTS
The grid (*overleaf*) was analysed by the GRAN program (Leach,1988). In this way how similarly the women perceived various aspects of themselves and other people in their lives to be to each other can be accessed. Some of the women's constructs were also compared by using non-parametric tests.

3. Dependency Grid

Many theorists as to why incest occurs hypothesise that socio-economic factors which increase stress play an important role. Thus to explore these issues Kelly's Situational Resources Repertory Test (1955, p.361), usually referred to as the Dependency Grid, was used. This enquires about who the person had in their world to whom they could refer when they had problems. She was asked to list the problems that she found that she most commonly experienced and also to add any

7	SELF NOW	FATHER	MOTHER	CHILD ETC.	IDEAL SELF	SELF AS CHILD	IDEAL FATHER	CHILDHOOD ABUSERS	IDEAL MOTHER	PARTNER/S ETC.	IDEAL CHILD	SELF AS AN ADOLESCENT	IDEAL PARTNER	SELF AS AN ABUSER	1
AFFECTIONATE															UNAFFECTIONATE
ABLE TO COPE ALONE															NOT ABLE TO COPE ALONE
CAN FORM CLOSE RELATIONSHIPS															CANNOT FORM CLOSE RELATIONSHIPS
I CAN TRUST															I CANNOT TRUST
IN CONTROL OF OWN LIFE															NO CONTROL OVER OWN LIFE
WANTING OF SEXUAL CONTACT															NOT WANTING OF SEXUAL CONTACT
AGGRESSIVE															NOT AGGRESSIVE
CARES FOR ME															DOES NOT CARE FOR ME

	FATHER	MOTHER	SIBLING	ABUSED CHILD	PARTNER	FRIEND	FRIEND	DOCTOR	PROFESSIONAL	PROFESSIONAL
MONEY										
PARENTS										
LONELINESS										
ANGER										
ILLNESS										
DEPRESSION										
PARTNER										
CHILDREN										
NEIGHBOURS/FRIENDS										
AT THE END OF YOUR TETHER										

other problems she experienced not on the list. The women were also asked to assess the frequency of those problems in their lives on a scale from ALMOST ALWAYS (4)–ALMOST NEVER (0).

4. Emotional Abuse

Each woman was asked to estimate on a four-point scale (0–3) the degree of emotional abuse she experienced in each of these categories during four periods of childhood: infancy, early childhood, school age and adolescence. (Min=0; Max=60).

DEFINITIONS AND EXAMPLES OF EMOTIONAL ABUSE (based on Garbarino, 1986)

REJECTION—behaviours that lead child to feel abandoned (active)
e.g. refusal to touch or acknowledge the child
e.g. adult does not talk or smile at the child, and/or actively refuses to meet the child's needs

e.g. refusing the child physical contact and comfort; placing child away from the family

e.g. constantly refers to the child negatively, name calling, belittling, scapegoating, verbal abuse and criticism

e.g. leaving the child or expelling from the family

IGNORING—parent being emotionally unavailable to the child; showing little or no attention to the child (*passive*)

e.g. fails to respond to child's needs; not noticing child

e.g. coldness to child; not responding to conversation; leaving child without engaged adult

e.g. non-protection of child from assault by siblings, peers or family members; no interest in child or child's life

e.g. ignoring the child and concentrating on other relationships

TERRORIZING—creating a climate of fear by threatening and scaring a child and by unreasonable discipline

e.g. teasing, scaring, subjecting the child to intense stimuli

e.g. verbal threats of extreme harm raging at the child; threats of the ghosts, monsters, etc.

e.g. place child in double-binds so that they can never get it right; changing the rules; constant criticism

e.g. public humiliation of the child, or the threat of exposure ridiculing the child

ISOLATING—preventing child's involvement in normal social experiences

e.g. leaving the child alone for long periods; denying child access to others

e.g. prevents child from being with other children

e.g. prohibit the child's play with other children; refuse to allow children into the home to play; withdraw child from school

e.g. prohibiting child from social and sports activities; keeping child home to fulfil household tasks; punishing child for normal social acts

CORRUPTING—rewards or reinforces anti-social behaviour, especially aggressive or sexual behaviour or substance abuse

e.g. creating drug dependence, encouraging illegal substance misuse

e.g. rewarding the child for aggression or inciting child to be aggressive to other children

e.g. involving child in sexual behaviour; encouraging sexually aggressive behaviour; exposing child to pornography; rewarding child for sex; involving child in prostitution

e.g. rewarding delinquent behaviour

APPENDIX 4: CARERS

Carers are the interpreters through which children learn about themselves, their feelings and the interactions between them and the world. We take as an example a child who falls over and cuts her knee while wearing a clean pair of long white socks which become covered in blood.

RESPONSE—PARENT 1

Empathetically: 'You poor thing, what a nasty accident that must really have hurt. Come and let me clean it up for you. It'll be a bit sore when I do this but we have to

get any dirt out or else it'll be worse. There, the worst is over. Let me give you a hug. Now we'll change your socks. Don't worry, the blood will come out in the wash and they'll be as good as new.'
RESPONSE—PARENT 2
Angrily: 'You stupid, clumsy child, look what you've done. You've ruined those socks. They were clean on today. Get them off and give them here.' (Wipes knee) 'Stop whining, or I'll give you something to whine for. It's your own fault for being so clumsy and giving me extra washing to do. I'll never get those clean.'

In both scenarios the same events took place but what the child learnt was dramatically different. In the first scenario the child learnt that it was good and cared for and that the pain was part of the accident and not attributed to some negative internal characteristic within the child. The child also learnt the source of the pain that she was experiencing and that it would soon end and that comfort was available in times of distress.

In the second scenario, the child learnt that she had done something that upset her carer, that it was her fault and that she had no right to feel pain; her feelings were not valid. Any pain she did feel was her fault, no comfort was available, and she had in fact done something irreparable and in the process hurt and alienated her carer. The pain of the child would therefore be exacerbated with feelings of fear of abandonment. There is no way that a child constantly subjected to an environment in which responses to her needs were of the kind described in the second scenario, would be able to accurately interpret her feelings of arousal. This of course would be even more profound if she had been physically and sexually abused by people who were in the position of carer towards her.

Appendix 5: AREAS TO BE COVERED IN ASSESSMENT

Issues Related to the Offending Behaviour

- When her offending behaviour began, the number of victims, the degree of her sexual conditioning and arousal to children, i.e. how central sexual offending is in her life.
- Level of responsibility taken for perpetration of the sexual abuse, including minimisation, denial and/or justification of offences committed.
- Level of responsibility taken for the effects of the sexual abuse on the child/ren, including minimisation, denial and/or justification of the effects.
- The degree of sadism in her offending behaviour.

The Formative Years: Infancy to Adolescence

- Genogram (family tree) to look for patterns of relationships within her family history.
- Details of relationship with her mother/maternal figure and her model of mothering. Any real alternative models that were available to her and whether these had been internalised.

- Details of relationship with her father/paternal figure and her model of fathering. Any real alternative models that were available to her and whether these had been internalised.
- Her own history of abuse: physical, sexual and emotional; and intervention, if any, that occurred. The degree of empathy the woman has for herself as a child enduring the abuses.
- The cognitive distortions the woman holds about herself as a result of her own abuse (hence the cognitive distortions that she is likely to make in relation to the child).
- Relationships with siblings and/or peers throughout childhood, including both possible alternative positive models and/or negative figures.
- Estimation of the kind of attachments she had in her early life, and the degree to which she repeats these as an adult.
- Her experience of adolescence, particularly issues of separation and individuation; was it possible for her to separate from the family model, or was it further reinforcement of her childhood experience?

Relationships with Self and Others

- Her self-esteem and level of control she feels she has over her own life.
- How aggressive she perceives herself to be.
- Degree of impulsivity in her reactions and behaviours.
- Her perception of her ability for closeness/intimacy.
- Adult peer relationships, and her experience of non-sexual, emotionally intimate relationships.
- Her adult partners with whom she has sexual relationships. Her feelings about these partners and those relationships.
- The involvement any of these partners still has in her life, and the ability of that partner to be a non-abusive partner and an adult protector of children (a full independent assessment of a permanent partner is recommended).

Stresses, Social Support and Coping Mechanisms

- The levels of stress in her life at the time of offending and currently.
- Degree of social isolation, her current and present social support network, and her ability to realistically and effectively use social support.
- Ability to understand, recognise and label her emotions. How she deals with her own stress and physiological arousal.
- Her current and past mental health history.
- Use of alcohol and other disinhibitors (e.g. child pornography).
- Whether she uses any 'extreme' belief systems to explain her behaviour.

The Children the Women Targeted

- The beliefs and expectations the woman specifically holds about child/ren she targeted and their inter-relationship/s.

- The cognitive distortions the woman holds about the children's experience of the sexual abuse, in particular how 'sexual' she perceives the child to be, and the control she attributes to the child in relation to the abuse.
- The beliefs and expectations the woman generally holds about children and their relationships to adults.
- The woman's understanding of child development.
- The degree of identification she feels generally with children and her ability to separate from those children she abuses.
- Whether or not the woman has tried to severely physically assault the child/ren.

The Woman's Experience of Sex

- The woman's perception of her sexuality.
- Her sexual feelings within adult relationships.
- Her sexual feelings while sexually abusing a child.
- Her use of 'sexual fantasy', 'sexual daydreaming' and masturbatory fantasies.
- Alternative sources through which her biosocial goals could be met.

General

- Her ability to recognise and describe her cycle of abuse.
- Her motivation and commitment to undergo the therapy necessary for her to change her patterns of behaviour.

During the interview details of the woman's emotional and behavioral responses should be noted, along with any difficulties, reluctance or refusal to answer any questions.

REFERENCES

Abramson, L. Y., Seligman, M. E. P. & Teasdale, J. D. (1978). Learned helplessness in humans: Critique and reformulation. *Journal of Abnormal Psychology*, **87**, 49–74.

Ainsworth, M. D., Blehar, M. C., Waters, E. & Wall, S. (1978). *Patterns of Attachment: Assessed in Strange Situations and at Home*. Hillsdale, NJ: Lawrence Erlbaum.

Akil, H., Watson, S. J., Young, E., Lewis, M. E., Khachaturian, H. & Walker, J. M. (1984). Endogenous opioids: Biology and function. *Annual Reviews of Neuroscience*, **7**, 223–255.

Allen, C. (1962). *A Textbook of Psychosexual Disorders*. London: Oxford University Press.

Allen C. M. (1991). *Women and Men Who Sexually Abuse Children: A Comparative Analysis*. New York: The Safer Society Press.

Amir, S. (1986). Catalepsy induced by body pinch: Relation to stress-induced analgesia. *Annals of the New York Academy of Science*, **467**, 226–237.

Anderson, C. & Mayers, P. (1982). Treating family sexual abuse: The Humanistic Approach. *Journal of Child Care*, **1**, 31–45.

Anisman, H. (1978). Neurochemical changes elicited by stress: Behavioral correlates. In H. Anisman, & G. Bignami (Eds), *Psychopharmacology of Adversely Motivated Behaviour*. New York: Plenum.

Araji, S. & Finkelkhor, D. (1983). *Explanation of Paedophilia: Review of Empirical Research*. Durham, NH: University of New Hampshire Press.

Araji, S. & Finkelkhor, D. (1986). Abusers: A review of the research. In D. Finkelkhor, *A Sourcebook on Child Sexual Abuse*. Beverly Hills, CA: Sage.

Argyle, M. (1983). *The Psychology of Interpersonal Behaviour*. (4th edn). Harmondsworth:Penguin Books.

Armstrong, L. (1978). *Kiss Daddy Goodnight*. New York: Pocket Books.

Averill, J. R. (1973). Personal control over aversive stimuli and its relationship to stress. *Psychological Bulletin*, **80**, 286–303.

Bagley, C. (1988). *Child Sexual Abuse in Canada: Further analysis of the 1983 National Survey*. Ottawa: National Health and Welfare.

Bagley, C. & King, K. (1990). *Child Sexual Abuse: The Search for Healing*. London: Routledge.

Bagley, C. & Ramsey, R. (1986). Sexual abuse in childhood: Psychosocial outcomes and implications for social work practice. *Journal of Social Work and Human Sexuality*, **4**, 33–47.

Baisden, M. J. & Baisden, J. R. (1979). A profile of women who seek counselling for sexual disfunction. *American Journal of Family Therapy*, **7**, 68–76.

Baker, A. W. & Duncan, S. P. (1985). Child sexual abuse: A study of prevalence in Great Britain. *Child Abuse and Neglect*, **9**, 457–467.

Bandura, A. (1977), *Social Learning Theory*. Engelwood Cliffs, NJ: Prentice-Hall.

Bandura, A. (1979). Self-efficacy: Towards a unifying theory of behaviour change. *Psychological Review*, **84**, 191–215.

Banning, A. (1989). Mother–son incest: Confronting a prejudice. *Child Abuse and Neglect*, **13**, 563–570.

Bass, E., & Thornton, L. (1983). *I Never Told Anyone: Writings by Women Survivors of Child Sexual Abuse*. New York: Harper & Row.

Beckett, R. (1994). Assessment of sex offenders. In T. Morrison, M. Erooga & R. Beckett (Eds), *Sexual Offending Against Children*. London: Routledge.

Beckett, R., Beech, A., Fisher, D. & Fordham, A. S. (1994). Community-based treatment for sex offenders: An evaluation of seven treatment programmes. London: HMSO.

Belenky, M. F., Clinchy, B. M., Goldberger, N. R. & Tarule, J. M. (1986). *Women's Ways of Knowing*. New York: Basic Books.

Benton, D. & Brain, P. F. (1988). The role of opioid mechanisms in social interaction and attachment. In R. J. Rodgers & S. J. Cooper (Eds), *Endorphines, Opiates and Behavioral Processes*. Chichester: Wiley.

Bentovim, A. (1991). Significant harm, quoted in M. Adcock, R. White and A. Hollows (Eds), *Significant Harm: Its management and outcome*. Croydon: Significant Publications.

Benward, J. & Densen-Gerber J. (1975). Incest as a causative factor in anti-social behaviour: An exploratory study. *Contemporary Drug Problems*, **4**, 323–340.

Berkowitz, L. (1969). The Frustration-Aggression Hypothesis revisited. In L. Berkowitz (Ed.), *The Roots of Aggression*. New York: Atherton.

Bliss, E. L. (1984). A symptom profile of patients with multiple personalities including MMPI results. *Journal of Nervous and Mental Disease*, **172**, 197–202.

Block, J. H. & Block, J. (1980). The role of ego control and ego resiliency in the organisation of behaviour. In W. A. Collins (Ed.), *Development of Cognition, Affect and Social Relations*. Hillsdale, NJ: Lawrence Erlbaum.

Bloom, K. (1981). *Prospective Issues in Infancy Research*. Hillsdale, NJ: Lawrence Erlbaum.

Blumberg, M. L. (1978). Child sexual abuse: Ultimate in maltreatment syndrome. *New York State Journal of Medicine*, **78**, 612–616.

Bolton, F. G., Morris, L. A. & MacEachron (1989). *Males at Risk: The Other Side of Sexual Abuse*. London: Sage.

Bowlby, J. (1969). *Attachment and Loss*, vol. 1: *Attachment*. London: Hogarth Press.

Bowlby, J. (1980). *Attachment and Loss*, vol. 3: *Loss, Sadness and Depression*. London: Hogarth Press.

Bowlby, J. (1988). *A Secure Base: Clinical Applications of Attachment Theory*. London: Routledge.

Boyd, A. (1991). *Blasphemous Rumours: Is Satanic Ritual Abuse Fact or Fantasy? An Investigation*. London: Fount Paperbacks.

Brady, K. (1979). *Father's Days: A True Story of Incest*. New York: Dell.

Bremer, J. (1989). Addressing the sexual abuser: Components of treatment. Paper presented at Mental Health Aspects of Sexual Abuse Conference, Huddersfield.

Bretherton, I. (1985). Attachment theory: Retrospect and prospect. In Bretherton, I. and Waters, E., Growing points of attachment theory and research. *Monographs of the Society for Research in Child Development*, **50**, Nos 1–2, Serial no. 209.

Bretherton, I. & Waters, E. (1985). Growing points of attachment theory and research. *Monographs of the Society for Research in Child Development*, **50**, Nos 1–2, Serial no. 209.

Brewin, C. R. (1988). *Cognitive Foundations of Clinical Psychology.* London: Lawrence Erlbaum.

Briere, J. (1984). The effects of childhood sexual abuse on later psychological functioning: Defining a post-sexual abuse syndrome. Paper presented at the Third National Conference on Sexual Victimisation of Children, Washington, DC.

Briere, J. (1988). The long term clinical correlates of childhood sexual victimisation. *Annals of the New York Academy of Sciences,* **528,** 27–34.

Briere, J. & Runtz, M. (1985). Symptomology associated with prior sexual abuse in a non-clinical sample. Paper presented at the annual meeting of the American Psychological Association, Los Angeles.

Briere, J. & Runtz, M. (1993). Childhood sexual abuse: Long-term sequelae and implications for psychological assessment. *Journal of Interpersonal Violence,* 8(3), 312–330.

Brown, G. L. & Goodwin, F. K. (1984). Diagnostic, clinical and personality characteristics of aggressive men with low 5-HIAA. *Clinical Neuropharmacology,* 7(1), 756–757.

Brown, G. W. & Harris, T. (1978). *Social Origins of Depression.* London: Tavistock.

Brown, G. W., Andrews, B., Harris, T., Adler, Z. & Bridge, L. (1986). Social support, self-esteem and depression. *Psychological Medicine,* **16,** 813–831.

Brown, M. E. (1979). Teenage prostitution. *Adolescence,* **14** (56), 665–680.

Browne, A. & Finkelhor, D. (1986). Initial and long-term effects: A review of the research. In D. Finkelhor (Ed.), *A Sourcebook on Child Sexual Abuse.* Beverly Hills, CA: Sage.

Brownmiller, S. (1975). *Against Our Will: Men, Women and Rape.* Harmondsworth: Penguin Books.

Burgess, A., Groth, N., Holstrom, L. & Sgroi, S. (1978). *Sexual Assault of Children and Adolescents.* Lexington MA: Lexington Books.

Burgess, A. W., Hazelwood, R. R., Rokous, F. E., Hartman, C. R. & Burgess, A. G. (1987). Serial rapists and their victims: Re-enactment and repetition. Presented at the Annals of the New York Academy of Science Conference on Human Sexual Aggression. New York City: Current Perspectives.

Burgess, A. & Holmstrom, L. (1979). Adaptive strategies and recovery from rape. *American Journal of Psychiatry,* **136,** 1278–1282.

Buss, D. M. (1987). Sexual differences in human mate selection criteria: An evolutionary perspective. In C. Crawford, M. Smith & D. Krebs (Eds), *Sociobiology and psychology: Ideas, Issues, and Applications.* Hillsdale, NJ: Lawrence Erlbaum.

Butler, S. (1978). *Conspiracy of Silence* San Francisco: New Gilde.

Butler, S. (1985). *Conspiracy of Silence: The Trauma of Incest* (2nd edn). San Francisco: Volcano Press.

Cameron, D. & Fraser, E. (1987). *The Lust to Kill.* Cambridge: Polity Press.

Canada (1984). Sexual offenses against children, vols 1–2. (Report of the Committee on Sexual Offenses Against Children and Youth.) Ottawa: Federal Department of Justice, Health and Welfare.

Carmen, E., Rieker, P. P. & Mills, T. (1984).Victims of violence and psychiatric illness. *American Journal of Psychiatry,* **141,** 378–383.

Casement, P. (1985). *On Learning From The Patient.* London: Tavistock.

Casement, P. (1990). *Further Learning From The Patient.* London: Tavistock.

Cavanagh-Johnson, T. (1989). Female child perpetrators: Children who molest other children. *Child Abuse and Neglect,* **13,** 571–585.

Chasnoff, I. R., Burns, W. J., Schnoll, S. H., Burns, K., Chisum, G. & Kyle-Spore, L. (1986). Maternal–neonatal incest. *American Journal of Orthopsychiatry*, **56** (4), 577–580.

Check, J. V. P., Perlman, D. & Malamuth, V. M. (1985). Loneliness and aggressive behaviour. *Journal of Social and Personal Relationships*, **2**, 243–252.

Chesler, P. (1972). *Women and Madness*. New York: Doubleday.

Christie, M. J. & Chesher, G. B. (1982). Physical dependence on physiologically released endogenous opiates. *Life Science*, **30**, 173–177.

Cicchetti, D. & Rizley, R. (1981). Developmental perspectives on the etiology, intergenerational transmission and sequelae in child maltreatment. In R. Rizley and D. Cicchetti (Eds), *New Directions in Child Development*. Washington, DC: Jossey-Bass.

Coe, C. L., Wiener, S. G., Rosenberg, L. T. & Levine, S. (1985). Endocrine and immune responses to separation and maternal loss in non-human primates. In M. Reite, & T. Field, (Eds), *The Psychobiology of Attachment and Separation*. London: Academic Press.

Cohen, S. & Wills (1985). Stress, social support and the buffering hypothesis. *Psychological Bulletin*, **98**, 310–357.

Cole, P. M. & Putnam, F. W. (1992). Effect of incest on self and social functioning: A developmental psychopathology perspective. *Journal of Consulting and Clinical Psychology*, **60**, 174–184.

Condy, S. (1987). Parameters of sexual contact of boys with women. *Archives of Sexual Behaviour*, **16**, 379–394.

Coons, P. M. (1984). The differential diagnosis of multiple personality. *Psychiatric Clinics of North America*, 7:1, 51–67.

Coons, P. M. (1986). Child abuse and multiple personality disorder: Review of the literature and suggestions for treatment. *Child Abuse and Neglect*, **10**, 455–462.

Coons, P. M. & Milstein, V. (1986). Psychosexual disturbances in multiple personality: Characteristic etiology and treatment. *Journal of Clinical Psychiatry*, **47**, 106–110.

Cooper, A. J., Swaminath, S., Baxter, D. & Poulin, C. (1990). A female sexual offender with multiple paraphilias: A psychologic and endocrine case study. *Canadian Journal of Psychiatry*, **35**, 334–337.

Dancia, E. (1988). *Don't: A Woman's Word*. London: The Women's Press.

Darke, J. L. (1990). Sexual aggression: Achieving power through humiliation. In W. L. Marshall, D. R. Laws & H. E. Barbaree (Eds), *Handbook of Sexual Assault*, New York: Plenum Press.

Dawkins, R. (1976). *The Selfish Gene*. Oxford: Oxford University Press.

Dawson, J. & Johnson, C. (1989). When the truth hurts. *Community Care*, 30 March.

Depue, R. & Spoont, M. (1986). Conceptualising a Serotonin Trait: A Behavioral Dimension Of Constraint. *Annals of the New York Academy of Sciences*, The Psychobiology of Suicide, pp. 47–62.

DeYoung, M. (1982). *The Sexual Victimisation of Children*. Jefferson, NC: McFarland.

Dietz, P. Hazelwood, R. & Warren, J. (1990). The sexually sadistic criminal and his offenses. *Bulletin of the American Academy of Psychiatry & Law*, **18**, 163–178.

DSM III (1987) *Diagnostic and Statistical Manual of Mental Disorders*, 3rd edn revised. Washington DC: American Psychiatric Association.

Duck, S. W. (1973). Similarities and perceived similarity of personal constructs as influences on friendship choice. *British Journal of Social and Clinical Psychology*, **12**, 11–6.

Dunn, J. (1988). Sibling influences on childhood development. *Journal of Child*

Psychology and Psychiatry, **29**, 119–128.

Egeland, B., Jacobvitz, D., & Sroufe, L. A. (1988). Breaking the cycle of abuse: Relationship predictors. *Child Development,* **59**, 1080–1088.

Egeland, B. & Sroufe, L. A. (1981). Developmental sequelae of maltreatment in infancy. In R. Rizley & D. Cicchetti (Eds), *Developmental Perspectives in Child Maltreatment.* San Francisco: Jossey-Bass.

Eldridge, H. (1991) (1992) (1994). Personal Communications.

Eldridge, H., (1995). *Maintaining Change: A Relapse Prevention Manual for Adult Male Perpetrators of Child Sexual Abuse.* Birmingham: The Faithfull Foundation.

Eldridge, H. & Fairfield, J. (1993). Personal Communication.

Elliot, M. (1993). *Female Sexual Abuse of Children: The Ultimate Taboo.* Harlow, Essex: Longman.

Epstein, S. (1980). The self-concept: Review of the proposal of an integrated theory of personality. In E. Staub (Ed.), *Personality: Basic Issues and Current Research.* Englewood Cliffs, NJ: Prentice-Hall.

Erikson, E. H. (1950). *Childhood and Society.* New York: Norton.

Erikson, E. H. (1968). *Identity: Youth and Crisis.* New York: Norton.

Erikson, E. H. (1977). *Toys and Reasons.* New York: Norton.

Fairbairn, R. (1952). *Psychoanalytic Studies of the Personality.* London: Routledge.

Faller, K. (1987). Women who sexually abuse children. *Violence and Victims,* **2**, 4, 263–276.

Faller, K. (1988). *Child Sexual Abuse. An Interdisciplinary Manual for Diagnosis, Case Management and Treatment.* New York: Columbia University Press.

Fehrenbach, P. A. & Smith. W., Montaskersy, C. & Deisher, R. W. (1986). Adolescent sexual offenders: Offender and offense characteristics. *American Journal of Orthopsychiatry,* **56**, (2), 225–233.

Finkelhor, D. (1979). *Sexually Victimised Children.* New York: Free Press.

Finkelhor, D. (1984a). *Child Sexual Abuse: New Theory and Research.* New York: The Free Press.

Finkelhor, D. (1984b). How widespread is child sexual abuse? *Children Today,* **13**, 18–20.

Finkelhor, D. (1986). *A Sourcebook on Child Sexual Abuse.* Beverly Hills, CA: Sage.

Finkelhor, D. (1988). *Nursery Crimes: Sexual Abuse in Day Care,* in association with Williams, L. & Burns, N. Newbury Park, CA: Sage.

Finklehor, D. & Russell, D. (1984). Women as perpetrators. In Finklehor, D., *Child Sexual Abuse: New Theory and Research.* New York: The Free Press.

Fisher, D. (1994). Personal Communication based on unpublished MSc thesis carried out with women who self-mutilate.

Flavin, P. (1991). quoted in the article 'Not Men Only' by S. Barwick in *The Spectator,* 1 June.

Fogel, A., Melson, G. F. & Mistry, J. (1986). Conceptualising the determinants of nurturance: A reassessment of sex differences. In A. Fogel & G. F. Melson (Eds), *Origins of Nurturance: Developmental, Biological and Social Perspectives on Caregiving.* Hillsdale, NJ: Lawrence Erlbaum.

Forward, S. & Buck, C. (1978). *Betrayal of Innocence: Incest and its Devastation.* Harmondsworth: Penguin Books.

Franselow, M. S. & Bolles, R. C. (1982) Conditioned fear-induced opiate analgesia. *Behaviour and Brain Science,* **5**, 320–323.

Fraser, S. (1989). *My Father's House; A Memoir of Incest and of Healing.* London: Virago.

Freud, A. & Dann, S. (1951). An experiement in group upbringing. In Rackbill &

Thompson (Eds), *Behaviour in Infancy and early Childhood*. New York: Free Press.

Freud, S. (1930). *Civilization and its Discontents*. New York and London: Pelican Freud Library (1963).

Friedman, S. & Harrison, G. (1984). Sexual histories, attitudes and behaviour of schizophrenic and 'normal' women. *Archives of Sexual Behaviour*, **13**, 555–567.

Fritz, G. T., Stroller, K. & Wagner, N. (1981). A comparison of males and females who were sexually molested as children. *Journal of Sex and Marital Therapy*, **7**, 54–59.

Furniss, T. (1991). in 'Not Men Only' in *The Spectator*, 1 June.

Gagnon, J. (1965). Female child victims of sex offence. *Social Problems*, **13**, 176–192.

Garbarino, J. (1986). *The Psychologically Battered Child*. New York: Jossey-Bass.

Garfield, S. L. & Bergin, A. E., (1986). *Handbook of Psychotherapy and Behaviour Change*. 3rd edn. New York: Wiley.

Gergen, K. J. (1987). Towards self as relationship. In K. Yardley & T. Honess (Eds), *Self and Identity: Psychological Perspectives*, Chichester: Wiley.

Gilbert, P. (1984). *Depression: From Psychology to Brain State*. London: Lawrence Erlbaum.

Gilbert, P. (1988). Emotional disorders, brain state and psychological evolution. In W. Dryden & P. Trower (Eds), *Developments in Cognitive Psychotherapy*. London: Sage.

Gilbert, P. (1989). *Human Nature and Suffering*. London: Lawrence Erlbaum.

Gilligan, C. (1982). *In a Different Voice*. Cambridge: Harvard University Press.

Goodwin, J. (1994). Sadistic abuse: definition, recognition and treatment. In V. Sinason (Ed.), *Treating Survivors of Satanist Abuse*. (pp. 33–44). London: Routledge.

Goodwin, J. (1993). *Rediscovering Childhood Trauma. Historical Case Book and Clinical Applications*. Washington, DC: American Psychiatric Press.

Goodwin, J. & Divasto, P. (1979). Mother–daughter incest. *Child Abuse and Neglect*, **3**, 953–957.

Gorst-Unsworth, C. (1992). Adaptation after torture: Some thoughts on the long-term effects of surviving a repressive regime. *Medicine and War*, **8**, 164–168.

Greaves, G. (1992). Alternative hypotheses regarding claims of satanic cult activity: A critical analysis. In D. Sakheim and S. Devine (Eds), *Darkness and Light: Satanism and Ritual Abuse Unveiled* (pp. 45–72). Lexington, MA: Lexington Books.

Gross, R. J., Doerr, H., Caldirola, D., Guzinski, G. M. & Ripley, H. S. (1980). Borderline syndrome and incest in chronic pelvic pain patients. *International Journal of Psychiatry in Medicine*, **10**, 79–86.

Groth, N. (1979). *Men who rape*. New York: Plenum.

Groth, N. (1982). The incest offender. In S. M. Sgrogi (Ed.), *Handbook of Clinical Intervention in Child Sexual Abuse* (pp. 215–239). Lexington, MA: Lexington Books.

Groth, N. (1983). Treatment of the sexual offender in a correctional institution. In J. Greer & I. Stuart (Eds), *The Sexual Aggressor: Current perspectives on Treatment* (pp. 160–176). New York: Van Nostrand Reinhold.

Guillemin, R., Vargo, J., Rossier, S., Minick, S., Ling, N., Rivirt, C., Vale, W. & Bloom, F. (1977). β-endorphin and adrenocorticotropin are secreted concomitantly by the pituitary gland. *Science*, **197**, 1367–1369.

Haley, J. (1990). *Strategies of Psychotherapy*, 2nd edn. Rockville, MD: Triangle Press.

Hanks, H. (1989). Personal Communication.

Hanks, H., Hobbs, C., & Wynne J. (1988). Early signs and recognition of sexual abuse in the pre-school child. In K. Browne, C. Davies & P. Stratton, (Eds), *Early Prediction and Prevention of Child Abuse*. Chichester: Wiley.

Hanks, H., Hobbs, C. & Wynne J. (1989). Article in the *Observer* newspaper.

Hanks, H. & Saradjian, J. (1991). Women who abuse children sexually: Characteristics of sexual abuse of children by women. *Human Systems: The Journal of Systematic Consultation and Management*, **2**, 247–262.

Hanks, H., & Stratton, P. (1988). Family perspectives on early sexual abuse. In K. Browne, C. Davies and P. Stratton (Eds), *Early Prediction and Prevention of Child Abuse*. Chichester: Wiley.

Harlow, H. F. & Mears, C. (1979). *Primate Perspectives*. New York: Wiley.

Harper, R. C. (1985). Power, dominance and non-verbal behaviour: An overview. In S. L. Ellyson & J. F. Dovidio (Eds), *Power, Dominance and Non-verbal Behaviour*. New York: Springer-Verlag.

Hartup, W. W. (1983). Peer relations. In P. H. Mussen (Ed.), *Handbook of Clinical Psychology*, vol. 4. *New York: Wiley*.

Hartup W. W. (1986). On relationships and development. In W. Hartup and Z. Rubin (Eds), *Relationships and Development*. Hillsdale, NJ: Lawrence Erlbaum.

Helfer, R. E. & Kempe, C. H. (Eds) (1968). *The Battered Child*. Chicago: University of Chicago Press.

Henderson, S. (1974). Care eliciting behaviour in man. *Journal of Nervous and Mental Diseases*, **159**, 172–181.

Herman, J. L. (1981). *Father–Daughter Incest*. New York: Harvard University Press.

Herman, J. L. (1986). Histories of violence in an outpatient population: An exploratory study. *American Journal of Orthopsychiatry*, **56**, 137–141.

Herman, J. L. (1990). Sex offenders: A feminist perspective. In W. L. Marshall, D. R. Laws & H. E. Barbaree (1990). *Handbook of Sexual Assault. Issues, Theories and Treatment of the Offender*. New York: Plenum Press.

Herman, J. L. (1992). *Trauma and Recovery*. London: Pandora.

Hill, S. & Goodwin, J. (1989). Satanism: Similarities between patient accounts and pre-Inquisition historical sources. *Dissociation*, **2**(2), 39–43.

Hinde, R. A. (1979). *Towards Understanding Relationships*. London: Academic Press.

Holubinskyj, H. & Foley, S. (1986). Escape or rescue: Intervention in a case of mother/daughter incest with an adolescent girl. *Australian Journal of Sex, Marriage and the Family*, **8**, (1), 27–31.

Hopper, E. (1991). Encapsulation as a defence against the fear of annihilation. *International Journal of Psychoanalysis*, **72**, 607.

Howell, D. C. (1986). *Statistical Methods for Psychology*, 2nd edn. Boston: Duxbury.

Hudson P. S., (1991). *Ritual Child Abuse: Discovery, Diagnosis and Treatment*. Saratoga: CARE.

Hunter, M. (1990). *Abused Boys—the Forgotten Victims of Child Sexual Abuse*. New York: Jossey-Bass.

Jacobs, M. (1988). *Psychodynamic Counselling in Action*. London: Sage.

Janoff-Bulman, R. (1992). *Shattered Assumptions*. New York: Free Press.

Janssen, M. (1983). *Silent Scream: I Am a Victim of Incest*. Philadelphia: Fortress Press.

Jehu, D. (1988). *Beyond Sexual Abuse: Therapy with Women who were Childhood Victims*. Chichester: Wiley.

Johnson, R. L. & Shrier, D. (1987). Past sexual victimisation by females of male patients in an adolescent medicine clinic population. *American Journal of Psychiatry*, **5**, 650–652.

Jonker, F. & Jonker-Bakker, P. (1991). Experiences with ritualistic child sexual abuse: A case study from the Netherlands. *Child Abuse and Neglect*, **15**, 191–6.

Kahn, R. L. & Antonucci, T. C. (1980). Convoys of social support: A life-course approach. In P. B. Baltes and O. G. O'Brien (Eds), *Life Span Development and Behaviour*, vol. 3. New York: Academic Press.

Kaplan, A. G. (1990). How normal is normal development? Some connections between adult development and the roots of abuse and victimisation. In Martha B. Straus (Ed.), *Abuse and Victimisation across the Lifespan* (pp. 127–139). Baltimore and London: Johns Hopkins University Press.

Kelley, S. J. (1989). Stress responses of children to sexual abuse and ritual abuse in day care centres. *Journal of Interpersonal Violence*, **4**, 502–513.

Kelley, S. J. (1993). Ritualistic abuse of children. In C. J. Hobbs & J. M. Wynne (Eds), *Bailliere's Clinical Paediatrics International Practice and Research. Child Abuse*, **1** (1), 31–46. London: Bailliere Tindall.

Kelly, G. (1955). (1963). *A Theory of Personality. The Psychology of Personal Constructs.* New York: Norton.

Kempe, R. (1979). *Child Abuse Within the Family*. CIBA Foundation, London: Tavistock.

Kempe, R. & Kempe, C. H. (1978). *Child Abuse*. London: Fontana.

Kercher, G. & McShane, M. (1984). The prevalence of child sexual abuse victimisation in an adult sample of Texas residents. *Child Abuse and Neglect*, **8**, 495–502.

Kinsey, A. C., Pomeroy, W. B., Martin, C. E. & Gebhard, P. H. (1953). *Sexual Behaviour in the Human Female*. Philadelphia: W. B. Saunders.

Knopp, F. H., & Lackey, L. B. (1987). Female Sexual Abusers: A summary of data from 44 treatment providers. The Safer Society Program of the New York State Council of Churches, Orwell, VT.

Kohut, H. (1985). *Self Psychology and the Humanities: Reflections on a New Psychoanalytic Approach*. New York: Norton.

Komisaruk & Whipple, B. (1986). Vaginal stimulation produced analgesia in rats and women. *Annals of the New York Academy of Sciences*, **467**, pp. 30–39.

Kramer, S. (1980). Object cohesive doubting: A pathological defensive response to maternal incest. *Journal of the American Psychoanalytic Association*, **31**, 325–351.

Krug, R. S. (1989). Adult male report of childhood sexual abuse by mothers: Case descriptions, motivations and long term consequences. *Child Abuse and Neglect*, **13**, 1111–1119.

LaFontaine, J. S. (1993). Defining organised sexual abuse. *Child Abuse Review*, **2**, 223–231.

LaFreniere, P. & Sroufe, L. A. (1985). Profiles of peer competence in the preschool: Interrelations between measures, influence of social ecology, and relation to attachment history. *Developmental Psychology*, **21**, 58–68.

Lambert, M. J. (1989). The individual therapist's contribution to psychotherapy process and outcome. *Clinical Psychology Review*, **9**, 469–485.

Larson, N. R. & Maddock, J. W. (1986). Structural and functional variables in incest family systems. In T. S. Trepper & M. J. Barrett (Eds), *Treating Incest: A Multimodal Systems Perspective*. New York: The Haworth Press.

Larson, N. R. & Maison, S. R. (1987). *Psychosexual Treatment Program for Women Sex Offenders in a Prison Setting*. Minnesota: Meta Resources.

Laub, D. & Auerhahn, N. C. (1993). Knowing and not knowing massive psychic trauma forms of traumatic memory. *International Journal of Psycho-Analysis*, **74**, 287–302.

Laws, D. R. & Marshall, W. L. (1990). A conditioning theory of the etiology and maintenance of deviant sexual preference and behaviour. In W. L. Marshall, D. R. Laws & H. E. Barbaree (Eds), *Handbook of Sexual Assault. Issues, Theories and*

Treatment of the Offender. New York: Plenum Press.

Lawson C. (1993). Mother-on sexual abuse: Rare or underreported? A critique of the research. *Child Abuse and Neglect*, **17**, 261–269.

Lazarus, R. S. (1966). *Psychological Stress and the Coping Process*. New York: McGraw-Hill.

Lazarus, R. S., Kanner, A. D. & Folkman, S. (1980). Emotions: A cognitive phenomenological analysis. In R. Plutchik & H. Kellerman (eds), *Emotion: Theory, Research and Experience*, vol. 1. New York: Academic Press.

Leach, C. (1988). GRAN: A computer program for the cluster analysis of a repertory grid. *British Journal of Clinical Psychology*, **27**, 173–174.

Leavy, R. L. (1983). Social support and psychological disorder: A review. *Journal of Community Psychology*, **11**, 2–21.

Lewis, I. A. (1985). [*Los Angeles Times Poll* #98] Unpublished raw data cited in D. Finkelhor, *A Sourcebook of Child Sexual Abuse*. Beverly Hills, CA: Sage.

Lidz, R. W. & Lidz, T. (1969). Homosexual tendencies in mothers of schizophrenic women. *Journal of Nervous and Mental Diseases*, **149** (2), 229–235.

Linnoila, M. et. al. (1983). Low cerebrospinal fluid 5-hydroxyindoleacetic acid concentration differentiates impulsive from non-impulsive violent behaviour. *Life Sciences*, **33**, 2609–2614.

Longdon, C. (1992a). Quoted in an article by S. Young in the *Observer*, 1 March.

Longdon, C. (1992b). Paper given at the Conference on Female Sexual Offenders, held at Central Hall Westminster, 31 March 1992.

Los Angeles County Commission for Women. Ritual Abuse Task Force (1989). Ritual abuse: Definitions Glossary, The Use of Mind Control. 15 September.

Lukianowicz, N. (1972). Incest: I Paternal incest. II Other types of incest. *British Journal of Psychiatry*, **120**, 301–313.

McCarty, L. (1986). Mother–child incest: Characteristics of the offender. *Child Welfare*, **65** (5), 447–458.

McFadyen, A., Hanks, H. & James, C. (1993). Ritual abuse: A definition. *Child Abuse Review*, **2**, 35–41.

McKellar, P. (1989). *Abnormal Psychology: Its Experience and Behaviour*. London: Routledge.

McNaron, T. A. H. & Morgan, Y. (Eds) (1982). *Voices in the Night: Women Speaking out about Incest*. San Francisco: Cleis Press.

MacFarlane, K. (1982). Personal Communication, quoted in Russell, D. E. H. & Finkelhor, D. (1984) Women as perpetrators: Review of the evidence, in D. Finkelhor, *Child Sexual Abuse*. New York: Free Press.

MacFarlane, K. & Waterman, J. (1986). *Sexual Abuse of Young Children*. London: Holt, Reinhart and Winston.

Mahler, M., Pine, F. & Bergmann, A. (1975). *The Psychological Birth of the Human Infant*. London: Hutchinson.

Main, M. & George, C. (1985). Responses of abused and disadvantaged toddlers to distress in agemates: A study in daycare setting. *Developmental Psychology*, **21** (3), 407–412.

Main, M. & Goldwyn, R. (1984). Predicting rejection of her infant from mother's representation of her own experience: Implications for the abused–abusing intergenerational cycle. *Child Abuse and Neglect*, **8**, 203–217.

Mair, M. (1977). The community of self. In D. Bannister (Ed.), *New Perspectives in Personal Construct Theory*. London: Academic Press

Margolin, L. (1986). The effects of mother–son incest. *Lifestyles: A Journal of Changing Patterns*, **8**, 104–114.

Margolis, M. (1977). Preliminary report of a case of consummated mother-son incest. *Annual of Psychoanalysis*, **5**, 267–294.

Marris, P. (1975). *Loss and Change*. Garden City,: Anchor/Doubleday.

Marvasti, J. (1986). Incestuous mothers. *American Journal of Forensic Psychiatry*, 7 (4), 63–69.

Marshall, W. L. (1989). Intimacy, loneliness and sexual offenders. *Behaviour Research and Therapy*, **27**, 5, 491–503.

Marshall, W. L. & Barbaree, H. E. (1990). An integrated theory of the etiology of sexual offending. In W. L. Marshall, D. R. Laws & H. E. Barbaree (1990). *Handbook of Sexual Assault. Issues, Theories and Treatment of the Offender*. New York: Plenum Press.

Marshall, W. L., Laws, D. R. & Barbaree, H. E. (1990). *Handbook of Sexual Assault. Issues, Theories and Treatment of the Offender*. New York: Plenum Press.

Masson, J. M. (1984). *Assault on Truth: Freud's Suppression of the Seduction Theory*. London: Faber & Faber.

Mathis, J. L. (1972). *Clear Thinking about Sexual Deviation*. Chicago: Nelson-Hall.

Matte Blanco, I. (1975). *The Unconscious as Infinite Sets*. London: Duckworth.

Matthews, J. (1992). Paper given at Female Sexual Offenders Conference, March 1992, Central Hall, Westminster, London.

Matthews, J. (1993). Working with female sexual abusers. In M. Elliott, (Ed.), *Female Sexual Abuse of Children: The Ultimate Taboo*. Harlow, Essex: Longman.

Matthews, J., Mathews, R. & Speltz, K. (1991). Female sexual offenders: A typology. In P. Q. Patton (Ed.), *Family Sexual Abuse*. New York: Sage.

Mayer, A. (1983). *Incest: A Treatment Manual for Therapy with Victims, Spouses and Offenders*. Florida: Learning Publications.

Mead, G. H. (1934). *Mind, Self and Society*. Chicago: University of Chicago Press

Megargee, E. I. (1966). Uncontrolled and overcontrolled personality types in extreme anti-social aggression. *Psychological Monographs: General and Applied* (no. 611).

Mehan, H. & Ward, H. (1975). *The Reality of Ethnomethodology*. New York: Wiley.

Meiselman, K. C. (1978). *Incest: A Psychological Study of Causes and Effects with Treatment Recommendations*. San Francisco: Jossey-Bass.

Meissner, W. W. (1988). *Treatment of Patients in the Borderline Spectrum*. Northvale, NJ: Jason Aronson.

Messing, R. B. (1988). Opioid modulation of learning and memory: Multiple behavioral outcomes. In R. J. Rodgers & S. J. Cooper (Eds), *Endorphines, Opiates and Behavioral Processes*. Chichester: Wiley.

Miller, A. (1990). *Banished Knowledge: Facing Childhood Injuries*. London: Virago.

Miller, A. (1991). *Breaking Down the Wall of Silence*. London: Virago.

Montagu, A. (1976). *The Nature of Human Aggression*. Oxford: Oxford University Press.

Moyer, K. E. (1976). *The Psychobiology of Aggression*. New York: Harper Row.

Mrazek, P. B. (1981). The nature of incest: A review of the contributing factors. In P. B. Mrazek & C. H. Kempe (Eds), *Sexually Abused Children and their Families*. Oxford: Pergamon.

Mrazek, P. B. & Kempe, C. H. (Eds) (1987). *Sexually Abused Children and their Families*. 2nd edn. Oxford: Pergamon.

Mrazek, P. B., Lynch, M. & Bentovim, A. (1981). Recognition of child sexual abuse in the United Kingdom. In P. B. Mrazek & C. H. Kempe (Eds), *Sexually Abused Children and their Families*. Oxford: Pergamon.

Neisser, U. (1976). *Cognition and Reality: Principals and Implications of Cognitive*

Psychology. San Francisco: Freeman.

Nelson, S. (1982). *Incest—Fact and Myth*. Edinburgh: Stamullion.

Obholzer, A. (1992). On relating to vulnerable adolescents. In V. P. Varma (Ed.), *The Secret Life of Vulnerable Children*. London: Routledge.

Oppenheimer, R., Palmer, R. L. & Brandon, S. (1984). A clinical evaluation of early abusive experiences in adult anorexic and bulemic females: Implications for preventative work in childhood. Paper presented to the Fifth International Congress on Child Abuse and Neglect, Montreal.

Panskepp, J. (1979). A neurochemical theory of autism. *Trends in Neuroscience, 2*, 174–177.

Panskepp, J., Herman, B. H., Vilberg, T., Bishop, P. & DeEskinazi, F. G. (1978). Endogenous opioids and social behaviour. *Neuroscience and Behavioral Reviews, 4*, 473–487.

Panskepp, J., Siviy, S. M. & Normansell, L. A. (1985). Brain opioids and social emotions. In M. Reite & T. Field (Eds), *The Psychobiology of Attachment and Separation*. London: Academic Press.

Parker, H. & Parker, S. (1986). Father–Daughter sexual abuse: An emerging perspective. *American Journal of Orthopsychiatry, 56*, 531–549.

Patton, M. Q. (1990). *Qualitative Evaluation and Research Methods*, 2nd edn. Newbury Park, CA: Sage.

Paykel, E. S. (1974). Recent life events and clinical depression. In I. K. E. Gunderson and R. D. Rahe (Eds), *Life Stress and Illness*. Springfield, IL: C. C. Thomas.

Perry, B. D. (1991). Neurobiological sequelae of childhood trauma. Post traumatic stress disorders in children. In M. Murberg (Ed.), *Catecholamines in Post-traumatic Stress Disorder:Emerging Concepts* (pp. 100–128). Washington, DC: American Psychiatric Press.

Peters, J. J. (1976). Children who are victims of sexual assault and the psychology of offenders. *American Journal of Psychotherapy, 30*, 395–421.

Peters, S. D. (1984). The relationship between childhood sexual victimisation and adult depression among Afro-American and white women. Unpublished doctoral dissertation, University of California at Los Angeles.

Petrovich, M. & Templar, D. (1984). Heterosexual molestation of children who later become rapists. *Psychological Reports, 54*, 810.

Pithers, W. D. (1990). Relapse prevention with sexual aggressors. In W. L. Marshall, D. R. Laws & H. E. Barbaree (Eds), *Handbook of Sexual Assault. Issues, Theories and Treatment of the Offender*. New York: Plenum Press.

Plutchik, R. (1986). *Emotion: A Psychoevolutionary Synthesis*. New York: Harper & Row.

Porter, R. (Ed.) (1984). *Child Sexual Abuse within the Family*. Publications for the CIBA Foundation, London: Tavistock.

Post, R. M., Pickar, D., Ballenger, J. C., Naber, D. & Rubinow, D. R. (1984). Endogenous opioids in cerebrospinal fluid: Relationship to mood and anxiety. In R. M. Post and J. C. Ballenger (Eds), *Neurobiology of Mood Disorders* (pp. 356–368). Baltimore: Williams & Wilkins.

Putnam, F. W. (1985). Dissociation as a response to extreme trauma. In R. P. Kluft (Ed.), *The Childhood Antecedents of Multiple Personality*. Washington, DC: American Psychiatric Press.

Putnam, F. W. (1991). Commentary: The satanic ritual abuse controversy. *Child Abuse and Neglect, 15* (3), 175–180.

Putnam, F. W. Guroff, J. J. Silberman, M. D. (1986). The clinical phenomenology of Multiple Personality Disorder. *Journal of Clinical Psychiatry, 47*, 293–298.

Ratner, S. C. (1977). Immobility in vertebrates: What can we learn? *Psychological Records*, **1**, 1–14.

Rawlings, E. T. & Carter, D. K. (1977). Feminist and non-feminist psychotherapy.In E. T. Rawlings and D. K. Carter (Eds), *Psychotherapy for Women*. Springfield, IL: C. C. Thomas.

Reite, M. & Field, T. (1985). *The Psychobiology of Attachment and Separation*. London: Academic Press.

Renshaw, D. (1982). *Incest: Understanding and Treatment*. Boston: Little, Brown.

Ricks, M. H. (1985). The social transmission of parental behaviour: Attachment across generations. In I. Bretherton & E. Waters, *Growing Points of Attachment Theory and Research*. Monographs of the Society for Research in Child Development, 50, Nos. 1–2, Serial no. 209.

Risin, L. I. & Koss, M. P. (1987). Sexual abuse of boys: Prevalence and descriptive characteristics of childhood victimisation. *Journal of Interpersonal Violence*, **2** (3), 309–319.

Rodgers, R. J. & Cooper, S. J. (Eds) (1988). *Endorphines, Opiates and Behavioral Processes*. Chichester: Wiley.

Rodgers, R. J. & Randell, J. I. (1988). Environmentally induced analgesia: Situational factors, mechanisms and significance. In R. J. Rodgers & S. J. Cooper (Eds), *Endorphines, Opiates and Behavioral Processes*. Chichester: Wiley.

Rose, E. S. (1993). Surviving the Unbelievable. Unpublished MS, January/February 1993, pp. 10–15.

Rosenberg, D. (1984). The Quality and Content of Pre-school Fantasy Play. Unpublished Doctoral Thesis, University of Minnesota.

Rosenfeld, A., Nadelson, C., Kreiger, M. & Backman, J. (1979). Incest and sexual abuse of children. *Journal of the American Academy of Child Psychiatry*, **16**, 327–339.

Rotter, J. B. (1966). Generalised expectancies for internal verus external control of reinforcement. *Psychological Monographs*, **30** (1), 1–26.

Rowan, E. L., Rowan, J. B. & Langelier, P. (1990). Women who molest children. *Bulletin of the American Academy of Psychiatry and the Law*. **18** (1), 79–83.

Rubin, Z. & McNeil, E. B. (1983). *The Psychology of Being Human*, 3rd edn. London: Harper Row.

Rumelhart, D. E. & Norman, D. A. (1985). Representation of knowledge. In A. M. Aitkenhead and J. M. Slack (Eds), *Issues in Cognitive Modelling*. Hillsdale, NJ: Lawrence Erlbaum.

Rush, F. (1980). *The Best Kept Secret*. New York: McGraw Hill.

Russell, D. E. H. (1983). The incidence and prevalence of intrafamilial and extrafamilial sexual assault on female children. *Child Abuse and Neglect*, **8**, 15–22.

Russell, D. E. H. (1986). *The Secret Trauma: Incest in the Lives of Girls and Women*. New York: Basic Books.

Russell, D. E. H. & Finkelhor, D. (1984). Women as perpetrators: Review of the evidence. In D. Finkelhor, *Child Sexual Abuse*. New York: Free Press.

Rutter, M., (1984). Continuities and discontinuities in socioemotional development. Empirical and conceptual perspectives. In R. Emde and R. Harmon (Eds), *Continuities and Discontinuities in Development*. New York: Plenum Press.

Rutter, M. (1989). Intergenerational continuities and discontinuities in serious parenting difficulties. In D. Cicchetti and V. Carlson (Eds), *Child Maltreatment*. New York: Cambridge University Press.

Salter, A. C. (1988). *Treating Child Sex Offenders and Victims*. Beverly Hills, CA: Sage.

Salter, A. C. (1995). *Transforming Trauma*. Beverly Hills, CA: Sage.

Sameroff, A. J. (1989). Principles of development and psychopathology. In A. J.

Sameroff & R. N. Emde (Eds), *Relationship Disturbances in early Childhood*. New York: Basic Books.

Sameroff, A. J. & Chandler, M. J. (1975) Reproductive risk and the continuum of caretaking casualty. In F. D. Horowitz, M. Hetherington, S. Scarr-Salapatek & G. Siegel (Eds), *Review of Child Development Research*, vol. 4. Chicago: University of Chicago Press.

Sandler, J., Dare, C. & Holder, A. (1970). Basic psychoanalytic concepts: III Transference. *British Journal of Psychiatry*, **116**, 667–672.

Saradjian, J. (1990). Probing the antecedents of mother–child sexual abuse: A controlled study. Unpublished undergraduate thesis, Department of Psychology, University of Leeds.

Saradjian, J. (1992). Typologies of female perpetrators of child sexual abuse: An emerging perspective. MSc Thesis, University of Leeds.

Schechter, M. D. & Roberge, L. (1976). Sexual exploitation. In R. E. Helfer & C. H. Kempe (Eds), *Child Abuse and Neglect: The Family and the Community*. Cambridge, MA: Ballinger.

Schreiber, F. R. (1973). *Sybil*. Harmondsworth: Penguin Books.

Schulz, R. (1976). Effects of control and predicability on the psychological well-being of the institutionalised aged. *Journal of Personality and Social Psychology*, **33**, 563–573.

Sedney, M. A. & Brooks, B. (1984). Factors associated with a history of childhood sexual experience in a non-clinical female population. *Journal of The American Academy of Childhood Psychiatry*, **23**, 215–218.

Seghorn, T. K., Prentky, R. A. & Boucher, R. J. (1987). Childhood sexual abuse in the lives of sexually aggressive offenders. *Journal of The American Academy of Child and Adolescent Psychiatry*, **26** (2), 262–267.

Serra, G., Collu, M. & Gessa, G. L. (1988). Endorphins and sexual behaviour. In R. J. Rodgers & S. J. Cooper (Eds), *Endorphines, Opiates and Behavioral Processes* Chichester: Wiley.

Sgroi, S. M. & Sargent, N. M. (1993). Impact and treatment issues for victims of childhood sexual abuse by female perpetrators. In M. Elliot (Ed.), *Female Sexual Abuse of Children: The Ultimate Taboo*. Harlow, Essex: Longman.

Shengold, L. (1980). Some reflections on a case of mother/adolescent son incest. *International Journal of Psychoanalysis*, **61**, 461–476.

Sholursh, L. P. (1988). Combat addiction. *Psychiatric Journal of Ottawa*, **13**, 17–20.

Sinason, V. (1988) Smiling, swallowing, sickening, and stupefying: The effect of sexual abuse on the child. *Psychoanalytic Psychotherapy*, **3** (2), 97–111.

Sinason, V. (1993). Talk given at Childline conference on 'Women who sexually abuse children'. London, October 1993.

Sinason, V. (1994). Treating survivors of Satanist abuse. London: Routledge.

Sinason, V. & Svensson, A. (1994). Going through the fifth window: Other cases rest on Sundays. This one didn't. In V. Sinason (Ed.), *Treating Survivors of Satanist Abuse*. (pp. 13–21) London: Routledge.

Smith, G. (1993, 1994). Personal Communications.

Snow, B. & Sorenson, T. (1990). Ritualistic child abuse in a neighbourhood setting. *Journal of Interpersonal Violence*, **5** (4), 474–487.

Speltz, K., Matthews, J. K. & Mathews, R. (1989). *Female Sexual Offenders: An Exploratory Study*. Orwell, VT: Safer Society Press.

Spiegel, D. (1988). Dissociation and hypnosis in post-traumatic stress disorders. *Journal of Traumatic Stress*, **1**, 17–33.

Spring, J. (1987). *Cry Hard and Swim: The Story of an Incest Survivor*. London: Virago.

Sroufe, L. A. (1983). Infant–caregiver attachment and adaptation in the preschool: The roots of competence and maladaptation. In M. Perlmutter (Ed.), *Development of Cognition, Affect and Social Relations*. Hillsdale, NJ: Lawrence-Erlbaum.

Sroufe, L. A. (1989). Relationships, self and individual adaptation. In A. J. Sameroff & R. N. Emde (Eds), *Relationship Disturbances in early Childhood*. New York: Basic Books

Sroufe, L. A. & Fleeson, J. (1986). Attachment and the construction of relationships. In W. Hartup and Z. Rubin (Eds), *Relationships and Development*. Hillsdale, NJ: Lawrence Erlbaum.

Staub, E. (1984) A conception of the determinants and development of altruism and aggression: Motives, the self and the environment. In C. Zahn-Waxler, E. M. Cummings and R. Ianotti (Eds), *Social and Biological Origins of Altruism and Aggression* (pp. 135–163). Cambridge: Cambridge University Press

Stern, D. (1985). *The Interpersonal World of the Infant: A View from Ppsychoananlysis and Developmental Psychology*. New York: Basic Books.

Stoller, R. (1975). *Perversion*. New York: Parthenon.

Storr, A. (1966). Human aggression. Harmondsworth: Penguin Books.

Stratton, P. (1990). Personal Communication.

Suarez, S. D. & Gallup, G. G. (1979). Tonic immobility as a response to rape in humans: A theoretical note. *Psychological Record*, **29**, 315–320.

Sullivan, H. S. (1953). *The Interpersonal Theory of Psychiatry*. New York: Norton.

Sullivan, H. S. (1950). Tensions interpersonal and international: A psychiatrist's view. In *The Fusion of Psychiatry and Social Science*. New York: Norton.

Summit, R. C. & Kryso, J. (1978). Sexual abuse of children: A clinical spectrum. *American Journal of Orthopsychiatry*, **48**, 237–251.

Summit, R. (1989). Ritual Child Abuse: A Professional Overview, Ukia. Cavalcade Productions (Videotape).

Tajfel, H. (1972). Experiments in a vacuum. In J. Israel and H. Tajfel (Eds), *The Context of Social Psychology: A Critical Assessment*. London: Academic Press.

Tate, T. (1994). Press, policitics and paedophilia: A practitioner's guide to the media. In V. Sinason (Ed.), *Treating Survivors of Satanist Abuse* (pp. 182–194). London: Routledge.

Travin, S., Cullen, K. & Protter, B., (1990). Female sex offenders: Severe victims and victimisers. *Journal of Forensic Sciences*, **35**, 140–150.

Trepper, T. S. & Barrett, M. J. (Eds) (1986). *Treating Incest: A Multimodal Systems Perspective*. New York: Haworth Press.

Troy, M. & Sroufe, L. A. (1987). Victimisation among preschoolers: The role of attachment relationship history. *Journal of the American Academy of Child and Adolescent Psychiatry*, **26**, 166–172.

Tufts' New England Medical Centre, Division of Child Psychiatry (1984). Sexually exploited children: Service and Research Project (final report for the Office of Juvenile Justice and Delinquency Prevention) Washington, DC: US Department of Justice.

Ussher J. (1991). *Women's Madness*. London: Harvester Wheatsheaf.

van der Kolk (1988). The trauma spectrum: The interaction of biological and social events in the genesis of the trauma response. *Journal of Traumatic Stress*, **1** (3), 273–290.

van der Kolk (1989). Pain perception and endogenous opioids in Post-Traumatic Stress Disorder. *Psychopharmacology Bulletin*.

Vietze, P., Falsey. S., Sandler, H., O'Conner, S. & Altemeier, W. A. (1980).

Transactional approach to prediction of child maltreatment. *Infant Mental Health Journal*, **1**, 248–261.

Wahl, C. W. (1960). The psychodynamics of consummated maternal incest. *Archives of General Psychiatry*, **3**, 188–193.

Wallnau, L. B. & Gallup, G. G. (1977). A serotonergic midbrain—Raphe Model of Tonic Immobility. *Behavioral Reviews*, **1**, 35–43.

Walters, D. (1975). *Physical and Sexual Abuse of Children*. Bloomington, IN: Indiana University Press.

Waterman, J., Kelly, R. J., McCord, J. & Oliveri, M. K (1990). Reported ritualistic and non-ritualistic sexual abuse in preschools: Effects and mediators. Final Report, National Center on Child Abuse and Neglect. Grant Number 90CA1179.

Waterman, J., Kelly, R. J., Oliveri M. K. & McCord, J. (1993.) *Behind the Playground Walls: Sexual Abuse in Preschools*. New York: Guilford Press.

Welldon, E. V. (1988). *Mother, Madonna, Whore: The Idealisation and Denigration of Motherhood*. London: Free Association Books.

Wilkins, R. (1990). Women who sexually abuse children. *British Medical Journal*, **300**, 5 May, 1153–1154.

Wilson, A. (1994). Personal Communication.

Wisconsin Female Juvenile Offender Study (1982). Sex Abuse among Juvenile Offenders and Runaways (Summary Report), Madison: WI.

Wolf, E. S. (1988). *Treating the Self: Elements of Clinical Self Psychology*. London: Guilford Press.

Woodward, J (1988). *Understanding Ourselves: The Uses of Therapy*. London: Macmillan.

Wyatt, G. E. (1985). The sexual abuse of Afro-American and white women in childhood. *Child Abuse and Neglect*, **9**, 507–519.

Wyatt, G. E. & Peters, S. D. (1986). Issues in the definition of child sexual abuse in prevalence research. *Child Abuse and Neglect*, **10**, 231–240.

Wyatt, G. E. & Powell, G. J. (1988). *Lasting Effects of child sexual abuse*. Beverly Hills CA: Sage.

Wyre, R. (1992). Personal Communication.

Yorukoglu, A. & Kemph, J. P. (1966). Children not severely damaged by incest with a parent. *Journal of the American Academy of Child Psychiatry*, **5**, 111–124.

Young, W. (1990). President's Report. International Society for the Study of Multiple Personality and Dissociation. Executive Council Meeting Ottawa, Ontario, Canada.

Youngson, S. (1989). All the world's a stage—But adolescence is a process. *Changes—Journal of the Psychology and Psychotherapy Association*, **7** (2), April.

Youngson, S. (1994). Ritual abuse. The personal and professional cost for workers. In V. Sinason (Ed.), *Treating Survivors of Satanist Abuse*. London: Routledge.

Zillman, D. (1984). *Connections between Sex and Aggression*. London: LEA.

de Zulueta, F. (1993). *From Pain to Violence: The Traumatic Roots of Destructiveness*. London: Whurr.

INDEX

Index compiled by Caroline Sheard

Related titles of interest from Wiley...

Cycles of Child Maltreatment
Facts, Fallacies and Interventions
Ann Buchanan

Easily accessible with clear summaries this book brings together both theories and research in the mechanisms of intergenerational transmission of child abuse.

Wiley Series in Child Care & Protection
0-471-95889-1   308pp   1996   Paperback
0-471-96174-4   308pp   1996   Hardback

The Emotionally Abused and Neglected Child
Identification, Assessment and Intervention
Dorota Iwaniec

Explores the definition, identification and treatment of the difficult problem of emotional abuse. Case studies are provided to illustrate the features of emotional abuse, and chapters are devoted to assessment and prediction, effects of emotional abuse as the child grows up, intervention and treatment and working with the family as a whole.

Wiley Series in Child Care & Protection
0-471-95579-5   222pp   1995   Paperback

Child Abuse Review
The Journal of the British Association for the Study and Prevention of Child Abuse & Neglect

Addresses current child protection and social welfare issues, and reflects the concerns and views of those working to prevent child abuse and neglect.

ISSN: 0952-9136

Children & Society

Presenting a range of provocative and challenging articles on all aspects of children's lives and services for children, this journal critically analyses significant developments in policy and practice, and stresses the importance of promoting and reviewing research.

Published in association with the National Children's Bureau
ISSN: 0951-0605